CLUB OPERATIONS AND MANAGEMENT

SECOND EDITION

CLUB OPERATIONS AND MANAGEMENT

SECOND EDITION

Ted E. White

Distinguished Lecturer
Florida International University
Miami, Florida

A N D

Larry C. Gerstner

Executive Director
Westview Country Club
Miami, Florida

 VAN NOSTRAND REINHOLD
_____ NEW YORK

Library of Congress Catalog Number 90–12169
ISBN 0-442-23528-3

Printed in the United States of America

Van Nostrand Reinhold
115 Fifth Avenue
New York, New York 10003

Chapman and Hall
2-6 Boundary Row
London, SE1 8HN, England

Thomas Nelson Australia
102 Dodds Street
South Melbourne 3205
Victoria, Australia

Nelson Canada
1120 Birchmount Road
Scarborough, Ontario M1K 5G4, Canada

16 15 14 13 12 11 10 9 8 7 6 5 4 3 2 1

Library of Congress Cataloging in Publication Data

White, Ted E., 1912–
    Club operations and management / by Ted. E. White and Larry C.
Gerstner — 2nd ed.
        p.   cm.
    Includes bibliographical references.
    ISBN 0-442-23528-3
    1. Clubs—Management.   I. Gerstner, Larry C., 1944–
II. Title.
TX911.3.M27W45   1991
367'.068—dc20   90-12169
                                                       CIP
                                                       Rev.

This book is dedicated to the
two persons most responsible for its completion
CHRISTINE H. KURTZ-WHITE
and
CHERYL I. GERSTNER
whose assistance, patience,
and understanding made this
work possible

Contents

vii

Preface

The purpose of this text is to record in detail the changes in club management that have taken place since I wrote the last edition of *Club Operations and Management*.

The greatest change has been in the attitude of club financial managers, who employ the latest business methods, and who understand that raising dues and prices is not the only answer to deficits. This text is written with the modern financial manager in mind.

To begin my planning and research for the second edition, I needed a co-author who was an active, successful club manager who had held progressively upward management positions throughout his or her career. He or she also needed to be able to express thoughts clearly and concisely in writing.

I found my co-author in Larry C. Gerstner, who has been a manager, a general manager, a teacher/consultant, and a president and chief executive officer of a club company which owned and operated five full-service country clubs.

Owners and managers of clubs, bars, and restaurants and real estate developers will all find this second edition a useful reference, covering all aspects of club management. Special topics covered include internal security, computerization, merchandising, insurance, renovation, and professional assistance. The second edition also includes more information than the first on clubs, both military and civilian, that are run by the United States Government.

Specifically, it is the intention of the authors to provide a comprehensive work that can be used as a text for students and a handbook for inexperienced managers. They also hope it will furnish a checklist and perhaps some new ideas and methods to anyone with an interest in the hospitality business.

Acknowledgments

The authors express their sincere appreciation and thanks to:

MR. ROBERT J. LAMB, JR., of the West Palm Beach, Florida, firm of Hillier, Wanless and Cherry, P.A., for providing information on equity conversions

MR. JOHN HUNGERFORD, president of the Stonebridge Country Club, McKinny, Texas, for pictures of his club

MR. RICHARD POOLE, JR., senior executive of the Club Corporation of America of Dallas, Texas, for his information, pictures, and advice

MR. ROBERT WILLIAMS, president of American Golf, Inc., of Santa Monica, California, for his assistance and advice on public golf course management

MR. PAUL DALY and MR. SCOTT GIDDINGS, associates of Larry C. Gerstner in Western Club Consultation and Management of San Ramon, California, for their input on management for the 1990s

MR. HARRY CHRIS of Chris Consultants, Inc., of Irving Texas for his advice and club pictures

MR. WILLIAM L. RIVERS, CPCU, of Dallas, Texas, for detailed information on club insurance; and American Business Computers for the use of the photograph of the micromotion Keyboards.

Ted E. White

CLUB OPERATIONS AND MANAGEMENT

SECOND EDITION

Introduction

Club Management in the nineties will differ greatly from club management in the eighties. The anticipated changes include:

1. More and more club functions will be controlled by computers, from timers and thermostats to cost accounting systems.
2. The dues structure of clubs will change as "unbundling" becomes increasingly popular: Instead of fixed dues, members will pay a flat fee plus fees for services and amenities they elect to use.
3. Clubs will be in serious competition with resort hotels; public golf courses, tennis courts, and swimming pools; corporate clubs (open to the public); and nationwide health clubs as the quality of these facilities continues to improve and their services are aggressively marketed.
4. Membership composition will change as restrictions to club enrollment, based on the First Amendment to the Constitution of the United States, are challenged. Though intended to protect "the right to free assembly," the First Amendment was not intended to promote racism and sexism and to bar persons of other than United States national origin from joining clubs of their choice.
5. Given trends in the eighties, numerous clubs may give up their nonprofit status in order to accept unlimited party business from nonmembers.

Club management is a challenging and exciting profession. For the purpose of this text a club is defined as a selected group of persons, gathered in a specific place, whose social and recreational needs are provided through professional management. The club business is distinguished by seven characteristics:

1. A club has an established, stable clientele. Unlike other businesses, a club must cope with the same customer on its premises who demands the same products day after day, week after week, month after month, and year after year.
   A fixed clientele requires that menus be recycled more frequently than is the norm for the rest of the hospitality industry—that they include daily specials

1

and changes in format and in types of dishes served. New innovative approaches must be developed for the celebration of the various holidays. The inventory in the various pro shops must be turned regularly and kept up to date with contemporary styles.

2. The privilege of using club facilities is obtained through the payment of dues. Members can expect the club dining room to be comparable to a four-star restaurant and the quality of all other facilities to be first class.

   Usually the menus are competitively priced, niceties being financed from dues or other sources. Niceties may include tablecloths (instead of bare tables or place mats), linen (instead of paper) napkins and matched china, silverware, and glassware. Also, goosenecks (instead of bottles) may hold the condiments; fresh flowers may grace tables; better-than-average service is offered (many times with a maitre d', captains, and hostesses); live entertainment is featured; furniture and fixtures are spotless.

   As for the grounds, they must be kept in immaculate condition. The golf course, tennis courts, and swimming pool must all meet professional standards.

3. The manager is expected to know more about the business of the club than its governing members, advisory group, or owners, together or severally.

   Members may be adequate judges of good food, drinks, and service; however, they may know nothing of the myriad details of management geared to producing quality results. In fact, managers in many clubs write their own operational manual to include: the basics of menu and drink planning, purchasing, receiving, holding, preparing, serving, and cost/waste control. In addition, managers may be called upon to assist the pros on staff in writing their recreational manuals.

4. Making a profit in each of the club's departments may not be a management objective; many clubs are subsidizing their food and golf departments with initiation fees and dues.

5. In clubs, managers almost always have an opportunity to use their full knowledge of the hospitality field. In hotel and restaurant chains, however, and even in most of the successful independents, managers are presented with an operations manual that must be strictly followed and that leaves little room for individual initiative.

6. There are many different types of clubs, each requiring a slightly different management approach.

7. Perhaps the most important aspect of club management—and this one characterizes the entire hospitality industry—is entertainment: the members (customers) are supposed to have fun. The club operation must be perceived as not being managed at all.

CLUB MANAGEMENT AS A CAREER

Club management as a career offers an exciting and rewarding life-style. Almost unparalleled in its variety and challenges, a general manager's position rivals its hotel counterpart. Likewise, the duties of a restaurateur in no way equal those of the club manager, for whom restaurant and bar operation are only one of many responsibilities.

Like hotel and restaurant managers, however, club managers must usually meet a round-the-clock schedule. In most clubs the busiest times are weekends and holidays; if management does get a day off, it will usually be a Monday.

For managers in most private clubs the path of advancement has two lanes: one, vertical, leading to general manager and the other, horizontal, to manager or general manager of another club. In corporate clubs and in some single-proprietary clubs, an adjunctive seat on the board is possible, with the title of vice president or treasurer, for example. The Club Managers Association of America (CMAA) and its local club chapters offer helpful referral services to their members. The association also has a referral list for managers seeking temporary employment.

The starting pay and fringe benefits for club managers are usually comparable to those offered by the rest of the hospitality industry, with the addition of one thing—the opportunity, at some clubs, to use the facilities. The three most important reasons for this extra benefit are: (1) the willingness of members to share club facilities with managerial staff, (2) the public relations experience this offers to managers and students alike, as well as (3) the chance for them to learn about the recreation activities of the club.

For students interested in the hospitality business as a career, a good place to start is club management. Before making any definite choice, however, they should have at least 800 hours of actual work experience in some facet of the hospitality industry. Two ways students can begin a career in club management are to obtain a part-time job in a club while still attending college and to join the college chapter of CMAA, if one exists. Either of these steps will give students valuable experience as well as a competitive edge.

1 The History of Clubs

CLUBS IN ANCIENT TIMES

It is a natural tendency for people to associate with their peers for social and recreational purposes. For many centuries these gatherings were limited to the specific locales in which people lived. They hunted, fished, and socialized together in groups.

The first records available on gatherings of civilized persons outside their immediate living area, for a purpose other than to obtain food, are of the baths of the ancient Romans and Greeks. Although the word *club* was not part of their vocabulary, baths fit the definition that is used today—that is, a selected group of persons, meeting for recreational, social, and sometimes political purposes in a place run by a manager.

The baths provided relaxation and an opportunity to associate in privacy with one's peers. The men and women had separate pools, tended by a favorite household slave. The attendants in the women's baths were male, and in the men's baths female. In addition to their other duties, the slaves were required to be prostitutes for the members. The emphasis was on total relaxation and privacy. Much of the government's behind-the-scenes business was conducted at the baths: Plots were conjured, assassinations planned, and influence swapped. Conduct at times was quite scandalous.

The Greek Army

Another type of gathering was originated by the Greek armies in the field. A Greek general is thought to be responsible for using the word *mesa* to indicate military personnel eating from a common pot, the officers separated from the common soldiers.

Mesa, translated into many languages, was widely used in medieval times to describe the sharing of a meal by military personnel. Later the British, then the

5

American military, adopted the word *mess* to designate the place where military personnel were fed. The term was also used to designate a military club and is still used in that sense by the Navy and Air Force; however, the other services now use the word *club*.

The Steward

The Bible records a step in club history: In the Gospels of Saint John and Saint Luke, the title *steward* is given for the person (always male) in charge of household duties. These included the daily preparation of food and drink, banquets and parties, housekeeping chores, and the maintenance of property. Significantly, although this man was a slave and a servant, he was the manager of his domain.

Today the title of steward is still used in some clubs in America and Europe to designate the manager and/or storekeeper, but it is no longer accepted as the proper title for the professional American club manager. In the transportation industry, stewards are persons who serve food.

CLUBS IN ENGLAND AND SCOTLAND

The next milestone in the history of the club business was reached in both England and Scotland in the seventeenth and eighteenth centuries with the importation of coffee from the East. In London in 1652 and in Edinburgh in 1731, coffee houses, later to become clubs, sprang up. Clubs featured conviviality, eating, drinking, and gambling as their attractions; many of the clubs set no limit to the gambling stakes.

Clubs in England

The first of the coffee houses were formed at three major English universities: Oxford, All Souls, and Cambridge. It was at Oxford that the coffee house was first called a club.

Gradually different houses attracted different types of clientele; for example, Lloyd's attracted marine insurers, Garraway's the city men, Young Man's the military, Old Man's the stockjobbers, Grecian the legal professionals, and Child's the clergymen. Also at White's Chocolate House, the Beau Brummels of their day gathered, and at Will's the literary set met. Some of the great literary figures of the times who frequented Will's were Samuel Pepys, the essayist; John Dryden, the poet, dramatist, and critic; Joseph Addison, the poet, essayist, and statesman; and Alexander Pope, the poet.

In clubs hard-to-get news was shared and many rumors started. Indeed, during the time of the Dutch Wars, the British government used Mr. Pepys to spread stories of Dutch atrocities, hoping to stir up some fighting spirit among club members. In 1660 Charles II, King of England, expressed concern about the freedom of speech enjoyed in the coffee houses and 5 years later suppressed them. Such a hue and cry rose that the King had to modify his order, stating they could continue to operate until a certain date. This was never enforced.

The London City Clubs

The London city clubs, from the time of their inception, have been, and still are, vastly different from their American counterparts. The British have always been more interested in the quiet, relaxed atmosphere of a lounge, where the current newspaper could be read and a softly voiced conversation could be held. In many American city clubs, the emphasis is more on the dining room and cocktail lounge. Most of the London clubs have extensive libraries. These are not generally found in American clubs.

Many of the London clubs founded in the nineteenth century are still very active today, having survived wars, political changes, and depressions. One club, White's, founded in the seventeenth century, spawned two other clubs, the Old Man's and the Young Man's, which functioned as subsidiaries within the larger club until 1753, when they moved into their own quarters. Every Prime Minister from Walpole to Peel was a member of White's. Playing cards was the most popular gambling activity, and although normally the stakes were low, at one session a London banker lost £20,000. Another member won £80,000 at cards at the club.

In the mid-Victorian era, White's, like many other clubs, was torn by the Great Smoking Dispute. In most clubs smoking was confined to certain areas and White's was no exception. A confirmed heavy smoker, the Prince of Wales (Heir Apparent to the British throne) expressed a desire to use the club and became a member. A general meeting of all of the members was held to change the no smoking rules, but the members voted to retain the old regulations. The Prince did not obey the rules and one of the staff requested that he stop smoking or leave the room. The Prince left the club very annoyed and founded the Marlborough Club, where smoking was allowed. After World War II the club was frequented by personalities such as Randolph Churchill and Evelyn Waugh. The latter used the club, very lightly disguised, as the setting of many of his novels. White's today has a 6-year waiting list and is one of London's finest clubs.

Clubs in Scotland

Many clubs were started in the eighteenth century in Edinburgh, Scotland. Some of these were the New Club, the Poker, the Club of the Crochallan Fencibles, the Boar Club, the Dirty Club, and the Cape. The Spendthrift Club established the first minumum charge: Members had to spend 41S. 2d. on each visit.

The Royal and Ancient Club of St. Andrews, established in Edinburgh in the eighteenth century, is still active and is now over 200 years old. This club, surrounded by five golf courses, is world-renowned for its contributions to the game of golf. The courses are open to the public and are very popular, particularly the first one built, called the "Old Course" and one built later, called the "New Course." In

1834, King William IV agreed to be a patron of the club and decreed that its name henceforth would be "The Royal and Ancient Golf Club."

The club's most important contribution to the game of golf is its committees, which have formulated and updated the rules of golf and managed the Open and Amateur tournaments. Through the influence of the American golfers who played in the Open, these rules became the standard for clubs in America and the rest of the world. The Americans who played in the Open have included almost every great golfer; to win the Open is the goal of every professional.

CLUBS IN AMERICA

The first clubs in America were established in the eighteenth century. The first club ever formally established is thought to be the Order of Free Masons in 1715. Lodges were formed in each of the thirteen colonies, with the exception of North Carolina, by 1750. Throughout the colonies loosely formed clubs were established in taverns. These were primarily social clubs, limited to men only, where the news of the day and topics of interest were discussed. According to Oliver Perry Chitwood, historian, "rum and other alcoholic beverages were generously absorbed."* Both city and country clubs, as they are known today, first appeared in New England, the mid-Atlantic areas, and on the West Coast. These clubs were formed primarily by individuals of the upper social strata, who pooled funds and purchased buildings and land. Primarily urban dwellers, they needed acreage to establish recreational facilities such as golf courses.

In the southeastern United States the affluent were mostly rural, owning plantations with homes large enough to do all of the indoor entertaining they cared to do. For a long time only a few clubs existed, primarily in the larger cities of Richmond, Atlanta, Charleston, Savannah, and New Orleans. It was well after the Civil War that clubs on a large scale, particularly country clubs, were established in the South.

American Tavern Clubs

Taverns in America were located along the transportation routes, which were traveled by horse, wagon, or boat. Imported into America by Great Britain in 1680, tea was popular in the taverns but did not promote conviviality the way hot rum and water did. It was not until after the Boston Tea Party, in the latter part of the eighteenth century, that coffee became a popular tavern drink. Clubs established in American taverns very rarely became as formal as their English and Scottish counterparts, however, even after coffee became available.

American Clubs in the Twentieth Century

In the early part of the twentieth century, clubs in America numbered about 10,000: 4500 in the city and 5500 in the country. By 1988 over 30,000 had been established. Throughout the teens, the twenties, and the thirties, country club membership was

*Oliver Perry Chitwood, *A History of Colonial America* (New York: Harper, 1961), p. x.

reserved for the more affluent members of the American population, and high society meant the "country club set." Clubs were low-key operations, with rigidly controlled public relations and powerful and arrogant membership committees. These committees carefully screened every application submitted (submission itself, in many cases, required tremendous influence).

Interestingly, mass-produced automobiles, instead of broadening club membership, encouraged exclusivity, for they allowed the old-line city clubs to expand into the country with little inconvenience to the members.

Millionnaires were separated from six-figure members and they, in turn, from the five-figure ones. The first real breakthrough in this caste system of clubs occurred in the late thirties, when business, stimulated by the wars in Europe and Asia, caused board rooms to overflow into the clubs. As a result of this movement, clubs found it necessary to open their doors to new moneyed and working groups.

Club Managers Association of America

A small group of progressive managers met in Chicago in 1927 to form an organization they called the Club Managers Association of America (CMAA). Their purpose was to make the position of club manager a professional one. At this meeting, nine women were present and were included as members in the original association. The association has in fact always included women, clubs being among the first businesses in America to have women in top management positions.

The First Amendment

Throughout their history clubs have practiced racial, sexual, and religious discrimination on the basis of the First Amendment to the Constitution of the United States. One of the nine amendments constituting the "Bill of Rights," the First guarantees freedom of worship, of speech, of the press, and of assembly. It also allows any citizen to petition the government for redress of grievances.

The "right of free assembly" is the legal peg clubs use for their segregation policies. The contention of segregated private clubs has been that citizens have a constitutional right to select those peers with whom they choose to associate. This interpretation of the First Amendment, however, is gradually being eroded.

For example, in 1988, the Supreme Court of the United States upheld a New York City local law that prohibited any club in that city from discriminating against women or minorities if the club had over 400 members, offered regular meal service, and received outside income such as employer-paid dues. The ruling terminated the privacy of clubs meeting these criteria. Among other states where legislation has been passed promoting nondiscrimination, the state of Minnesota has changed its property tax laws so that golf clubs filing for property valuation must meet certain criteria to maintain their low rates.

Nightclubs

Nightclubs in America, on both land and water, can be traced back to the early nineteenth century. England and Europe had nightclubs even earlier, but, unlike the "gentleman clubs" of Great Britain and Scotland, they seem to have left almost no record of their activities. The only proof of their existence is their portrayal in some early Dutch paintings.

On American waterways—the Mississippi, the Ohio, and other rivers—riverboats served three or more meals a day and offered evening entertainment. The latter usually consisted of gambling, dance-hall girls, and ragtime bands from Chicago, Memphis, and New Orleans.

The Volstead Act

When prohibition went into effect in 1917 with the passage of the Volstead Act, for the next 16 years "speakeasies" became the place to get a drink or a bottle. As alcoholic beverages were legal in Canada and throughout the Caribbean, "rumrunning," next to owning a speakeasy, became the most profitable business of the day in the States.

This was also the era of the great criminal mobs. Gangsters such as Al Capone in Chicago and his counterparts in Detroit, New York, and Los Angeles defied the law for many years with impunity. Their control of the importation and distribution of alcoholic beverages was made possible by the general public's contempt for the law and its desire for alcoholic beverages. Even law enforcement officers conspired with the crime syndicates, turning their backs on the illegal activities. Every city and hamlet had its own source of alcoholic beverages, supplied by persons called "bootleggers."

Franklin D. Roosevelt, elected President of the United States in 1932, had the Volstead Act repealed in 1933. Most of the speakeasies became neighborhood bars and some became nightclubs. Today nightclubs can be divided into two categories: nightclubs with disc jockeys or canned music, and show bars with live entertainment.

World War II and Golf

The next major event in the history of the club business was the impact of World War II. Many of the new military bases built during this period included golf courses as part of their recreation programs and these were available to all of the military officers. For the first time, any man who donned a uniform in the Armed Forces had an opportunity to play golf.

Prior to World War II many military establishments had golf courses but they had been primarily for the officers' use. Also, few public courses existed and only the more affluent of the American populace could join country clubs. After the war the returning military, most of whom were average workers, brought with them a demand for public golf courses and affordable clubs with golf facilities. This led to the vast construction programs of the sixties, seventies, and eighties. As clubs grew in number and prospered, businesspeople found that belonging to one could assist them in selling their wares, such as stocks, bonds, insurance, and automobiles, and might also be of help in securing job promotions. Clubs were a boon to outside industry, and vice versa.

The Real Estate Developer and the Country Club

With the coming of age in the early eighties of the "Baby Boom" generation and the opening up of job opportunities for women in every field, discretionary income became available and clubs became the "in" place to spend these funds.

First in California and then throughout the rest of the nation, real estate developers soon discovered that one of the best ways to sell homes was to build them around a country club. This was financially feasible because the cost of a club with all its facilities (golf courses, tennis courts, pools, club houses, and so forth) could be prorated through that of the four to five hundred individual homes surrounding the club. Thus at last affordable clubs were made available to average middle-class families, and golf has since become the most popular participatory sport in the country. In the state of Florida alone, there are over seven hundred golf courses ranging from nine to ninety holes.

Club Corporation of America

In 1957 Robert H. Dedman founded the first of several companies that ultimately would be consolidated into the Club Corporation of America (CCA). He had discovered that some club owners were looking for ways to enjoy their clubs without the continuous hassle of being responsible (despite having hired a manager) for the day-to-day operation of the club. He also had found that good management procedures could be applied to the club business with remarkable financial results. His efficient corporate structuring of CCA enabled other club companies to hold management contracts, administered by their corporation.

American Golf Corporation

In the late seventies David G. Price formed American Golf, Inc. (AGI) on the premise that "Golf is a business, not a sport." His company manages and/or owns over a hundred golf courses and country clubs and is the leading manager of municipal golf courses operating nationwide and expanding rapidly. Directors of the company base its success on efficiency, consistent quality, friendly service, and, most of all, volume. AGI's size allows it to spread the cost over many different revenue-producing facilities. Able to hire full-time agronomists, accountants, and golf teachers, it also can buy in bulk and offer discounts in its pro shops which feature a line of hats, gloves, and balls under its own label. Although AGI owns some country clubs, it is not in competition with CCA, as it intends to realize its expansion via the huge market of public-owned golf courses.

REVIEW QUESTIONS

1. Why do you think the study of the history of clubs is important to today's manager?
2. Why did *steward* denote a servile title?

3. How did the Ancient and Royal Club of Scotland influence the game of golf in America?
4. What was the basic reason behind the formation of the Club Managers Association of America?
5. How did the importation of coffee into Great Britain affect the club business?
6. What is the origin of the word *mess* used by many military clubs?
7. What role did the American tavern play in the history of the club business?
8. What was the rationale for the formation of Club Corporation of America?

2 Types of Clubs and Their Management Structure

TYPES OF CLUBS

Different types of clubs satisfy social, recreational, and financial needs.

Country Clubs

The term "country club" originally designated a club with enough acreage to include a clubhouse, golf course, tennis courts, one or more swimming pools, and other types of outdoor activities (Fig. 2.1). An eighteen-hole golf course generally requires a minimum of 110 acres for its construction, and with other outdoor amenities a 200-acre tract is not unusual. Some clubs maintain both a city and country location so their members can enjoy convenience of the city club and the recreational facilities of the country club.

In addition to the three main recreational activities of golf (Fig. 2.2), tennis, and swimming, country clubs may also offer:

Horseback riding (possibly with stabling privileges)
A polo field
Diving and wading pools
Driving, chipping, and putting areas
Archery, rifle, skeet, and pistol ranges
Cycling lanes
Skating rinks
Jogging lanes
Bocci, lawn, ten-pin, and duckpin bowling courts
Cross-country skiing
Deck and paddle tennis courts
Squash, racquetball, and handball courts
Volleyball courts

FIGURE 2.1 *Exterior view of the Reston Wood Country Club, Raleigh, North Carolina (Courtesy of Chris Consultants).*

Track-and-field facilities
Television lounges
Billiard rooms
Card rooms
Libraries
Exercise rooms, including facilities for aerobic dancing
Sauna and steam baths
Sleep rooms and guest quarters

There is in fact no limit to the activities that can be added if the members desire and can afford them (Fig. 2.3).

The 1990s will see rapid growth in the number of country clubs. As part of real estate deals to sell houses, clubs will become increasingly attractive to buyers and developers alike (Figs. 2.4 and 2.5). Options open to the buyer include:

- Purchasing a home in a development with a club, which may be joined immediately or at some time in the future. Even if the club has a cap on the number of persons who may join, most developers reserve a block of memberships for home owners. A sample of this type of development is the Old Marsh Club in West Palm Beach, Florida.
- Purchasing a home in a development where the purchase price of each home includes a portion of the purchase price of the club. A developer has established this type of contract at the Gleneagle Country Club in Delray Beach, Florida. When the 1600 units in the development are all sold, the home owners will own the country club.

FIGURE 2.2   *Members playing golf (Courtesy of Stonebridge Ranch).*

Real estate developers have played a large role in the development of country club communities. Not only does a country club located within a development increase the value of the surrounding residential property, it also allows the construction of high-priced residential units in areas where no other attractions exist. For the real estate developer options include the following:

- Including the price of the club in the home buyer's purchase price and operating the club until all of the homes in the development are sold. Membership dues must be low enough to attract buyers but high enough to help cover operating costs. The developer of the Kendale Lakes Golf and Country Club, in Florida, went the low route and charged only $10.00 a month for dues and lost a huge sum of money until a large percentage of the homes were sold. In the seventh year of the club's operation, the dues could only be raised to $17.75 and in the four-

FIGURE 2.3 *The outdoor patio at the Hollytree Country Club, Tyler, Texas (Courtesy of Chris Consultants).*

teenth to $25.50. Between the seventh and fourteenth year the club became very profitable and saleable. It was purchased by the American Golf Corporation.
- Selling the club to the home owners in the development after the homes have all been sold. Eventually, as lots and houses are sold, the country club loses

FIGURE 2.4 *Sonterra Country Club, San Antonio, Texas (Courtesy of Chris Consultants).*

FIGURE 2.5 *Entrance to the Glen Eagles Country Club, Dallas, Texas (Courtesy of Chris Consultants.)*

most of its marketing value, becoming a significant drain on the developer's resources.
- Keeping the club and hiring a professional management company to operate it.
- Retaining ownership and operating the club themselves. Many developers have discovered this to be a very poor option as club business is completely different from real estate.

Historically, disposition of country clubs has been by sale or rent to a professional club management organization that is able to run the club at a profit. This type of disposition arrangement, however, does not maximize the developer's return on investment and may create adverse publicity for the developer. Because the management organization will usually open the club to the general public to maximize demand for club services, the exclusivity associated with the development and the club is canceled.

As a solution to their problems real estate developers are increasingly disposing of country clubs through the implementation of equity membership programs. As discussed later in the chapter, an equity conversion when handled properly is an effective marketing tool that proves beneficial to the developer as well as to the home owners in the club community.

City Clubs

City clubs are usually located in the city or in the suburbs and hold all of their activities in one building or part of a building. Some of these clubs are limited to a restaurant, bar, and cocktail lounge and only serve luncheons and cater special parties for their members. Other city clubs, such as the Press Club in Washington, the Commerce Club in Atlanta, and the New York Athletic Club in New York, are able to offer indoor swimming pools, bowling lanes, racket and handball courts, gyms and complete fitness centers, as well as other facilities. Fitness centers with state-of-the-art exercise machines and free weights have become one of the major attractions in city clubs and a principal marketing device to increase membership.

City clubs are destined to become increasingly popular as "luncheon sites" (Fig. 2.6). With traffic problems worsening daily and commuting times lengthening, more and more city workers are choosing to have lunch within walking distance of their jobs. Even the very affluent are having to forego driving to their country clubs for lunch.

FIGURE 2.6 *Mixed Grill at the Town Club of Corpus Christi, Corpus Christi, Texas (Courtesy of Chris Consultants).*

Yacht Clubs

Located on a river or body of water, yacht clubs are associations of people who own boats or love boating. Some yacht clubs only dock sailboats, others powerboats. Many clubs will accommodate both. They may also provide full marina services, such as wet and dry storage, piers, mooring buoys, gasoline and diesel fuel, oil, water, electricity, and sewage connections to holding tanks. Clubs such as the Coral Reef Yacht Club on Biscayne Bay in Miami, Florida, have, in addition to the above, full-service clubhouses and can provide luncheons, dinners, a snack bar, and a swimming pool as well as cater private parties for their members.

Rowing and Paddling Clubs

Rowing and paddling clubs are located on rivers or protected waters. Very popular, these clubs feature crafts propelled by human energy, specifically single or crew sculls and canoes. Property is usually restricted to storage space for the boats; however, some clubs have a clubhouse and a full-time manager.

Fraternal Clubs

Fraternal clubs were formed for many different purposes. Usually their objectives are charitable, such as those of the Elks Club, which raises money for local charities; the Masons, who dedicate themselves to raising money for children's hospitals; and the Lions Club, which operates an eye bank and other services for the blind and those with impaired vision. The Hibernian Club, started by Irish immigrants to the United States, is interested in improving surrounding municipalities, as are the Rotary Clubs. The Kiwanis Clubs raise money primarily for the care and safekeeping of children through sports programs and athletic activities. The American Legion and Veterans of Foreign Wars are clubs that minister to the needs of veterans of all of America's wars and their families, assuring that veterans are properly cared for in veterans' hospitals and by the United States Veterans Administration. These clubs are also instrumental in raising money for local charities.

Many fraternal clubs own or rent buildings which they use as clubhouses. Some provide services similar to those of city clubs.

Government Clubs

The United States Government operates numerous clubs, those of the Department of Defense numbering 797 in 1988, with gross annual sales of $758 million. Clubs are also operated by the Departments of the Treasury, State, the Interior, and Agriculture.

The Defense Department has authorized the Army, Navy, Air Force, and Marine

Corps to operate clubs worldwide for the officers and enlisted men and women of the Armed Forces. The Treasury Department has established 43 clubs for the Coast Guard with a total business of $75.4 million in sales annually.

Most of these clubs offer facilities resembling those of city clubs. Some, however, offer much more. For example, the Sanno in Tokyo offers, in addition to the usual amenities of a city club, hotel rooms, travel and car rental agencies, a bookstore, a barber shop, and a complete beauty salon. Other clubs feature golf courses, swimming pools, and tennis courts.

Until the end of the eighties, the majority of military clubs were segregated according to rate (enlisted men) and rank (officers). Rates and ranks have been combined with some success, however, and the nineties will see a continuation of this trend. Also, the number of civilian managers at these clubs will probably increase.

Condominium and Apartment Complex Clubs

In order to rent or sell condominium and apartment complexes, realtors have discovered that a "recreation package" is an excellent marketing tool. Such a package usually features a restaurant, a bar or cocktail lounge, swimming pools, tennis courts, television, and card and exercise rooms. Where these types of amenities are offered, professional management is required.

Condominium owners, under most state laws, must form a condominium association. They elect officers, hold regular monthly meetings, and pay a fee for the upkeep of their property's facilities.

In apartment complex dwellings the cost for the maintenance of recreational amenities is included in the rent. This concept is new but growing as demand increases for "one-stop living."

Specialty Clubs

Specialty clubs center on a single activity—for example, swimming, tennis, rowing, or riding—and require professional management. The only difference between these clubs and others is the absence of a clubhouse.

Athletic Clubs

Athletic clubs were started by persons interested primarily in indoor sports activities. Located in urban areas, the clubs' principal attractions are gyms, swimming pools, racquetball and handball courts, and exercise rooms (Fig. 2.7). Many athletic clubs, however, have all the facilities of the city clubs, and many, like the New York Athletic Club, have hotel-style rooms for their members.

FIGURE 2.7   *The Vining Athletic Club, Atlanta, Georgia (Courtesy of Chris Consultants).*

Health Clubs

Health clubs are nothing new, but from the fifties to the seventies their use was limited to the very wealthy, and most offered live-in programs for the treatment of alcoholism, drug abuse, obesity, and stress. Although this type of health club still prospers, the eighties saw a major change in the meaning of the term "health club."

Counteracting the trend toward increasingly sedentary and stressful life-styles that are the product of an efficient industrial society, health clubs have proliferated. Allowing workers to expend the physical energy they no longer use on the job, health clubs are also responding to the tremendous numbers of people, young and old, who wish to get or stay "fit." The city of Miami, Florida, alone, boasts sixty-one health clubs.

In the better clubs, the manager instructs members and directs programs as a physical fitness professional. Other clubs train personnel to use the various machines, but instructors are not expected to know anything about their effects on the human body. Unfortunately, no state or other regulations control the type of programs offered. In many clubs, a general manager oversees both the fitness and business agendas.

To remain competitive in the nineties, health clubs will begin to offer more than just exercise. The big thrust is likely to be toward the social end of the entertainment package. For example, aerobic studios will become dance halls perhaps twice a week, and snack bars will become full-service restaurants with tables and chairs.

The national leaders in voluntary physical fitness in the eighties were the United States and Japan. Fitness clubs were introduced into Japan from America and 80 percent of their equipment is American-made. The number of Japanese sports clubs dedicated to physical fitness increased from 75 in 1977 to 705 in 1987, and the growth continues. Corporations in Japan, like their American counterparts, are finding that keeping their employees fit pays dividends. In 1987 63.0 percent of Japanese health clubs were owned by corporations, 26.9 percent were privately owned, 7.1 percent were owned by business partnerships, and 3.2 percent by other business concerns.

Hotel Clubs

In the 1950s some hotels realized that right outside their doors there was a multitude of people who might like to use the hotel's amenities, including swimming pools, exercise rooms, tennis courts and, in some instances, golf courses. Other hotels decided to set aside space for a nightclub, as was done for the Haymarket Club by the Hilton Hotel in Chicago. The Waldolf Astoria in New York at one time operated three clubs within the hotel.

Hotels sometimes charge an initiation fee, but the majority only charge dues or an admission fee. In some hotels the charge for admission to the club is part of the room charge or is offered to the hotel guest at a reduced rate.

Resort Hotels and Conference Centers

The latest bloomer in the hospitality field is the resort hotels and conference centers (Fig. 2.8), which have exploited the popular trend of mixing business and pleasure. The resurgence of resort hotels is largely due to the growth of discretionary income. The resort hotel is primarily a country club with hotel rooms and facilities large enough to handle a business conference.

Corporate Clubs

Clubs owned and managed by corporations are increasing in number as more and more of America's larger companies diversify into real estate development. An example of this is Alcoa's acquisition of Johnathon's Landing Country Club in Jupiter, Florida. The club management corporations are enjoying tremendous growth, which should continue into the nineties.

FIGURE 2.8 *The Doral Country Club in Miami, Florida: one of America's luxury resort hotels, with four eighteen-hole golf courses, nineteen tennis courts, a swimming pool, and facilities for ten other sports activities (Courtesy of Ted E. White).*

CLUB MEMBERSHIP

The reasons for which club-minded persons join a particular club are many and varied. Some of these include:

- To recreate with friends.
- To maintain one's social position.
- To recreate with business associates to enhance public relations or to further one's career. The proximity of a particular club to the office is a criterion of increasing importance as traffic problems mount.
- To use the special facilities offered by the club. Prospective members are impressed by complete service clubhouses with at least a minimum of an eighteen-hole golf course, swimming pools, and tennis courts.
- To join a club whose financial condition is sound.

Membership Promotion

The membership process starts by contacting prospective members. Clubs open to the public and real estate development clubs use all types of commercial advertising, including television, newspaper ads, radio, and direct mail. Privately owned non-profit clubs, however, must take a more dignified and subtle approach.

Private clubs have found that the best source of new members is existing ones. In some clubs a bonus is given, either in cash or merchandise, to those who bring in new members. Others simply give credit for good club spirit. Another tried-and-true method to ensure membership growth in clubs whose regular membership is limited to the members' households is to extend "junior memberships" to sons or daughters who have established their own residence, whereby they lose club privileges. The way many clubs handle this is to postpone the initiation fee and reduce the annual dues until the junior member reaches a certain age (for example, thirty-five), at which time he or she must join as a regular member. In some clubs, all or a portion of the dues that have been paid are credited toward the initiation fee.

The smartly managed club guarantees future members by assuring that children of all ages have a good time at the club. Popular menu and snack bar items and diverse sports programs and clinics serve to instill into the minds of members and their children that the club is the place to have a good time.

Types of Membership

The types of membership offered in clubs depend on their ownership. Equity clubs (those owned by the members) may offer some or all of the following:

- *Founder Membership.* Founder membership designates members who have provided the funds to build or purchase the club. The number of persons holding this type of membership is limited. A certificate is issued, which is transferable with the board's permission. Founding members have full voting rights on any item concerning their club. They pay monthly or annual dues, however, which in some clubs are reduced.

- *Regular Membership.* Regular members pay an initiation fee to join the club and monthly or annual dues. They have the right to vote on all issues with the exception of items, such as the sale of the club, that will affect the founders' equity.
- *Junior Membership.* Junior membership is reserved for persons under a particular age. Eligibility is sometimes based on whether one is the child of a club member (see "Membership Promotion" above).
- *Social Membership.* Social membership restricts the number of facilities that can be used by the member, who may use only the clubhouse or everything but the golf course, for example. The initiation fee and dues are reduced accordingly.
- *Associate Membership.* Associate membership is reserved for out-of-state members who only use the club seasonally or infrequently. In some clubs both the initiation fee and the dues are reduced.
- *Absentee Membership.* Absentee status is extended to members who are going to be out of the country for a year or more, during which time dues are suspended.
- *Temporary Membership.* Temporary memberships are offered to visiting dignitaries as a courtesy; neither an initiation fee nor dues are charged. This type of membership is also used in conjunction with hotels that do not have clubs but wish to make one available to guests. For example, the Royal Sonesta Hotel in Key Biscayne, Florida, has made arrangements for their guests to use the Key Biscayne Golf Course, about 2 miles from the hotel.
- *Miscellaneous.* The modern trend in the club business is to give prospective and existing members a wide choice in the types of membership offered. "Unbundling" of services so that members pay only for those they use has lead the club to all sorts of membership permutations. For instance, one club, with a $12,000 initiation fee for a full membership, will sell a membership without golf for $6,000 and reduce the dues of $3,000 by a third. A "non-golf" member may use the course (which is not open to the public) upon payment of a guest and cart fee.
- *Reciprocity Agreements.* Agreements can be made by clubs whereby their members share privileges with members of clubs in other cities, not only in the United States but in foreign countries. This gives members the opportunity to use other clubs while traveling. One Miami club has such a reciprocity agreement with a club in England and a club in New York. Reciprocity also allows members the use of another club when theirs must be closed for a considerable length of time, either to give the staff a vacation (many clubs close down for a month in the fall to do this) or in case of a disaster such as a fire.
- *Terminated Membership.* A club's bylaws usually cover the procedures to follow when a member resigns or dies. Resignations are always accepted with regrets in a letter from the board. If the resigning member is a founder, the bylaws stipulate the disposition of his or her founding certificate. Some clubs will buy back the certificate at a percentage of its cost. In others the certificate must be returned to the club, which will put it up for sale.

In the event of the death of a member, most clubs allow the surviving spouse, if one exists, to retain the membership at his or her discretion. In many private clubs where a founder's fee has been paid and there is no buy-back policy, an attempt will be made to sell the founder's certificate if requested.

New Memberships

The first step in joining a club is to fill out an application for membership. Prospective members may apply directly to the club or have a friend or acquaintance who is a member sponsor them. In the latter case, it is the sponsor's responsibility to acquire the necessary papers from the club and assist the applicant in preparing them. In most clubs the membership application (Fig. 2.9) requires that the original sponsor sign the application and attest to the character of the applicant. The completed application is then submitted to the club office and held there until it is reviewed by the membership committee. A letter to the applicant should acknowledge receipt of the application and indicate that it is being forwarded to the membership committee for action.

In many clubs, if there are numerous applications for membership, a letter is sent out to the general membership listing recent candidates and requesting comments both for and against their admission to the club. The reasons a member might give in objecting to an applicant might include personal dislike, religious affiliation, national origin, bad reputation in the community, or competition in business. However useful members' comments may be, the committee's actions must ultimately be governed by the bylaws of the club. Dissenting members may be requested to appear before the committee to assist them in their decision.

Clubs in England use the "black ball" system to indicate whether a candidate is acceptable. Every member is given two balls, one white and one black, to be used in a secret ballot. Every member votes once, placing the white ball in a basket to indicate approval, or the black in the basket to refuse the candidate. One black ball in the basket suffices to deny a candidate membership. In many clubs, sponsors of persons refused admittance to the club are forced to resign because of the poor judgment shown in proposing their candidates. Unlike their English cousins, most clubs in the United States give their membership committees much broader powers and, despite the disagreement of even several members, may admit a candidate.

EQUITY CLUBS

The term "equity" is used to designate clubs owned by the members. Equity clubs are usually established as "nonprofit" corporations so that no federal income tax need be paid. These types of clubs are true examples of the democratic process since all members vote on all rules and procedures applicable to the operation of the club. As noted in "Types of Membership," members who provide the funds to establish or purchase the club are called "founder" members. Usually the founders will establish other types of membership, some of which have voting privileges. In most clubs, regular members and, in some cases, one junior member, may serve on the board.

HEAVENLY HILLS COUNTRY CLUB

MEMBERSHIP APPLICATION

Date _____

Name _____ Spouse's Name _____

Address _____

_____

Telephone Number: Home _____ Business _____

Name/Names of children under 21 years of age and living at home _____

_____

Occupation _____

Type of membership desired: Full __ Golf __ Tennis __ Pool __

See enclosed sheet for fees and dues.

NOTE: Each sports membership carries clubhouse privileges.

Sponsored by _____

Endorsed by 1. _____

2. _____

3. _____

MEMBERSHIP COMMITTEE

Date _____

Approved __ Returned to Sponsor _____

Chairperson _____

FIGURE 2.9 *Membership application.*

As noted earlier in the chapter, equity clubs are often formed when real estate developers divest themselves of a country club, selling it to home owners in a development through equity conversion programs.

In an equity membership program, a separate nonprofit corporation is formed to sell memberships within a housing development. The proceeds from the sale of the memberships are used by the club to purchase the country club's assets. Through a properly structured equity membership plan, a developer is able to retain control of the club until most of the residential lots are sold. This assures that the club's operation and marketing value will not be adversely affected before completion of its sale.

Through equity membership conversion developers are usually able to at least double their financial investment in a club's assets while profiting from the enhanced marketability of the residential real estate. An equity membership plan may also increase both the value of the surrounding product being sold (i.e., the residential property) and the rate of absorption of the product.

An equity membership plan involves significant accounting and consulting services. The plan should include a review of financial projections to demonstrate that the club can operate with dues kept at a reasonable level. The plan should also set limits on the initial membership fee charged by the club. Comparison with other equity clubs will assist financial analysis, which should include inspection of the developer's federal and state income tax status.

Many equity clubs use a tiered membership program. Under this program a person desiring membership chooses from one of the available categories of membership and pays a membership fee accordingly. Tiered membership works well when the number of memberships available equals the number of homes in the development and the number of memberships does not exceed the perceived maximum capacity of the facilities (i.e., 400 golf members or less per eighteen-hole golf course and thirty members or less per each tennis court). When this perfect ratio cannot be met, a unitary membership plan may be desirable. In this plan everyone acquires the same interest in the club by paying the current membership fee and selecting each year from a club facilities menu of annual memberships. No limits are placed on any membership category, so that an annual dues–paying member in any one of them (i.e., a tennis membership) can hold an annual membership in any other category (i.e., golf).

An equity club conversion may be implemented at three different points in the evolution of a residential development: its inception ("up front"), after the sale of a portion of the residential units ("midterm"), or at a point near or after the completion of the project ("tail end").

If any membership conversion is implemented at any point other than at the inception of the development, a developer is subject to promises made with respect to the operation of the country club. Additionally, after inception the larger the number of homeowners within the development and the greater the number of members of the club, the greater the leverage they will have against the developer. Therefore, the earlier the developer starts the equity membership conversion program the easier the conversion will be. Also, the longer the developer waits, the fewer proceeds he or she can expect from the sale of the country club, as facilities depreciate in value over time. At whatever time it is implemented, however, an equity membership conversion is the most profitable and beneficial means whereby developers may divest themselves of club assets, guaranteeing a more substantial financial return over any other divestment method.

The Board of Directors/Governors

Private clubs are run by a board of directors or governors, which makes club policies and which has complete authority over club operations (see Fig. 2.10). The club's governing body (hereinafter referred to simply as "the board") is democratically elected in one of two ways. The membership may elect the board (filling its vacancies) and the board in turn elects the club officers from their group, or else a slate of

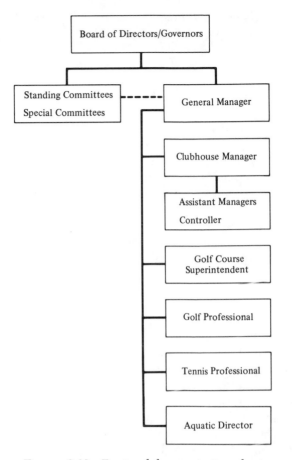

FIGURE 2.10 *Equity club organization chart.*

officers and directors/governors may be filled upon election among themselves. For example, a club's bylaws may call for a president, one or more vice presidents, a treasurer, a secretary, and a sergeant-at-arms. These officers may be elected by the members or elected among themselves.

The usual term of office is 2 years. In a new club half of the group would be elected for 1 year, the other half for 2 years, so that new faces and ideas are brought to the club without losing continuity in policy making. The board should be composed of an odd number of persons, which guarantees a majority. The duties of the board and the officers are spelled out in the bylaws of the club (see Appendix 1).

The board's responsibilities are many and varied and include all of the following:

1. The broad policies under which the club will operate.
2. The financial stability of the club. The board will usually meet once a month to review the financial statement and to check whether or not the club is operating within the established budget. If the approved budget is not being followed, it is the board's responsibility to take appropriate action.

3. The qualifications for membership. The board establishes guidelines under which applicants are admitted to membership.
4. The initiation fee and the dues members will pay.
5. Appointment of all of the club's committees.
6. Hiring of the general manager and sometimes the clubhouse manager as well as the various professionals such as the golf and tennis pros. The board appoints a search-and-screen committee to fill the positions they need. The committee may advertise positions through the local chapter of the CMAA or other sources and present the three or four best-qualified candidates to the board for their final selection. It is customary for the club to pay the travel expenses of the candidates they interview. The newest management concept is to hire a general manager who will then assist in hiring the various department heads such as the clubhouse manager; the golf, tennis, and aquatic (swimming pool management) professionals; and the controller (office manager). The old-fashioned way was to hire a club manager and department heads all at once and hope they could get along with each other.

Club Officers

The office of president of the club is its highest position and an honor not to be bestowed lightly. Sometimes this office, and others, are filled by persons who are popular rather than competent. Some clubs have an unwritten policy that the officers succeed to the top office in an unbroken chain. When there is more than one vice president, precedence is established by numbering them first, second, third, and so forth.

The treasurer needs some knowledge of accounting and finance, as the member in this position oversees the fiscal affairs of the club and provides advice and guidance to management on these matters.

The secretary will record, or have recorded, the minutes of all official meetings, prepare all confidential correspondence of the board, and be responsible for preserving all the records of the board.

The sergeant-at-arms will be the club's parliamentarian and be available at all meetings to assist the presiding officer, as necessary, in correct parliamentary procedure.

The Board and Management

It is the board's responsibility to make the policies and the management's responsibility to carry them out: Realization of this basic principle requires that the manager establish positive communication with the board and its individual members. Many problems between the board and management can be traced to a lack of communication. To communicate effectively management must acquaint itself with board members' interests, concerns, and anxieties. Without this understanding viable working relationships cannot be formed. For example, one board member may be very interested in the food department, another in the fitness programs. Management can use this knowledge when problems in the separate divisions arise.

The importance of the board and the committees to the club cannot be over-emphasized, as they can be "sounding boards" for ideas to improve its operation. It may be helpful to management to understand why the various board and committee members wished to volunteer as policy makers for the club. Their reasons might be among the following:

1. They enjoy sharing the "prestige" of being part of the policy team shaping the club's future.
2. They feel that the association with the top people in the club will perhaps add to their social standing.
3. They would like to be instrumental in maintaining a fine club. Universally, members concur that the finest include:

   • Top-quality membership.
   • First-class facilities, well maintained.
   • Personal recognition by all of the staff.
   • A limited number of members.

Aware of these concerns, however, management must also judge whether expectations are always realistic, based on budgetary requirements. For instance, it might be highly desirable to limit the membership from the point of view of their convenience in having facilities readily available. New members, however, bring in monies that may be necessary to maintain grounds and services.

Following are some additional ways that management can win the trust, respect, and confidence of the board.

• Get to know each board and committee member personally, if possible, developing a relationship whereby top-level officers can be approached with ease, yet with the respect and demeanor appropriate to their status.
• Ask for comments, constructive criticism, and advice. Point out management problems as they occur and explain how they will be handled.
• Do not give preferential treatment to any board or committee members. Remember, there will probably be new members next year.
• Never make promises that you are not absolutely positive can be kept; do not be intimidated by the board or the committees—learn to say "no" when necessary; and always remember that management is ultimately responsible for the day-to-day operation of the club. For example, if the board complains about poor service and this is caused by lack of personnel, recommend additional staff. Back the recommendation with a cost estimate and an opinion as to whether or not the existing budget can absorb it.

It is customary for the general manager to attend all of the board meetings which, except in emergencies, usually take place once a month. The agenda for each meeting is drawn up by the secretary. The general manager is consulted to ascertain if there are any items he or she wishes to discuss with the board. Each member of the board and the general manager are given copies of the agenda which usually gives an update on the overall state of the club and club business and indicates the date, time, and place for the meeting. The monthly financial statement is available for the members at the meeting, but it is a good idea for the general manager to prepare a digest, or summary, of the statement to present to the board upon which recommendations can be made. In the event there is no general manager, the clubhouse manager should present the digest, as the accounting department will be under his or her control.

The manager must also keep the board informed as to current trends in the industry. These are detailed in Chapter 3.

Equity Club Committees

A committee is a group of members who volunteer to serve in providing advice and guidance to the board on various aspects of the club's business.

The committees in equity clubs are very powerful; usually their recommendations are accepted by the board. The committees work with the general manager to carry out the policies and rules established by the board. Many clubs have some of the more important committees chaired by a member of the board. Committee size is determined by the board, who generally fix an uneven number so there will almost always be a majority vote (except in the case of abstaining members). Committees are formed by volunteers with an interest in the principal concern of the committee; for example, golfers place themselves on the golf committee.

The committee system works best when the members concentrate on fine-tuning the policies of the club with the general manager or on making policies relevant to their specific concern. For example, the house committee might establish the dress code for the clubhouse. Committees must work with management but not interfere in its functions. A smooth-running organization requires that the general manager have complete control of day-to-day operations.

There are two types of committees: (1) the standing committees, which are permanent and (2) the special committees, sometimes called "one-time" or "ad hoc," which are formed to assist in special events. For example, if a gala is being planned to celebrate a club's anniversary, a special committee could be designated by the board for this event. When the affair is over, the committee would be disbanded with a letter of thanks from the board.

There are usually five or more standing committees depending on the number of club activities and, whenever possible, these are chaired by a member of the board. These include the membership, finance and budget, house, entertainment, and athletic committees. Other committees, such as those for golf, tennis, bowling, skeet and rifle, fencing, chess, and bridge, elect their own leaders.

The following broad rules can serve as a guide to effective formation:

1. Membership is limited. Three is an ideal number with one member acting as chairperson. An old axiom states that "If you wish to delay action on an item,

refer it to a large committee." Unfortunately, club committees are considered prestigious and the chairperson usually equates the importance of the committee with its size.

2. Committees set policy only, according to guidelines set forth in the club's bylaws. Committee members should address management on specific issues, at no time being allowed to supervise staff.
3. Committees are encouraged to seek advice and guidance from the manager.
4. The board understands the meaning of "standing" and "special" committees. The standing or permanent committees are usually determined by the size and principle activities of the club.
5. Committees perform best when a policy has been established to determine who makes the final decision in a disagreement—the president, the board, or the full membership.
6. The manager works with the committees but only receives advice and guidance at committee meetings. This gives the manager the options and freedom of action that is needed.
7. The club may purchase a supply of "So You're On A Committee" and distribute this set of principles to each new committee member. These are published by CMAA and can be obtained by writing to: the Club Managers Association of America, 1733 King Street, Alexandria, Virginia 22314.

The Membership Committee

The Membership Committee controls membership and interprets the bylaws. Its specific duties include:

- Reviewing applications for membership and evaluating the qualifications of the applicants.
- Judging the moral and ethical conduct of the members and supporting management in maintaining the decorum of the membership. Problems frequently dealt with are abuse and harrassment of the employees, theft, drunkenness, and past-due bills. Members of this committee have the authority to recommend disciplinary action against club members for misconduct and to cancel their membership. In some clubs this committee has the authority to take independent action when it is deemed necessary.

The Finance and Budget Committee

The Finance and Budget Committee supervises the club's financial strategies and strives to make them financially sound. Its duties are as follows:

1. To recommend to the board the initiation fee and the dues structure for the club.
2. To recommend to the board the amount and timing of member assessments as these become necessary because of financial difficulties or special projects.
3. To provide advice and guidance to management and the controller on financial matters.

4. To assist departments in the preparation of their annual budgets and to review them for recommendation to the board.
5. To analyze the monthly financial statement and to review it with the management and the controller before its presentation to the board.
6. To set a limit on expenditures by the management and the individual departments. Usually a dollar limit will be placed on single expenditures even when the total is below the budget limit.

The House Committee

The House Committee is sometimes called the "Clubhouse Committee." In many clubs this committee is simply charged with maintenance of the clubhouse building; in others its responsibilities include clubhouse food and beverage operations. In a multifaceted role the committee would also be responsible for the following:

1. Maintaining the physical plant. The committee would work with management to see that the facility was kept clean, all its equipment kept in operating order, and all minor and major repairs were attended to promptly.
2. Consulting with management on the hours of operation of the clubhouse.
3. Consulting with management on menus, beverage and wine lists and on the selling prices.
4. Assisting management in preparing the annual budget and the 1-year and long-range capital improvement budgets.

The Entertainment Committee

The Entertainment Committee is responsible for the entertainment policy of the club. Aware of what the membership will enjoy, the committee assists management in making appropriate selections by serving as a panel of critics. In some clubs the Entertainment Committee also is responsible for sports events or assists the Sports Committee with tournaments and other special sports activities.

The committee also works with the manager in preparing the annual budget.

Athletic Committees

Athletic Committees establish and recommend to the board operational policies applying to their particular sports. The Golf Committee, for example, oversees the golf course, the locker rooms, and golf-related activities. In particular, Athletic Committees:

1. Establish the rules and regulations for their sport.
2. Work with professionals, the golf superintendent, and management in preparing the annual budget.
3. Assist in the operation and planning of tournaments and observe the conduct of the players.
4. Develop sports programs with management and the pros.
5. With the pros, control starting times on the golf course and the use of tennis courts and the pool, and set the hours of operation.

A large club may appoint committees for sports as diverse as cycling, racquetball, horseback riding, polo, bowling, track and field, and yacht racing. Each committee will have its own operating rules and regulations, incorporated in the club's bylaws.

Special Committees

As noted previously, special committees are appointed by the board for specific purposes such as assisting management in hosting parties, sponsoring big tournaments, and decorating the club for holidays. Although used in every type of club, these committees are hard to control because of the fine line that exists between policy makers and management. (For example, it takes a very strong manager to tell the chairperson of the "Mothers Day Special Committee" that it might have seemed like a good idea but the waiters cannot be ordered to dance with the unescorted mothers.) Special committees are disbanded by the board when their task is completed, usually with a letter of thanks.

EQUITY CLUB OFFSHOOTS

Yacht, Rowing, and Paddle Clubs

Yacht, rowing, and paddle clubs have the same organizational structure (if member-owned) as other equity clubs with the exception that the title of commodore is sometimes substituted for that of president to designate the top executive.

Corporate-owned Clubs

Clubs owned by a corporation not in the club management business are operated as a subdivision of a department, sometimes out of the controller's office (Fig. 2.11). Corporation clubs, like the Jonathan's Landing Club in Jupiter, Florida (owned by the ALCOA Corporation), will hire an accounting firm specializing in the club field to do the search and screen for management personnel or they will do it themselves. They will usually hire a general manager and allow this person to nominate the department heads subject to their final approval. The general manager operates the club under the policies established by the corporation.

The manager is usually directed to encourage club members to establish committees for the more important operations such as the golf, tennis, and clubhouse facilities. These committees have no power or authority but can make recommendations to the general manager or to the company for the company's review. The general manager is usually given the authority to operate the club, accept new members, purchase items for the club within certain dollar limits, and hire and fire personnel.

Fraternal Clubs

Fraternal clubs are part of a national chain of clubs controlled by a central headquarters. Each is chartered for a specific community purpose. Their charities range from the support of children's hospitals to orphanages, from assistance to the blind to the care of the aged. They operate like equity clubs with similar boards and committees but their management structure is determined by their charter. Clubs affluent enough to have a clubhouse will have a full-time manager.

FIGURE 2.11 *Corporate club organization chart.*

Military Clubs

Each branch of the Department of Defense (the Army, Navy, Marines, and Air Force) has a major command—called the Morale and Welfare Department or Recreation Management—that controls the overall policies of military club operation. These commands have established:

- A uniform system of accounts and obligatory accounting system
- Control over expenditures for capital improvements

- Operations manuals
- Personnel policies, which cover hiring and firing of personnel (not selection), salaries, and fringe benefits
- Audits and inspections
- Management consultant services as needed or when desired
- Three schools, one at Lackland Air Force Base in Texas, for the Air Force, one at Fort Benjamin Harrision in Indiana for the Army, and one at the Naval Air Test Center in Maryland, for the Navy, Marines, and Coast Guard

In every military club, an advisory group makes recommendations to the club's commanding officer, who establishes policy and operational procedures for the club. The Commanding Officer at each base, fort, center, station, or field may select any civilian personnel he or she chooses subject to only one rule, which states that if the position is a Civil Service one (salary paid with appropriated funds and tax dollars), then the person selected must be on the Civil Service Register.

Within the United States, military clubs are divided, for funding purposes, into two categories: clubs for officers and those for enlisted personnel. Because of budgetary constraints, more and more clubs are paying their staffs with club funds (called nonappropriated funds). Many clubs are still being supported by the placing of military personnel in key positions but this practice is frowned upon by the Congress and is definitely on the way out. Clubs outside the United States get almost unlimited support.

As for support, military clubs receive their building, equipment, the grounds, and some maintenance, paying no federal or state taxes, and in some states no alcoholic beverage or sales taxes. Within the United States all clubs get free use of water, trash and garbage disposal, sewage disposal, and some grounds maintenance. Only the enlisted clubs get gas and electricity from operating funds available to the establishment.

Officers' clubs may charge monthly dues in addition to receiving financial support, as do all military clubs, from their special services branch, the exchanges (military retail stores), and their headquarter commands. All clubs may purchase their supplies from commissary stores (military supermarkets) and the commissary and supply departments.

The Army and the Navy actively recruit at a number of colleges and universities for management trainees to fill both Government Civil Service (GS) and Nonappropriated Funded (NAF) positions. These positions are graded and salaried according to their responsibilities, and offer fringe benefits along with a generous retirement system. The NAF system gives its employees one additional benefit, disability insurance, to protect them from non-job-connected injuries or illnesses.

The Navy also runs a summer internship program for college and university juniors which offers outstanding pay and practical experience.

CLUB MANAGEMENT COMPANIES

As mentioned in the previous chapter, the two leading corporations engaged in owning and managing clubs are Club Corporation of America, Inc. (CCA), and American Golf, Inc. (AGI).

CCA, based in Dallas, Texas, with over 200 clubs worldwide in 1989, has divided the United States into five districts with a complete corporate setup in each. The district offices are each headed by an executive vice president, who reports directly to the president of CCA. Under the vice president are three to four regional managers (depending on the size of the region), a marketing director with two assistants, two contract designers (to discover and evaluate new properties), a food and beverage director, a controller, a service director, an executive chef, a human resources director, and an administration director. Regional managers are responsible for the clubs in their regions and have the general managers of these clubs report to them. In addition each regional manager supervises five management trainees for manager and general manager positions. General managers exercise enormous authority in running their clubs, which operate at a profit. The clubs are usually completely computerized and their functions are centralized at the district headquarters.

AGI is the world's leader in public golf course management, with well over 125 golf courses in 1989. Based in Santa Monica, California, AGI operates all over the United States. The corporation has been remarkably successful in improving the quality of the courses they manage and in saving tax dollars. For example, in managing seven golf courses for New York City they changed a $200,000 annual loss into a $175,000 profit for the city in just 2 years. Their success is primarily due to their dedicated professional personnel and to their management structure and expertise.

The AGI is structured as follows.

- *Construction Department.* The construction department supervises all design, construction, and renovation of new facilities and the renovation of existing buildings. The staff has extensive experience in landfill construction and drainage reconstruction. Constructing permanent buildings and courses on land that is filled requires the utmost engineering knowledge and experience. Also, proper drainage is a major golf course construction problem.
- *Agronomy Division.* The in-house agronomy expert supervises and advises golf superintendents nationwide in the proper care of turf and trees.
- *Training Department.* The training department ensures that all new employees are intensely trained in AGI procedures, policies, and philosophy.
- *Marketing Department.* All corporate marketing, advertising, promotion, and public relations are directed by the marketing department. It also supervises pro shop merchandise coordination and provides centralized purchasing when it is economical to do so.

Health Clubs

Corporate Health Clubs

The hundreds of corporations who run health clubs have as their objective the health and well-being of their employees. The cost of outfitting a section of the office building or factory and hiring a professional physical fitness director (PFD) and staff is more than offset by the gain in man-hours previously lost to employee illness.

Corporations both large and small have found that organized company fitness programs pay off in healthy employees and noticeably increased production.

To start a program, the company will take a poll of its employees to ascertain their interest and find out when they would be most likely to use the club. Operating hours usually set by the corporation include 2 hours before work, the lunch period, and 4 hours after work. The organizational structures of corporations differ, but many run the club through their human resources or administrative departments.

As soon as a health club is decided upon, a PFD is hired. The duties of the PFD are as follows:

1. Plans the space and the equipment needed based on their availability and the employee poll
2. Works with the design department in preparing plans to renovate the approved space
3. Works with the maintenance and purchasing departments in carrying out the renovation and in purchasing the exercise equipment
4. Writes job descriptions for one or two assistants, as necessary, and for an aerobic dance instructor, charging the human resources department to do the necessary search and screening of them
5. Hires and trains the employees
6. Makes sure the club carries proper insurance
7. Is responsible for the day-to-day operation of the club
8. Is available to demonstrate the club's equipment and to establish appropriate exercise programs for persons who desire them

The Chain Health Clubs

The chain health clubs are divided into two categories, those operated directly by the corporation and those to which the corporation has sold franchises. The big companies, Bally and Vic Tanny, operate franchises from a central headquarters using on-site managers and staff. In the Scandinavian Health Clubs, owned by Bally, in addition to the manager, there are aerobic instructors, physical fitness experts, and a clerical and sales force.

REVIEW QUESTIONS

1. What effect has real estate development had on the club business?
2. Why is a country club so important to a real estate developer?
3. Define what is meant by an "equity" club.
4. Name the various types of membership that an equity club may offer. Describe in detail their differences.
5. What is the meaning of the word "unbundling" as applied to club membership?
6. Describe the membership application process in equity clubs.
7. What are some of the methods management can use to further its relationship with the board of directors?

8. How has the management structure of the American Golf Corporation contributed to its success?
9. What is meant by a real estate developer's "equity conversion"?
10. Describe the different kinds of health clubs and explain why they have become so popular.

CASE STUDY 1

The Entertainment Committee at the Frozen Lake Country Club planned a special party to celebrate the club's anniversary. During the preparation of the annual budget, the board authorized $2,000 as the club's share of the expenses. The members were to pay $25 per person, which included dinner, drinks, entertainment, and dancing. The budget called for this party, with the $2,000 subsidy, to break even. The manager left every detail of the party except food and beverages in the hands of the entertainment committee, including the decoration of the club, the band, and the entertainment. The manager planned and served a dinner and provided an open bar within the budgeted allowance of $25 per attendee.

However, the party cost the club $3,500, $1,500 over budget. The board blamed the committee. The committee blamed the manager. . . .

What actions can the board take (1) to find where the fault lay and (2) to prevent a recurrence of such financial mismanagement in the future?

CASE STUDY 2

The Heavenly Hills Country Club was having financial difficulties. This is an equity club owned completely by the members. They had limited the membership to 400 so that their eighteen-hole golf course would not become too crowded. The original initiation fees were used to start the club. The mortgage and operating expenses exceed the dues, fees, and income from sales by $1,000 each month.

The members have the following options:

1. Raise the dues. There might be a problem as the dues are paid annually and the year is half over.
2. Unbundle the club and sell golf, swimming pool, tennis, and clubhouse memberships.
3. Have a membership assessment on each member to carry the club through the rest of the year so that a further study can be made.
4. Raise prices.
5. Hire a management company to take over the club.

Consider each option and decide the effect of each option on the membership.

3 The Role of the Club Manager

THE GENERAL MANAGER

"General manager" is finally being accepted by most club executives as the proper title for the person in charge of day-to-day operations of a club. Other titles are used, such as "director of club operations," "executive director," and "chief operating executive," but they all mean only one thing—supreme command.

First and foremost, managers must be answerable to a code of ethics and standards of conduct, which can be summed up as follows:

- They shall be judicious in their relationship with members. By their demeanor and behavior toward club members, they set an example for their employees.
- They shall become as active as possible in local community affairs.
- They shall participate in local and national associations that may assist them in their work.
- They must be above reproach. There can be no half measures of integrity in their obligations to their club, their members, their employees, and in their dealings with their purveyors. Honesty in all transactions is a basic requisite. They may not accept subsidies of any kind.
- They must not be deterred from speaking out if they observe any action that may be detrimental to the club.

Duties and Responsibilities

One of the first duties of the manager is to organize the club into operating departments or, if these have already been set up, to analyze their relative effectiveness. Each department will have a supervisor, as follows:

Department	Supervisor
Food production	Chef
Alcoholic beverages	Head Bartender
The dining room	Maitre d', Hostess, or (occasionally) Assistant Manager
Office management	Controller
Golf course operation	Golf Professional
Golf course maintenance	Golf Superintendent
Tennis	Tennis Professional
Pools and water sports	Aquatic Director

The general manager runs the separate departments of the club by means of supervisors who are responsible for the efficient conduct of their departments. The manager organizes his or her organization chart, if possible, so that no more than five persons report directly to him. The other supervisors would report to the assistant manager (see Fig. 3.1). The general manager's duties and responsibilities include:

- Supervise the day-to-day operation of the club.
- Control the hiring, promotion, and termination of the club's employees.
- Assign the duties, through job descriptions, of the manager, assistant managers, the professionals, department heads, supervisors, and all other employees.
- Be responsible for the safety of all employees and their safe working conditions.
- Be responsible for developing a fringe benefit package for the employees which is presented to the board. Study any existing fringe benefit program to be sure it is cost-effective.
- Be responsible for developing in-house training and career development programs.
- Be responsible for all the cash, inventory, physical property, and records of the club and for their safekeeping.
- Sign checks and all financial documents.
- Prepare the necessary budgets.

For specific details of departmental management, see Chapter 4.

Management Resources

Intelligence and Experience

The intelligence and experience of club managers is tested constantly in the day-to-day operation of the club. They need imagination, patience, and intuition to deal with the problems they encounter. The club business is composed of a thousand and one details which must be addressed and handled in an appropriate and timely fashion. For example, the desk reports that a female member of the club has snagged her hose on one of the dining room chairs. The manager apologizes to her for the mishap and has the chair replaced immediately, but the member is upset and does not seem to enjoy her luncheon. The manager could purchase a $5 gift certificate from a local store and enclose it in a letter to the member with his or her own personal apologies, also assuring the member that the particular chair was being fixed and that all chairs and table legs would be inspected. The manager would then see that this was done.

People
The club business is a "people business"; the people with whom management has daily contact are a resource that, if not handled properly, can easily become management's biggest problem. These people include the board; the committees; the club members; the employees; the purveyors; the delivery men and women; the local, state, and federal inspectors; outside auditors; and contacts in the local community. In addition, managers may be required for business and public relations purposes to join local and national organizations. As discussed in Chapter 2, the relationship with the board and the club committees is especially complex.

Property
Club property is an important resource and must be properly maintained. The upkeep of the golf course, to many members the most important property the club has (it may have been the only reason why they joined), requires an enormous amount of expertise on the part of management and a very close relationship with the golf superintendent (the title for the person in charge of golf course maintenance). Property resources also include other athletic facilities and the clubhouse. Usually managers and supervisors will communicate frequently with the janitorial supervisor so that management will be advised immediately of any problems that constitute potential danger to persons and/or damage to the property. Broken handrails and torn carpets, for example, should be repaired immediately.

Equipment, Furnishings, and Inventory
Equipment, furnishings, and inventory used by management represent a large investment. Equipment includes golf course machinery, kitchen equipment, golf carts, office machines, and any automobiles or trucks. Management must work closely with appropriate personnel to provide machinery and rolling stock for the various club departments and facilities.

Furnishings include all the furniture, drapes, pictures, displays, wall coverings, carpets, and any other decorative items. To use and protect this resource, management must prepare maintenance schedules and see they are adhered to. These schedules should address the polishing of furniture, cleaning of draperies, dusting of pictures and displays, washing and wiping of wall coverings, washing of windows and doors, and shampooing of carpets.

The inventories the manager has to work with are valuable and must be protected by various control systems. These inventories include food and beverages; china, glassware, silverware, and linen; materials in the pro shops; and the club's paper goods and supplies.

Time
Club managers, as much or more than other managers in the hospitality business, need time to think and plan. They gain time through organization and delegation of

COUNTRY CLUBS OF THE SOUTHWEST, INC.

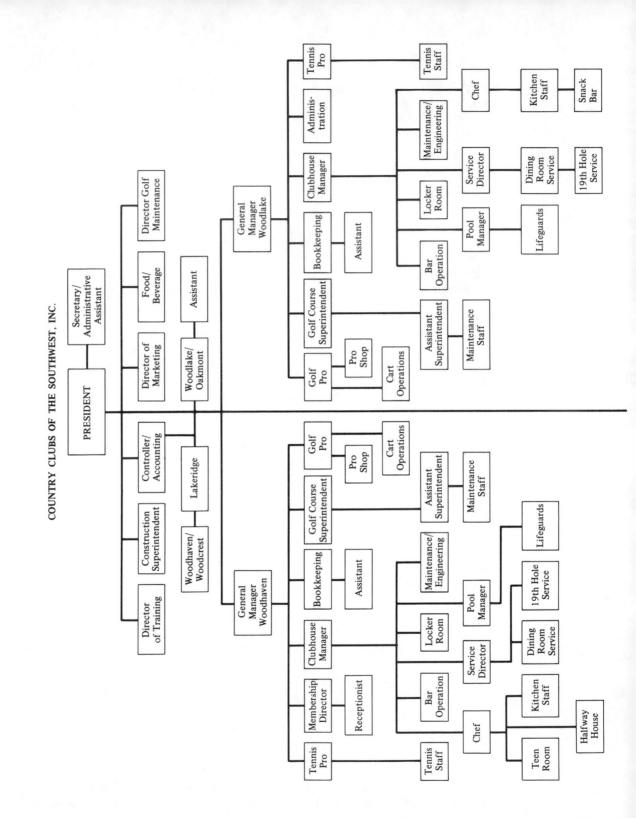

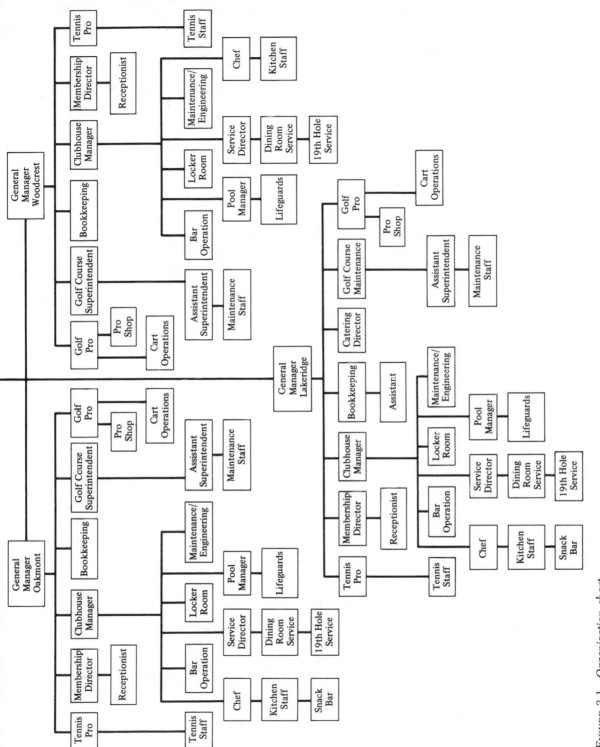

FIGURE 3.1   *Organization chart.*

authority. The time available is in direct proportion to the number of departments they must oversee: many departments, less time; fewer departments, more time.

Delegation of authority is based on the sound management principle that responsibility and authority are inseparable. However difficult, it is both necessary and advantageous. The reasons for this include:

- It gains managers valuable time.
- Managers owe it to themselves and their club. It is a form of insurance that the club will run more smoothly and efficiently by not having "all its management eggs in one basket."
- It gives managers peace of mind to know that if they should be absent from the club for any reason the members' needs will be satisfied.
- Delegation of authority builds the manager's image as a leader. Managers owe it to their subordinates to delegate. The latter must have an opportunity to exercise authority and manage directly.
- The manager can never hope to be promoted to the position of general manager in a privately owned club or to that of a district or regional manager in a commercial club unless some subordinate has had some experience in management.

The reasons for which some managers will not delegate authority are primarily based on personal insecurity. (Clubs are plagued with management insecurity, and one of the purposes of this text is to overcome this.) Many managers think that delegation of authority:

- Erodes their position
- Will show up their weaknesses if the subordinate does a better job than they
- Exposes poor management methods

In summary, managers fear competition—needlessly and counterproductively. The competence of every employee is a direct compliment to the manager's ability. Managers should praise their employees to the members and subtly take credit for their training.

In spite of all the reasons to delegate authority, many managers still may not be convinced that delegation is a good idea. The negative effects of this administrative lapse are:

- It puts the supervisors in an awkward position to have to consult the manager before making a decision. Also, they cannot gain the respect of their employees if they cannot supervise them directly.
- It undermines supervisors' morale.
- It could keep the manager from getting promoted.
- It creates jealousy and mistrust among the staff.
- It could indicate to supervisors and staff that management does not trust them. This lack of confidence can be contagious, eroding workers' performance.

Clearly, trust and confidence must be promoted. The steps to take to successfully delegate authority to subordinates are as follows:

1. Select the jobs that can be delegated and prepare them for turnover. For example, a manager who attended every standing committee meeting whether or not it interfered with more important duties finally delegated this duty to the assistant manager and only attended the meetings when it was convenient. The manager then explained to each chairperson that he/she was training the assistant manager and any time the committee wished to have him/her in attendance he/she would be available.
2. Pick the proper person for each job. Some jobs may go to the department heads, others to the supervisors. In one club the manager supervised the cleaning of the offices, thinking it necessary because of the confidentiality of some of the material there. Eventually the job was delegated to the controller, who had always thought the manager was usurping one of his duties and who was pleased to be put in charge.
3. Prepare and motivate personnel for the new assignment. Delegate work as a means of recognizing outstanding performance.
4. Turn over the task regularly, making sure that its scope and details are understood.
5. Encourage independence. However, final responsibility cannot be delegated: the manager remains ultimately responsible for everything that happens in the club.

Money

Money is essential to operation of the club and a vital resource to the manager. Working together, the board and management can increase "cash flow." For instance, many clubs have changed from monthly to annual dues, which of course gives the club the dues in advance but also allows it to invest a large portion of the money in short-term securities, such as 6-month bank certificates of deposit.

Another way to ensure cash flow is to have a strong policy on payment of monthly charges. Most clubs will suspend charge privileges after a member's account is 90 days past due, but some have dropped this back to 60. Also, managers can consider taking as much as a 5 percent discount for paying invoices within 10 days of receipt of goods or services.

Management Goals

Courtesy, Attention, and Service

When employees greet clientele by name, the people know they are in a very special place. In the club business, normal business courtesy is different from that of public establishments in that club members not only wish to be recognized by the management and the club's employees, but believe they should be. It is the duty of the club manager to assist supervisors and staff in accomplishing this task. The first step for all employees is to be able to recognize the club officers and gradually the members. This is a slow process, but remembering names is habit-forming. The more names an employee learns the easier it becomes. Here are some helpful tips for management:

- Post pictures of the officers with their names and titles on the employees' bulletin board. Eventually the manager, supervisors, and even observant employees can point out the members they know.
- Thank the member by name after the server picks up the signed guest check. Most equity clubs have in-house charging so that the member's name and club number are on the check.

    In military clubs, officer members should be addressed by their rank. Charts can be posted on the employees' bulletin board to make recognition of ranks easy. In civilian clubs, usually the only titles used are "Reverend" and "Doctor." Other members are addressed by "Mister" or "Ms." and their last name. Responses to them should be followed by "Sir" or "Ma'am."

Club employees must give their undivided attention to the members, even interrupting their duties to handle a request or problem. All employees should also be able to assist members with routine concerns. For example, janitors should know where the various segments of the club are and, in particular, where to find the club bulletin board giving detailed information such as dining room hours.

Attention to members in the dining room and cocktail lounge is especially important. Members should be greeted by name, if possible, and escorted to their tables. The maitre d' or hostess should provide the members with menus and the name of the server who will wait on them. Then the server for that table should establish eye contact with them as soon as possible, even if busy at another table. Once again, greeting by name is so important. If an order cannot be taken immediately, servers should tell members when they will be with them.

What results from the application of the principles of recognition and attention to members is *service*. An essential ingredient of service, and the most important to keep in mind, is cheerfulness. It is contagious and is bound to rub off on the members.

Finance

With the help of the manager and the finance committee, the board establishes the financial goals for the club, allocating the use of the various types of funds available. For example, the first of these are the founders' fees, used to purchase or build the club. If there is a mortgage on the club's property, this can be treated as a monthly expense. In some equity clubs, initiation fees are used to reduce the mortgage, or the money goes into a reserve for improvements and betterments. If these funds have to be used as income to meet current obligations the club could be in financial difficulty.

The next funds of crucial importance are the dues charged. Dues, even if charged annually, should be prorated monthly and this money plus the revenue from the various departments should exceed the total expenses for operating the club. If this is not the case, the year-to-date financial status of the club should be checked. Also, the previous years' financial statements should be checked to see if there was a pattern of losing months offset by profitable ones. If the club continues to lose money, there are several things the club can do. Any department not operating in accordance with its budget should be carefully inspected. (For details of departmental budgeting, see Chapter 4.) If the club's budget has simply failed and no department budget can be found at fault, then any or all of the following steps must be taken:

- *Raise Prices.* A very careful study must be made to assess competition. What are other clubs or fine restaurants in the vicinity charging? If prices are raised higher than members' expectations can allow, this step could adversely affect volume.
- *Raise the Initiation Fee.* This is an iffy measure, beause the number of new members who will join the club at any time is unknown.
- *Place a One-time Assessment on the Members.* Assessments should only be used in the event of an emergency and when the club knows the exact amount that is needed. Their repeated use to defray operating expenses would be a faulty business tactic that would ultimately alienate members.

Productivity

The productivity of club employees is always an important consideration. To receive a-day's-work for a-day's-pay, management must be totally aware of the duties of each worker, which are detailed in the club's job descriptions. It is the responsibility of the department heads and supervisors to see they are carried out. Measurement of productivity and standards of production are discussed in Chapter 4.

Operating Policies

As mentioned in Chapter 2, the club should be organized so an excellent working relationship exists between the manager, the board, and the committees. The board and the committees establish the policies controlling the club's operations. Usually the broad policies are spelled out in the bylaws of the club, such as those covering qualifications for membership, initiation fees, and dues. Other important operating policies are sometimes conveyed to the manager orally or are published as "house rules" in the club roster. Policies covered there might include:

- The club's operating hours. Subentries would give the hours for the dining room, snack bar, or coffee shop; bar and cocktail lounge; card rooms; library; and all sports facilities.
- The dress code at various hours and times of year.
- Parking and valet service.
- Members' responsibility for their valuables.
- Members' check-cashing privileges.
- The club's reservation and party cancellation policy.

Oral instructions to the manager on these matters are promulgated to the members through the club's monthly bulletin. Usually separate rules and regulations for the sports activities are written by their committees with the assistance of the manager and the various professionals.

Compensation for the Manager

The manager's salary and benefits are generally based on the size of the club and the manager's experience but are always negotiable, as no positive rule of thumb exists on which to base salaries. Some accountants use a percentage of gross sales for administrative salaries, ranging anywhere from 7 to 9 percent. The support and maintenance department personnel and the manager and any assistants are paid from this total. The major accounting firms and the national hospitality associations all publish comparative salary listings for personnel in these departments.

Fringe Benefits

Fringe benefits are anything of value given to a manager other than salary and are given for only one reason, to help the club. In evaluating the fringe benefit package, the following questions should be considered:

- Will they help to attract a better type of employee?
- Will they boost the manager's morale? Some voluntary benefits, which psychologists call "sanitary benefits," do not affect morale if given but hurt morale if not. Most industries give these benefits today—vacations with pay and health insurance.
- Will they keep the manager from seeking employment elsewhere?

Management fringe benefits are spelled out in the employment contract (see Appendix 3). The most popular ones are:

- *Vacations with Pay.* Usually managers are given 2 to 4 weeks off each year with pay. Part or all of this might be taken while and if the club is closed for a definite period annually. If the club is very busy, it will often pay the manager the leave money to stay on the job or allow the leave to be carried over into the following year.
- *Sick Leave with Pay.* Sick leave may or may not be part of the management contract but is not usually included. Whether to give this benefit or not is left to the board's discretion.
- *All Types of Insurance Programs.* This could include health, disability, life, and pension plans. It is important for the board to note that no longer can pension plans be given to management personnel alone. If the club has a plan, it must be given to all employees.
- *Stock Options or Warranties.* These are offered by the corporate-owned clubs.
- *An Automobile.* The automobile would have no club markings.
- *Living Quarters.* This usually includes all expenses.
- *Use of the Club's Facilities.* Allowing the manager to use the facilities is considered beneficial to the club as this gives the manager a chance to see them in operation.
- *Paid Membership in the CMAA.* The club would also pay the manager's expenses to attend the CMAA monthly chapter meetings and the annual conference.

- *Education*. Sometimes the club will pay for courses in club-related subjects at a nearby college or university. Also, the CMAA has workshops that give management a way to learn more about the club business.
- *Expenses*. Managers are customarily allowed to charge certain expenses to the club to promote good will. The amount is recommended by the finance committee and approved by the board.

Employee Compensation

Reimbursement and Responsibility

Steps that management can take to organize the staff are as follows:

1. Analyze job salaries according to the responsibilities each job entails.
2. Compose a chart listing salaries and responsibilities for all positions.
3. Grade the jobs.
4. Establish the salaries for each grade.
5. Work to bring the staff reimbursement in line with responsibilities.

Preparing a responsibility and reimbursement chart could be the first step in personnel evaluation for the new manager or the first step in personnel control for the old one (Table 3.1).

The responsibility and reimbursement chart is prepared by listing the job titles of all department heads and supervisors in numerical order in accordance with their responsibilities and importance to the club. Then the salary ranking is posted for each job next to the job title. The goal of every club is to have salaries match responsibilities.

TABLE 3.1   Prioritization of Supervisors' Responsibilities and Reimbursement

Job Title	Responsibilities	Salary
General manager	1	1
Assistant manager		
Night manager		
Golf professional	2	3
Food and beverage manager	2	4
Chef	3	2
Golf superintendent	3	4
Controller	4	4
Banquet manager	4	5
Tennis professional	5	5
Maitre d'	5	5
Retail sales manager	6	6
Aquatic director	6	6
Maintenance manager	6	6

In the example provided by Table 3.1, the manager has decided that the golf professional and the food and beverage manager have equal responsibility, yet their salaries are different and neither one is paid as much as the chef.

In the event that analysis reveals that salaries are not in line with responsibilities, the general manager must consider steps to get them in line. The easiest step, if the budget will allow it, is to raise salaries lower on the scale. Unfortunately, this may not be practical if higher salaries have not been based on responsibilities but on longevity, nepotism, favoritism, or error. Thus, it might take time to make adjustments. Salaries might only be adjustable when cost-of-living increases, bonuses, or raises are given.

Wage and Hour Chart

In setting up wage controls for hourly employees, an entirely different procedure is used. For these employees jobs are graded in accordance with the skills required to perform them. The principles to be applied here are that each job in the club will have a starting wage and for satisfactory service every employee may expect regular increases in pay. The grades can be as numerous as the jobs requiring different skills. The skill factor determines the grade not the job title. Many grades are usually necessary. These can be:

1. Food and drink service personnel, janitors, buspersons, lifeguards, helpers, gardeners, dishwashers, doormen, and elevator operators
2. Office clerks, telephone operators, automotive drivers, helpers, golf starters, and locker room attendants
3. Hostesses and hosts, receptionists, dining room captains
4. Senior life guard, security guards, ground maintenance personnel, cashiers, storekeepers, special clerks (such as accounts receivable, payable, and payroll clerks; and second cook)
5. Bookkeeper, pantryperson, tractor and equipment drivers, head janitor, bartender, social director, proshop managers, computer operator
6. Butcher, baker, garde-manger, first cook, and sous chef
7. Purchasing agent, head of security, computer technician, and automotive and equipment mechanics

These jobs are just a sampling of those a club may have. For example, the CMAA, in their booklet "Job Descriptions in the Private Club Industry," lists almost two hundred different jobs a club might have.

After each job is assigned a grade, a chart is made up (Table 3.2).

Grade 1, Step 1, is the minimum wage established by the Fair Labor Standards Act as amended. The steps may be an annual percentage increase or a flat monetary figure. Step 4 in the preceding grade is used as the first step in the next grade. The U.S. government uses the monetary system $.12 to $.20 per hour. Clubs using job grading and step increases have used from 5 to 10 percent as the annual increase, others have used from $.25 to $.50 per hour for theirs. An employee with a satisfactory evaluation could advance one step each year for the first 5 years, to steps 6, 7, and 8 at the seventh, ninth, and eleventh years, to step 9 at the fifteenth year of

TABLE 3.2 Hourly Employees' Wage Scale

Grade	1	2	3	4	5	6	7	8	9	10
1										
2										
3										
4										
5										
6										
7										

service, and to step 10 after 20 years. The grading system is an excellent management tool, as it does a number of things:

1. It assures every employee that the club pays equal wages for equal work.
2. It deters employees from seeking wage increases as the club policies arc clearly spelled out.
3. It promotes a feeling of security in the employees to know the club has a 20-year plan.
4. It assists in establishing the payroll at budget time.

When this wage-scale system is put into effect, it may include some overpaid employees. For example, a dishwasher is making an hourly rate exceeding that of the tenth grade on the wage scale. He is an excellent employee and previous managers have continually raised his wages. Management must take action to amend this disparity. The first corrective step is to hold a meeting with the employee and explain the wage scale. Emphasize that he is being paid at a higher rate than the scale allows and something has to be done about it. The manager has, in fact, five options:

1. If the employee has been getting excellent or outstanding evaluations, it may be because he is in effect running the dish room, breakage is at a minimum, clean dishes are always available, and he gets along with the other employees very well. The manager could let him retain his wage but make him dish room supervisor so his wage level can be explained to new employees.
2. Give him an opportunity to increase his skill level by training for another job. It just might be that because of his competence, no one has ever thought to

promote him. In this situation if the employee is agreeable, he spends 7 hours at his job instead of eight and spends 1 hour each day in training at another. For example, a bartender's position. Once trained, he could be promoted to the first opening and would be expected to train someone to take his place. This employee, while waiting for an opening, can now be used for special events such as parties. He must be paid the bartender's rate and his schedule adjusted so that the overtime rate need not be paid. Every employee in the club will be informed about the plan. Promoting from within is a sure employee morale booster.

3. Drop the employee's wage to step 10. This may have a serious effect on morale, but many conglomerates do just this when they take over businesses. Club operation is a serious business and must be operated as one.
4. Release the employee. This also may affect morale, but the situation, unless corrected, will only deteriorate if allowed to continue.
5. Retire the employee.

The manager may also consider bonuses as part of the wage scale. These are not to be used as profit incentives in the same direct way as in hotels and restaurants, but as stimulants to achieve percentage goals. The only worthwhile bonus is one which benefits the club. Christmas and other bonuses must be tied to attendance, performance, visible courtesy, or other club objectives to be of any value. If the club is trapped into an unproductive bonus system by tradition, it should be changed to a constructive one as rapidly as possible.

Bonuses can be based on many things. However, those based on percentage goals are the most beneficial to the club. For example, management has decided that the food department will strive for a 30 percent food cost but 35 percent will be acceptable. The head of the department will get a bonus if the cost is less than 35 percent. Bonuses should never be easy to achieve and, to repeat, must always be of benefit to the club. It is a good idea to allow department heads to control their bonuses completely. Bonuses are taxable; therefore management can monitor their distribution.

TYPES OF CLUB MANAGEMENT

Management of the various types of clubs differs in many ways and may even differ for the same type of club. The most efficient level of management is achieved when the board and the club committees establish policy that the manager has sole responsibility to carry out through club employees. The manager must have complete charge of day-to-day operations. In addition, in a well-organized club the manager should have to report to only one boss at a time, getting directions from the board and the committee members in the areas of their responsibility. This is not always possible, which causes managers to lose some of their management effectiveness.

Equity Clubs

In the opinion of top-notch professional club managers, the most pleasant position in club management is as manager of an equity club. The personal contacts and the appreciation for a job well done in this type of club is often missing in the other types. The equity clubs however have a unique type of problem—that posed by members giving orders and taking up complaints with the employees. Most of these members own the club and therefore carry a great deal of weight. The manager must prepare for this problem well in advance by taking the following actions.

- Take time to develop a cordial relationship with the board and all committee members.
- Emphasize to all members that there can only be one manager and stress the harm that could result if management's authority were undermined. It is very bad for employee morale when employees do not know who is really their boss. It is also impossible for the manager to maintain his or her authority.

In certain equity clubs, the relationship of the board, committees, and management is further complicated by the addition of an Executive Committee. This committee originated when membership on the board was an honorary position and the committee was appointed to run the club. Now most boards are operative, and unless the duties of the board and their committees' members are very carefully detailed, deadlocks and confusion are bound to result.

Corporate Clubs

In corporate clubs the manager is the sole on-site boss and runs the club by policies set by the corporation. Committees have no authority but are simply advisory.

Military Clubs

Military clubs are managed by local commanding officers who have complete authority and responsibility in operating the clubs and who discharge their duties through the appointment of an advisory group. The head of this committee usually acts as the manager's liaison with the commanding officer. On some military installations, however, an officer may be given the collateral duty (meaning part-time and not primary) of supervising the manager. The advisory group meets monthly and forwards the minutes of the meeting (which will contain any recommendations they or the manager care to make) and a digest of the audited financial statement to the commanding officer and, in some commands, to the ultimate authority. The commanding officer returns the minutes to the group, indicating his or her approval or disapproval of their recommendations.

Military clubs are audited monthly by a board which is composed of personnel not connected with the club. This audit board is appointed by the commanding officer and, unlike auditors of civilian clubs, also takes and verifies the monthly inventories. Military clubs require skilled professional management because, as is often the case in civilian clubs, the ruling authority may know nothing of the complexities of the business. Their managers, however, do not have quite the freedom of operation that the equity club and other civilian managers have.

PERSONNEL

Recruiting

The manager must keep the club fully staffed in order to provide proper service to the members. Also, now and again and for many different reasons, the board may need a new manager. Although turnover is not a serious problem, replacement of employees is always necessary, and every club needs part-time personnel and some backup applications. In recruiting for management personnel, a number of sources can assist the board. The local chapter of the CMAA usually has a placement officer who keeps a list of available managers. Also the national association may be of help. The association also has a list of experienced managers who are interested in interim positions until the club can hire a manager. Additional sources include accounting companies that specialize in the hospitality field. For assistant managers, food and beverage managers, and for part-time personnel, colleges and universities are the place to look.

Recruiters for the club should give each person who seems interested an employment application to either complete at once or return by mail.

Screening Job Applicants

After a sufficient number of applicants have been recruited, the next step to be taken in hiring personnel is the screening process.

Although selection of the right applicant is the club's ultimate objective, elimination of unqualified applicants is of primary importance. This saves time during the employment process and reduces turnover later. The basic tools to use in screening are:

1. Preliminary interviewing. This is covered under "Interviewing" later in the chapter.
2. References and work history checks. The most important part of the screening process is in the verification of the work and educational history provided by the applicant in the job application. An applicant's work and school record can be checked through several sources:
   a. Previous employers: The club may call and ask any question of a previous employer listed by an applicant. The Invasion of Privacy Act may inhibit the former employer from answering questions that might impinge on the

applicant's character; however, the hesitation or the enthusiasm shown by the former employer can be revealing. The law does allow the verification of employment.

    b. Official college transcripts: The applicant will usually have to request these as they are also considered privileged information.

    c. School authorities.

    d. Service discharge papers.

    e. Credit reports.

    f. Police and Federal Bureau of Investigation reports.

It is very important to make the above contacts because the Civil Rights Act of 1964, Title VII, designed to protect young minorities seeking employment, legally bars the interviewer from asking many types of questions.

Testing

More and more clubs, like Country Clubs of the Southwest for example, use tests to screen out unqualified or undesirable applicants. The tests also assist in placing qualified persons in the right jobs. The following are some of the most popular tests used.

1. *The Manual Dexterity Test* is a series of simple manipulative tests used for food service personnel to test their dexterity. These tests quickly eliminate applicants who are not able to handle jobs in which a certain degree of manual dexterity is required.
2. *The Mental Ability Test* measures an applicant's ability to understand and solve problems.
3. *The Aptitude Test* measures the particular skills or abilities an applicant has to do a particular job.
4. *The Knowledge Test* measures the general or specific knowledge an applicant has gained through study or experience.
5. *The Personality Test* attempts to measure an applicant's attitudes, interests, behavior patterns, and motivations. It is sometimes referred to as a Psychological Test. Personnel experts point out that tests for manual dexterity, mental ability, job aptitude, and job knowledge are most helpful in determining what an applicant can do, whereas personality tests are helpful in determining what an applicant will do. They also point out, however, that any worthwhile insight into an applicant's personality must be based on test information, information from previous employers, plus information from a personal interview. One of the things that management must understand is that the personality tests, unless administered by an expert and licensed psychologist, are just as worthless as the old polygraph tests. In 1988 the Congress of the United States banned pre-employment polygraph tests because they were convinced that the tests were not accurate. Immediately the polygraph companies started marketing written tests that were supposed to be able, if the employee filled in the blanks, to tell whether an employee was honest.

Interviewing

The applicants for club jobs and positions will be given an application to complete before the interview starts (Fig. 3.2). Persons applying for supervisory positions will generally have a resume to present to the interviewer along with the application. The interviewer must also have a form called a position description, which details the exact duties of the position, indicates under which department the position falls, and gives the title of the employee's supervisor. (*Note:* Updated in 1979, the CMAA's publication listing jobs used in the club business remains a very useful tool. Although computerization of many functions may have changed the method of accomplishing the duties of a particular position, the duties themselves have remained unchanged.)

The interview consists of both visual and oral components. The appearance of the candidate, the "visual interview," gives the interviewer certain kinds of information about the applicant's suitability for the position for which he or she is applying. The interviewer should keep in mind, first of all, whom the applicant will come in contact with on a daily basis. If the position calls for contact with members, as in the position of assistant manager, social secretary, receptionist, bartender, server, or pro shop clerk, a particular set of physical standards must apply. Applicants must be neat and pleasant, smile frequently, and have excellent communication skills. For other types of jobs, such as the food production positions (not used on the buffet line) these attributes would not be as critical. If lifting, carrying, and setting up bandstands, tables, and so forth, are requirements, as in the position of storekeeper or in the janitorial force, still other physical attributes would affect employability. However, the interviewer must beware of the "halo effect," whereby an applicant is favored because of a preconceived notion of what he or she should look like.

The oral part of the interview provides more complete information on the candidate as long as the interviewer can get the applicant talking. This can be done in a number of ways, one of which is to make an effort to talk about personal topics and areas of interest. In other words, the interview should be a conversation not simply a question-and-answer session. This conversational thrust has one great advantage—it allows the interviewer to gather indirectly information that otherwise could only be gained by questions prohibited by the Civil Rights Act of 1964, Title VII.

Any questions concerning the following subjects may not be asked unless they are an integral part of the job:

- Arrest and conviction
- Credit references
- Height and weight
- Education
- Contraception usage, plans to have children, and unwed motherhood

The rationale behind prohibition of these questions is as follows:

1. *Arrest and Conviction.* An arrest could be a mistake for as small a thing as a traffic violation. A conviction means an individual may or may not have com-

---

Application for Employment

(Please Print Plainly)

PERSONAL   Date: _____

Name _____ Social Security No. _____
           Last   First   Middle Initial

Present address _____
           No.   Street   City   State   Zip

How many years have you lived at this address? _____ Telephone No. (   ) _____
                                               Area

Previous address _____ How long did you live there? _____
           No.   Street   City   State   Zip

Job(s) applied for 1. _____ Rate of pay expected $_____ per_____

               2. _____ Rate of pay expected $_____ per_____

Are you 18 years of age or older?   ☐ Yes ☐ No

If under 18, can you, after employment, submit a work permit?   ☐ Yes ☐ No

Do you want to work   ☐ Full-Time or ☐ Part-Time. Specify days and hours if part-time_____ _____

Have you worked for us before?_____ If yes, when? _____

List any friends or relatives working for us _____

_____

If hired, on what date will you be available to start work? _____

If hired, do you have a reliable means of transportation to get to work? _____

Do you have a valid driver's license? _____ Number _____

Do you have any physical condition which may limit your ability to perform the job applied for? _____

If yes (describe) _____

_____

Have you ever been convicted of a crime, excluding misdemeanors and summary offenses?   ☐ No ☐ Yes

If yes, describe in full. _____

_____

_____

_____

Person to be notified in case of accident or emergency
Phone Number _____ Name _____
Relationship _____ Address _____

FIGURE 3.2 *Application for employment*.

mitted a crime (innocent persons do get convicted and minorities more than most), but in any event his or her debt to society has been paid.
2. *Credit References*. In this age of plastic dollars iffy credit ratings are common.
3. *Height and Weight*. Unless height and weight have direct bearing on how the job will be performed, such questions are an invasion of privacy.

EDUCATIONAL BACKGROUND

TYPE OF SCHOOL	NAME AND ADDRESS	How Many Years Attended	Graduated	COURSE OR MAJOR
GRAMMER OR GRADE			☐ Yes ☐ No	
HIGH SCHOOL			☐ Yes ☐ No	
COLLEGE			☐ Yes ☐ No	
POST GRADUATE			☐ Yes ☐ No	
BUSINESS OR TRADE			☐ Yes ☐ No	
OTHER			☐ Yes ☐ No	
			☐ Yes ☐ No	

WORK EXPERIENCE

LIST EXPERIENCE FOR LAST 5 YEARS.
INCLUDE MILITARY, IF APPLICABLE.
(LIST IN ORDER, LAST OR PRESENT EMPLOYER FIRST)

DATES FROM	TO	NAME AND ADDRESS OF EMPLOYER	RATE OF PAY START	FINISH	SUPERVISOR'S NAME AND TITLE	REASON FOR LEAVING

Describe in detail the work you did.

DATES FROM	TO	NAME AND ADDRESS OF EMPLOYER	RATE OF PAY START	FINISH	SUPERVISOR'S NAME AND TITLE	REASON FOR LEAVING

Describe in detail the work you did.

DATES FROM	TO	NAME AND ADDRESS OF EMPLOYER	RATE OF PAY START	FINISH	SUPERVISOR'S NAME AND TITLE	REASON FOR LEAVING

Describe in detail the work you did.

DATES FROM	TO	NAME AND ADDRESS OF EMPLOYER	RATE OF PAY START	FINISH	SUPERVISOR'S NAME AND TITLE	REASON FOR LEAVING

Describe in detail the work you did.

May we contact the employers listed above?   If not, indicate below which ones(s) you do not wish us to contact _____

FIGURE 3.2 *Application for employment (continued).*

4. *Education.* The education level of the applicant can be ascertained from the application. For most club employees, the ability to read and write English is necessary. Even a dishwashing job requires the washer to read directions and follow instructions.

5. *Contraception Usage, Plans to Have Children, and Unwed Motherhood.* Questions on these topics are very personal and discriminate against women and although they may have some bearing on job performance, they may not be asked.

Are there any other experiences, skills, or qualifications which you feel would especially fit you for work with this company?

_____

_____

_____

PERSONAL REFERENCES
(Excluding Former employers or Relatives)

Name and Occupation	Address	Phone Number
1. _____	_____	
2. _____	_____	
3. _____	_____	

Thank you for completing this application form and for your interest in employment with us. We would like to assure you that your opportunity for employment with this company will be based only on your merit and on no other considerations.

DO NOT WRITE BELOW THIS LINE

INTERVIEW ☐ YES ☐ NO Date _____ Hour _____

Result of Interview _____

_____

_____

_____

_____

Interviewed by: _____

Acceptable for Employment? _____ Starting Rate _____ Starting Date _____

Job Title _____ Dept. No. _____ Full or Part-Time _____

No. of Regular Hours to work per week _____

Employed by (Department Head) _____

Approved by (General Manager) _____

FIGURE 3.2   *(continued)*

Hiring

The actual hiring of a job candidate is done by the prospective supervisor. When the supervisor has made a selection, he or she submits the necessary papers to the personnel office. The supervisor informs the personnel office of the date, day, and time the employee is to report for duty, and this information is passed on to the employee.

Orientation

All new employees must be given the information necessary to start to work—what is called "employee orientation." This information helps them get their bearings in a new environment. It also tells them what they are supposed to do and where to do it.

A printed handbook of general information is given to the new employee before he or she reports to work. A meeting is then scheduled with the supervisor to answer any questions the employee might have. The orientation handbook could include the following suggested subjects, tailored to fit the individual club's needs:

- A short history of the club.
- An organization chart.
- A wage scale.
- Whether or not a physical examination is required.
- Hours of work. The job starts on whatever day the club decides and runs for 7 consecutive days. The work week for nonsupervisory personnel is generally 40 hours, for which the wage-scale rate is paid. If any employee is required to work over 40 hours in one calendar week, the pay is 1½ times the regular rate.
- Days off. Many clubs are open 5 to 7 days a week and frequently employees may have to work at night and on Saturday or Sunday.
- A statement should be included in the handbook that the club is an "Equal Opportunity Employer." The statement could be worded as follows: "It is the policy of this club to seek out and employ the best-qualified personnel in all positions and to provide equal opportunities to all employees without regard to age, race, color, religion, sex, national origin, or handicaps."

Another type of orientation is given orally by the supervisor when the employee reports to work. If possible, the supervisor should schedule the time the employee reports so that as much time as necessary can be spent with the new employee. The subjects to be covered include:

1. A welcome to the employee.
2. Where the employees park their cars.
3. Whether a sticker or an identification card is needed to get onto the grounds on a permanent basis and where the employee goes to get one. Also the employee is informed if there is any public transportation available.
4. The work schedule: what it is, where and when it is posted, and where the employee's name is on it.
5. What to wear to work. The employee is informed about the club's dress code for its employees. The employee is told whether the job requires a uniform, furnished by the club, or if the work will be done in the clothes worn to work. If uniforms are required and furnished, the employee is told where they are located and how frequently they are changed.
6. Which club entrance to use in reporting to work. (*Note:* It is always a good idea to have all employees check in at a central place. The exception may be the

golf course maintenance personnel. The club should have a time clock or a sign-in sheet, an employees' bulletin board, and if possible, a supervisor's office close by so that the employees can be observed.)

7. Where the lockers and restrooms are located.
8. Where to find the time clock and how to use it.
9. Where to obtain supplies and equipment.
10. When and where to obtain and eat meals.
11. Where smoking is allowed.
12. Where the pay phones are located if the employee needs to make a personal call.
13. When and where to get the pay check and how to cash it.
14. The person to call and the telephone number if arriving to work at the scheduled time is not possible.

The last orientation duty of the supervisor is to introduce the new employee to the manager and to his or her fellow workers. Then the supervisor assures the new employee that he or she is a most welcome addition to the team.

Compensation and Fringe Benefits

Compensation

Employees would be compensated according to the salary scale of the club. (See managerial guidelines for employee compensation presented earlier in the chapter under "The General Manager.")

Fringe Benefits

Most clubs provide an excellent fringe benefit program for their full-time employees in addition to benefits required by law (a full-time employee is one who works at least 37½ hours a week).

Benefits fall into two categories, those mandated by law, called involuntary, and all others, called voluntary. Those mandated by law are the employer's share of Social Security, Worker's Compensation, and federal and state unemployment tax. Voluntary benefits are of two kinds, those that represent no cost to the club and those that do. (*Note:* The fringe benefit program is *not* a give-away. Its sole purpose is to motivate and retain the best employees. It is expensive and should be reviewed at specific intervals.) A fringe benefit package may include all or some of the following:

VACATION LEAVE   Generally after 1 year of satisfactory service, an employee will receive 1 week of vacation with pay, after 2 years 2 weeks, and after 5 years 3 weeks. Vacations hours are accumulated each payday and the total, at the end of the year, are the hours earned (40, 80 or 120). Vacation leave, unless specifically authorized, is usually taken in the year earned or the time is lost.

Note: Vacation leave, for other than the top management employees, may not be carried over from one year to the next unless the club has an emergency. The "take it or lose it" policy should be enforced for many reasons. Some of these are:

1. The employee, if a hard worker, needs the rest for renewal of enthusiasm.
2. The employee may accumulate more earned time than can be spared.
3. Management may wish to find out how well the club operates without the employee.

SICK LEAVE   Sick leave is earned to protect the employee if he or she is unable to come to work because of illness or a non-job-related accident. Sick leave is generally accumulated each payday so that the hours earned total forty at the end of each year. The total sick leave that is earned may be carried over from year to year. To encourage employees not to abuse the sick leave privilege some clubs have a policy allowing any unused sick leave to be redeemed for cash when the employee retires. Clubs that do not offer sick leave can establish a reporting-time requirement involving 1 or 2 hours of pay. Although not required by law, this requirement is a good business policy.

JURY DUTY   If an employee is called for jury duty, most clubs will continue to pay his or her salary in full. If paid any fee, the employee may be expected to give this money to the club.

ADMINISTRATIVE LEAVE   In special cases and to outstanding employees, leave with pay may be granted to take care of emergencies.

INSURANCE PLANS   After employees have worked in the club a certain number of months, they are eligible to join the various insurance plans. After 6 months employees may join the health, dental, and disability plans (to protect them from non-job-connected illness or injuries). After 12 months they are usually eligible to join the pension plan. *Note:* The club has two options for handling these insurance programs. The club may pay the total amount of the premium or any portion of the cost, or the employee may pay the total cost. In the latter event, the plan must be voluntary. Even if the employee pays the whole premium, it is still a fringe benefit, as the club can negotiate a group rate and forward the premiums to the insurance company through a payroll deduction.

EMPLOYEE MEALS   Employees may purchase meals at the club at the hours set by the club. The meals should be sold to the employees at cost.

Note: Until just a few years ago, all eating establishments furnished meals free to the employees. Wages were low, workers were transient, and feeding them was a necessity. Many clubs, because it was the policy of the hospitality industry, followed suit. Today clubs have an option. Any charge for food is highly recommended, as the fringe benefit packages are getting expensive. Assuredly, selling the food at cost is still a nice fringe benefit. The employee prepares a guest check, blanks are kept by the chef, and the cost of the meal furnished is deducted from the employee's pay. If free meals are furnished, it is important that guest checks still be used, as the value of a meal is considered pay under Social Security regulations and both the employee and the club must pay this tax.

LODGING   In the event it is necessary to provide lodging to employees, it should be provided without cost. (*Note:* The fair value of the lodging is considered pay and the Social Security tax must be paid.)

Savings on the club's fringe benefit program that will help and not hurt morale can be made by doing the following:

1. Have new employees serve at least a 3-month probationary period before they get the benefit package.
2. As health insurance costs soar each year, have the employee pay part or all of the increased expense.
3. If the club does not have health insurance, disability insurance (to protect the worker from non-job-connected injuries or illness) and/or group life insurance, offer to have a representative visit the club and explain these programs to the employees. The program or programs would be voluntary and paid for through payroll deductions so the insurance companies could give the employees a group rate.
4. Under the Tax Reform Act of 1986, the club that does not have a pension plan can offer their employees SEP (simplified employee pension). Booklets explaining the plan are available from the major insurance companies at no cost.
5. Have the manager use the employees' bulletin board to publicize events that are important to them. These events could be birthdays, weddings, births, graduations, dependents' achievements, and so forth. Management attention is a (no- or low-cost) fringe benefit that is often overlooked.
6. Start an "Employees' Beneficial Suggestion Program" with a monthly cash award (based on the value of the suggestion to the club). The amount should be decided by a committee composed of a member of the board, a member of the committee involved, and the manager. If the suggestion cannot be adopted, a warm and friendly letter of thanks explaining why should be delivered to the employee. He or she should also be encouraged to try again.
7. Organize low- or no-cost sporting and entertainment events. For example a bowling team, a visit to a theater or an amusement park cost little, and management may be able to get a group or team rate. A softball team could be formed at little expense and perhaps at no expense if a business member would sponser the team. Such efforts would help to promote team spirit that could carry over into the club. To start group programs, pick out the most outgoing, extroverted types on the club staff and encourage them to start thinking about club employee recreation.
8. Make arrangements with the bank the club uses to cash employees' payroll checks whether or not they have accounts there.

Training

The training of club employees and its constant review is perhaps the most difficult task the manager has to perform. Training and review (which is another name for supervision) are needed in all departments. As well as the training of new employees, the manager and supervisors must provide additional training to staff as needed.

Today the old method of telling persons in a stern voice to do things and assuming they will get it done is no longer advisable. The modern manager must think of him- or herself as a coach, the supervisors as assistant coaches, and the staff as a team.

When AT&T wanted to teach 3500 consumer-products division managers about leadership, teamwork, and trust, it had them scale cliffs, shinny up poles, and balance on beams in the remote reaches of Vermont and Texas. The purpose: to teach and demonstrate teamwork.

One management team at Aetna Life and Casualty Insurance company boosted its productivity by sending two of its employees to a sensitivity session with a consultant. They ironed out their differences in a highly emotional session. The differences between these two persons had been disrupting an entire department.

These two examples illustrate how management's concern for the mental state of its employees encourages teamwork in the workplace.

In a club the training priority would be given to those persons meeting and/or serving the members. This would include the following jobs:

Assistant managers
Professionals of golf, tennis, aquatics, etc.
Golf starters and range marshals
Hosts and hostesses in the dining rooms
All waiters and waitresses
All buspersons
Kitchen personnel who work on the buffet line
The receptionist
The telephone operator
The central cashier
The janitorial staff

The catch words of job analysis, sometimes called job simplification, are "work smarter, not harder." The task of figuring out how to train an employee can be made much easier by remembering this principle.

Back in the fifties Standard Brands Sales Company devised a training plan that still works very well today. The plan can be outlined as follows:

1. Before starting training:
   a. Prepare a training plan. This means that the complete details of how to do a job would be written out and discussed with a knowledgeable individual. If the manager delegates this task to a supervisor, the manager may wish to review the plan before it is implemented.
   b. Have everything ready to teach the job. This means that if a job requires tools or supplies, see they are on hand when the training starts.

2. When training:
   a. Prepare the employee for instruction. Employees must be confident they can do a job when trained. It is the responsibility of the trainer to instill this confidence in trainees. This will put them at ease and make them more receptive to training.
   b. Explain the job and its importance. The employee must believe that the job is important and that he or she will be of greater value to the club once the job is mastered. This definitely helps to create interest in the job and adds to the trainee's comfort and ease in learning a new job.

    c. Present the job:
      (1) Follow the job breakdown.
      (2) Explain and demonstrate one step at a time.
      (3) Stress the key parts of the job.
      (4) Do not try to do too much at one time. Time the training sessions to the employee's endurance.
      (5) Use simple language.
      (6) Do not do all the talking. Try to get feedback that will show what the trainee is learning.
      (7) Set high standards.
      (8) Give reasons for methods and procedures.
      (9) Show one thing at a time.

3. After training:
    a. Have the employee tell the "why" and the "how" of the job.
    b. Make sure the employee can stress the key points.
    c. Correct errors and omissions as they are made.

4. Throughout training keep in mind the following:
    a. No criticism is ever necessary.
    b. Let trainees correct their mistakes.
    c. Do not overdo correcting.
    d. Do not correct in front of others.
    e. Do not be too quick to blame the trainee.
    f. Encourage the trainee.
    g. Get back everything that has been given to the trainee. This feedback is a crucial part of the training program.
    h. Trainers should continue until trainees knows what they do.

5. Follow-through:
    a. Put the employee on the job.
    b. Encourage questions from the trainee and be sympathetic to him or her.
    c. Check frequently the performance of the trainee.
    d. Let the employee know how he or she is doing.
    e. Watch the employee do the job in its entirety.

Evaluation

The evaluation of the club employees is a review of their total attitude, interest, and performance on the job. The evaluation process is a vital part of personnel management.

The club could have new employees serve a probationary period at the end of which their performance is evaluated. The length of the probationary period depends on the type of job the employee is required to perform. For example, it would take a much shorter time to know if a waitress was going to become a satisfactory employee than it would to learn whether an assistant manager could do the job. Usually clubs set a probationary period of 3 months for the blue collar worker and 6 months to 1 year for supervisors. The probationary period for the granting of fringe benefits is usually 3 months for workers and immediately for the supervisors.

The evaluation sheets are different for the supervisors and the workers (see Figures 3.3 and 3.4).

Termination

People either voluntarily or involuntarily terminate their employment. Voluntary terminations happen for many reasons. Some of these are:

- Transfer of a spouse to a distant city
- Illness of a family member in a distant city
- Boredom or frustration with the job and the desire to make a change
- Dissatisfaction with their supervisor or fellow employees
- Poor adaptation to the environment either at the club or at home
- Dissatisfaction with salary or benefits
- Retirement

The manager should hold an exit interview with every worker whose employment has been terminated either voluntarily or involuntarily, as the reputation of the club might be at stake or a good employee could be lost because no one cared. In some cases management must get more involved than in others, for example:

1. The employee is bored with the job. Many times the person is overqualified for the position. The job he/she is doing offers no challenge. To many intelligent persons, those factors could become intolerable. It just might be possible to add additional duties to the position, find another job for this employee, or recommend him or her to another club manager in the vicinity.
2. The job is too easy or too hard. If the job is too easy, additional duties may be added. If the job is too hard physically, perhaps there is not proper equipment for the job or the hours are too long. Also, there could have been an error in hiring. If the job is too much of a mental strain, then additional training might be helpful in retaining the conscientious employee.
3. The employee is unhappy with the supervisor. Management must be very tactful and strive to get the disgruntled employee to talk. Sexual harassment is not uncommon in clubs, though management might first find out about it in a court of law. The culprit might be the supervisor, a fellow employee, or a member.
4. The employee is dissatisfied with fellow employees. Supervisors and employees make the work place a happy and tolerable one, or an unhappy and intolerable one. Management must understand that it is not always possible to make every employee happy, as happiness is not in everyone's nature. If, however, what is causing dissatisfaction is within the manager's province, then management should know about it.
5. The employee is maladapted to the environment. If the employee has been

Evaluation

Employee's Name _____ Date _____

DOES THE EMPLOYEE: *Satisfactory*   *Unsatisfactory*

  1. Report for work at the scheduled time?   _____   _____

  2. Start work at the scheduled time?   _____   _____

  3. Perform assigned work in a safe manner?   _____   _____

  4. Perform assigned work efficiently?   _____   _____

  5. Have an even temper?   _____   _____

  6. Work well with employees?   _____   _____

  7. Get along with other employees?   _____   _____

  8. Get along with his/her supervisor?   _____   _____

  9. Work well under pressure?   _____   _____

10. Work well without constant supervision?   _____   _____

11. Carry out the tasks of the job?   _____   _____

12. Make few or no errors?   _____   _____

13. Produce food of good quality?   _____   _____

14. Follow required procedures?   _____   _____

15. Learn things quickly?   _____   _____

16. Appear neat and clean?   _____   _____

17. Ever volunteer to help other employees?   _____   _____

18. Perform work within the time allotted?   _____   _____

19. Take criticism well and correct the problem?   _____   _____

20. Follow the rules and regulations of the company?   _____   _____

21. Correct problems quickly?   _____   _____

22. Make any suggestions that will help the company?   _____   _____

Employee consultation held (date) _____ by _____

Employee has read and received a copy of the evaluation.

Signature of employee _____

(Signature does not imply agreement with this evaluation.)

Revision Date _____

FIGURE 3.3 *Employee evaluation form.*

Date _____ Supervisor's Name _____
Department _____

	Yes	No
1. Gets along well with peers.	_____	_____
2. Sets example for other supervisors.	_____	_____
3. Understands and takes complicated orders well.	_____	_____
4. Is a leader.	_____	_____
5. Accomplishes work on schedule.	_____	_____
6. Schedules workers satisfactorily.	_____	_____
7. Uses part-time workers.	_____	_____
8. Keeps overtime pay at a minimum.	_____	_____
9. Provides adequate training or workers.	_____	_____
10. Sets good example for workers.	_____	_____
11. Employee turnover rate is acceptable.	_____	_____
12. Handles problems well.	_____	_____
13. Handles emergencies well.	_____	_____
14. Has good personal habits.	_____	_____
15. Has the respect of the workers.	_____	_____
16. Gets along well with management.	_____	_____

This evaluation was discussed with employee on _____(date) by _____.
I have read my evaluation and my supervisor has discussed it with me.
Employee's signature _____

FIGURE 3.4 *Supervisor evaluation form.*

working in the club he or she may be happier with an outdoor job when one becomes available. If living conditions are the problem, the manager could allow the employee to put a notice on the employees' bulletin board requesting information on housing.

6. The employee is dissatisfied with the salary or fringe benefits. The manager could discuss the wage scale and explain how the skill level works (see "Employment Compensation" earlier in the chapter). As to fringe benefits, the manager may get an opportunity to learn what other businesses and clubs are offering. If their benefits are better than the club's, perhaps it would be appropriate to discuss this with the board.

7. The employee wishes to retire. Any employee in good health can retire and draw Social Security at age 65 and if they are ill or disabled, even earlier. Also, if the club has a pension plan, there may be a compulsory retirement age. If the person is in good health and just does not want to work as hard, they may draw Social Security benefits and work part time at the club. The manager should explore this possibility if the employee is an outstanding worker.

Employment can be terminated involuntarily for two reasons. These are:

- Mandatory retirement forced on the employee by a company pension plan. Employees may become too ill or too old to perform the duties of the jobs they are assigned. Regrettably, few clubs are affluent enough to carry this "dead wood" for any great length of time. Management should do everything in its power to make the transition to retirement as painless as possible. This could include assistance in filing the necessary papers for Social Security and Medicare.
- Termination for cause. In a well-managed club an employee may be summarily terminated for misconduct but never for bad workmanship, tardiness, or absenteeism. These may indeed constitute reasons for termination but not until an employee evaluation (discussed previously) has been filled out and a probationary period has expired.

EMPLOYEE AND EMPLOYMENT LAWS

The laws that apply to employees and employment are enacted by both state and federal authorities. There are two general rules that a manager must know concerning these laws. The first is that if any state has a law providing greater benefits to employees than the Fair Labor Standards Act (FLSA), the state law will prevail. The second is that any business conducted on club property becomes a concessionaire and all the laws that apply to the club apply to it. For example, if the golf professional is managing the pro shop and receiving income, or an outside group is operating the beauty salon, the golf pro and the outside group are both governed by the laws that govern the club.

If the state has no laws on a specific case, federal laws prevail. For example, the state of Florida has no minimum wage law, so the FLSA prevails.

The Federal laws pertaining to employees and employment are:

- The Fair Labor Standards Act, as amended
- The Equal Opportunity Employment Act
- The Equal Pay Act of 1963
- The Age Discrimination Act of 1973, as amended
- The Immigration and Control Act of 1986

The Fair Labor Standards Act

The Fair Labor Standards Act, as amended in 1985, applies to all businesses that gross $365,500 annually, with the exception of nonprofit clubs, where the gross is $250,000. The FLSA covers the following:

1. *Minimum Wage*. The law establishes the minimum wage that may be paid an employee for 1 hour's work. This need not all be in cash but may be reduced

by furnishing meals or lodging for the employee's convenience and/or by a tip credit. If, for example, a meal was furnished worth $.80 and the employee worked an 8-hour shift, the hourly wage could be reduced by $.10 an hour. The employer's tip credit is 40 percent of the minimum wage, which may be deducted from the wage if the employee is guaranteed to receive at least the 40 percent back in tips.

The tip credit is in addition to any other deduction. In the event the employee works at two jobs, only one of which involves tips, the tip credit can only be applied to that job. If the employee takes a tip credit, it must be disclosed to the members by a printed notice on the menu in letters at least as large as the smallest print used.

2. *Tip Distribution.* Tips given to employees on credit cards or on in-house charge tickets may be distributed daily or at the next regular pay period.

3. *Service Charges.* A service charge posted to a member's check, whether voluntary or not, is handled completely differently.
   a. All or any portion of the service charge, or none of it, may be distributed to the employees.
   b. In the event any of the service charge is given to the employees, it is considered wages and all taxes apply.
   c. If a club has a service charge and if an employee works more than 40 hours and is entitled to overtime pay, the pay is figured differently. For example, if the employee earned $4 per hour and worked 50 hours, the regular pay would be 40 hours times $4, plus 10 hours times $6 for a total of $220. If the service charge paid the employee and the regular pay earned totaled $300 or more (the total hours worked times the overtime rate) then the employer's out-of-pocket expense is $200 instead of $220.

4. *Overtime Pay.* All employees, with the exception of management, administrative, and professional personnel are entitled to 1½ times their regular hourly rate after they have worked 40 hours in any work week. The law further states that exempt employees be divided into two groups, called "long form" and "short form."
   a. Long Form. The employee must be in charge of a department, supervise two or more employees, and have the authority to hire and fire them. The supervisor must not engage in "hands-on work" more than 40 percent of the time.
   b. Short Form. These employees must be paid a minimum of $250 per week and hold a bona fide management position. In addition, they must have complete control over two or more employees and must not engage in "hands-on-work" more than 50 percent of their time.
   c. Regular Hourly Rate Not Applicable to:
      (1) Money given as a gift or as a reward.
      (2) Money paid for periods when no work is performed, such as holidays or

vacations. For example, if an employee started the work week with Monday, worked Tuesday and Wednesday, and did not work Thursday but was paid for it, for purposes of overtime pay the employee only worked 24 hours that week.

(3) Sums paid in recognition of services performed if the amounts paid are determined at the sole discretion of the employer or pursuant to a benefit profit-sharing plan.

(4) Contributions to a benefit plan.

(5) Premium pay for holidays or hours in excess of daily or weekly standards. This may be provided by employment contracts. This extra compensation may be credited toward overtime payments.

(6) Extra compensation (at least time and a half). Pursuant to an applicable employment contract or collective bargaining agreement for work outside the regular workday or workweek, this may also be credited to the overtime payments.

5. *The Workweek.* The workweek is any continuous 7 days of 24 hours each for a total of 168 hours. Every employer has the right to set the workweek the employees will work. This should be done in writing in the form of a work schedule. If at all possible the employees should initial the schedule. The workweek may be different for some or all of the employees.

   If an employee is hired to work a regular workweek over 40 hours, the law will allow the employer to calculate the pay in a different way. The normal way would be to pay straight time for 40 hours and overtime for the additional hours. Assuming the employee worked 10 hours of overtime, an employee earning $5 per hour would receive $275. Under the alternate plan the wages due the employee are computed by dividing the 50 hours into the dollar amount of the 40-hour week (40 × $5 divided by 50). The hourly rate becomes $4 per hour and the overtime rate $6. The pay is reduced to $260. The manager must give serious consideration to the effect this method has on the morale of employees. Is it worth the amount of money saved?

6. *Tipped Employee's Overtime.* The overtime rate for tipped employees is 1½ times the minimum wage rate. Whether or not the employer is taking a tip credit does not change this.

7. *Employees on a Guaranteed Salary for a Fluctuating Workweek.* When an employee on a guaranteed salary works in excess of 40 hours in one workweek, the pay is the salary divided by the total hours worked. For example, if the employee worked 50 hours and the guaranteed salary was $250 per week, the base would be $5 and the employee would be paid, in addition to the $250, time and a half for the 10 hours overtime, or $7.50. The total pay for the week would be $325.

8. *Employee Uniforms.* The general rule for the hospitality industry is that if the employee is required to work in any clothes that are not normally street wear,

they must be furnished by the employer. In the event the employee is required to maintain a washable uniform, the time required to care for this garment is considered work time. An hour's pay at the minimum wage is considered adequate.

9. *Record Keeping.* Basic records such as payroll must be kept for 3 years. Supplementary records, such as time cards, must be kept for 2 years. It is a sound business practice to establish a monthly disposal time so that storage space can be better utilized.

10. *Notice of Tip Credit.* Any club that uses the tip credit to reduce its employees' wages and whose servers are paid less than the minimum wage should publicize the percentage deducted on any menu.

    The lettering must be the common size used in the menu, and if the club has a snack bar or other facility where a posted sign or a blackboard is used, the same rule applies.

    The notice of tip credit does not apply to other tipped employees who receive tip credit, such as valet car parkers, golf starters, and so on.

11. *600-Hour Employees and Independent Contractors.* The law recognizes that from time to time it may become necessary to hire employees for a short time. These are called "600-hour employees," or casual labor. The club may hire persons for a maximum of 600 hours without deducting Social Security or federal withholding tax.

    Another category of employment is called the "independent contractor." The law covering independent contractors is very explicit and must be obeyed. The penalty for not deducting withholding tax, Social Security, and state and federal unemployment taxes is severe. The definition of an independent contractor is as follows:
    a. The worker is paid on a job basis and must take care of all expenses.
    b. The worker furnishes all tools and equipment needed to do the job. There can be some exceptions to this. For example, if the club had a contract with an agronomist to inspect and cure some problems on the golf course, the contract could legally include the professional's use of the club's equipment.
    c. The worker has a considerable investment in the tools and equipment used. Legitimate exceptions can be made to this when a bona fide contract is involved.
    d. The worker is in a position to realize a profit or a loss on the job.
    e. The worker offers the same service to the general public.
    f. The worker can not be fired.

The employer has broad discretionary powers to handle the following items not covered by the FLSA. They are not covered by the law and management should only grant the privileges concerned when it is to the club's best interests.

1. An advance discharge notice or any severance pay.
2. A holiday, Saturday, Sunday or, nighttime pay differential.
3. Report time or show time.
4. Time off for vacations or rest periods. In some states rest periods are mandated by state law.
5. Overtime pay for hours worked in excess of 8 hours per day.
6. Pay raises, including cost-of-living allowances, and fringe benefits not required by law.
7. A limit to the hours an employee 16 years of age or older can work in one 24-hour day. There are also state laws that limit the hours that women may work.

Other Labor Laws

The Equal Opportunity Employment Act
The Equal Opportunity Employment Act covers interviewing practices. Only three categories of persons are not employable: illegal aliens, persons awaiting trial for the commission of a crime, and persons in prison.

The Civil Rights Act, Title VII
The Civil Rights Act, Title VII, bans all discrimination in employment because of race, color, religion, sex, or national origin.

The Equal Pay Act of 1963
The Equal Pay Act of 1963 bans salary discrimination on the basis of sex. The law clearly states the principle of equal pay for equal work.

The Age Discrimination Act of 1979
The Age Discrimination Act of 1979 bans discrimination because of age in the hiring, retirement, or dismissal of anyone 40 years of age or older. However, a bona fide executive whose retirement pay would be a minimum of $27,000 a year, excluding Social Security, may be involuntarily retired.

The Immigration Reform and Control Act
The Immigration Reform and Control Act was passed in an attempt to discourage illegal immigration into the United States. Any club that hires an employee after November 6, 1986, must verify that the applicants are either U.S. citizens or are lawfully authorized alien workers. Clubs hiring after this date are required to have on file documentation establishing employees' identity and legal status. This means that every club must have on file Form 1-9 put out by the Immigration and Naturalization Service.

EMPLOYEE HYGIENE

The health of the club's employees is of major concern to the manager. Not only are healthy employees more productive but club members must be protected from even very minor illnesses such as the common cold. In many states a physical examination is required for all food handlers. Even if not legally mandatory, it is highly recommended as a preemployment requirement for club personnel. Most club health insurance policies require an annual physical.

It is the manager's responsibility to train the supervisors on personal hygiene. A supervisor's checklist should be made available for them to use. A checklist for daily use could include the following:

Outward signs of illness. Specifically, check for sneezing, coughing, runny nose, red eyes, and open sores of any kind

Hair neatly combed and arranged

Working costume neat and clean

Fingernails trimmed and clean

Hands clean

Hose neat and shoes shined

Supervisors must be taught to be alert and hardnosed concerning employees' appearance. If it is slovenly, then sending offenders home, without pay, is the only proper solution. If an employee appears ill and the club offers a sick leave policy as a fringe benefit, the employee must be asked to use it.

EMPLOYEE SAFETY

The average club employee never thinks of work in the club as dangerous, yet in some areas it definitely is. The National Safety Council has gathered figures proving that supervisors and employees are accident prone and careless. Many accidents are possible and do occur in the receiving, preparing, and serving of food.

Accident Prevention

It is management's responsibility to discover and eliminate potential causes of accidents. Safety and being safe are not a matter of luck. As far as safety is concerned, people make their own luck.

Receiving

In the receiving area, goods should be moved to the proper holding areas as soon as possible to prevent tripping or slipping. Then the receiver should inspect the area to see that there are no remaining hazards, such as wet spots. Another safety concern involves the handling of heavy items in the holding areas. This is covered in great detail later in this section.

Kitchens and Dining Rooms

In kitchens and dining rooms accidents can happen in numerous ways.

BURNS AND SCALDS   Because intense heat is needed to cook food, there is always danger of servers getting burned when food is being prepared. The following rules will ensure safety:

1. Use pot and pan holders when picking up hot pans or containers.
2. Make very sure that a pan holder is completely dry, as water in a damp holder will conduct heat.
3. When a pot or a pan has a handle, pick it up by the handle with the stronger hand. Use a dry holder in the other hand to steady the pan.
4. Before lighting a gas oven that has been recently used, leave the door open for about a minute to rid the oven of fumes.
5. Before putting hands in any liquid, test the temperature.
6. Make sure the steam cooker, if the club has the old-fashioned kind, is completely free of steam before opening the door.
7. Be especially careful around the deep-fat fryer, as one drop of boiling fat can cause a severe burn.
8. Always turn the handles of pots and pans on ranges inward.
9. Special care must be taken in pouring hot liquids such as soups and gravies. Pour them very slowly to prevent splashing.
10. Avoid overfilling containers with hot foods or liquids.

SLIPS AND FALLS   As preparing and serving food requires the movement of people and equipment from place to place, extra precautions must be taken to prevent slips and falls.

1. If a tray must be carried up or down a flight of stairs, only carry as much as can be handled by one hand. This leaves the other hand free to grasp the banister.
2. When heavy items must be moved up or down stairs, always ask the supervisor for the additional help of one or more persons.
3. Food or equipment may have to be carried through an unlighted area, for example, in serving at a nighttime pool or garden party. A temporary solution to the lack of light is to have a supply of disposable flashlights on hand to use in illuminating the servers' path. Use the same precautions in carrying hot food as were mentioned above.
4. Wearing comfortable shoes helps prevent slips and falls. The wearing of open-toed shoes and sandals could be hazardous, as there is always the possibility that items may be dropped or spilled.
5. Clean up spills promptly. Spills could make working areas slippery and slippery floors can cause accidents.
6. Keep all floors clean and dry.
7. Do not litter. Place all trash in the trash containers.
8. Use a ladder to reach high places.
9. Never run in the kitchen or dining room. Keep a steady pace at all times; hurrying can cause accidents.
10. If there are separate doors leading in and out of certain areas, all persons must use the proper door.

11. Boxes, crates, cartons, and equipment must be kept off of the floor and out of the aisles.

GETTING HIT OR HITTING SOMEONE   Carried items can always be dropped. A dropped item can hit the person carrying it or hit someone else.

1. In placing items on a tray, employees should never stack them higher than their waist.
2. When using a cart, push it, do not pull it. A pushed cart is much easier to control than a pulled one.
3. A cart should never be stacked so high that the visibility of the pusher is impaired.
4. Do not stack bottles, cans, cartons, and so forth, so close to the edge of a shelf that they could accidentally be brushed off.
5. If items are to remain in boxes or cartons, place the heavier ones on the lowest shelves.
6. When passing through double swinging doors, go through very slowly. In passing through a single swinging door, push it open and observe that the way is clear before passing through.

Transport and Displacement

In every club things have to be moved around—cartons, boxes, crates, equipment, etc. These items are sometimes very heavy, so precautions must be taken by all employees against sprains and strains.

1. In moving heavy objects of 50 pounds or more, two or more persons should be involved.
2. Stoop to pick up any object; this uses the legs rather than the back. The legs are much stronger.
3. Before lifting, get a firm grip on the object to be lifted. Wipe off the hands or the object if either is slippery. Place the fingers under the object if possible. Wear heavy work gloves if the object is rough or has sharp edges.
4. Have the feet firmly planted on a nonskid surface when lifting.
5. Keep the arms straight. This allows the use of shoulder muscles.
6. Lift gradually and steadily; any jerking puts an unnecessary strain on the muscles.
7. Avoid any twisting motion when lifting. Shift the position of your feet so that any movement is up and down.
8. When putting objects down, stoop, using the leg muscles, keep the back straight, and do not twist the body.

Housekeeping

A clubhouse requires special housekeeping procedures for both the safety of the club employees and the members. Some checklist items are:
1. Keep utensils and equipment off the floor.
2. If an item is spilled in the dining room, a chair should immediately be placed

over the spillage until it can be cleaned up. This will prevent either a member or an employee from stepping in it and perhaps falling.

3. Lighting in all areas, particularly in areas with stairs or protrusions, must be relamped immediately.
4. Any furniture that has rough or torn places must be removed.
5. Torn or scuffed spots in carpeting should be repaired.
6. Servers must serve dishes from the proper side, i.e., members' left, as members are expecting the food and drinks to arrive in this manner. Any deviation from the norm could result in an accident.

Valet Parking

Valet parking is a luxury service a club may offer. It should be handled in one of two ways: by contract or by the club hiring personnel. It is a very dangerous practice to allow parkers to work just for tips. If they should get injured, the club may be liable and they would not be covered by workmen's compensation insurance. Also, if a member's car is damaged, the club may have an implied liability not only to repair the car but to pay incidental expenses.

Many clubs are too isolated or do not want an outside contractor providing a service they cannot control and thus hire their own parkers. In addition to the usual employment procedures, the club must examine the applicants' driving records. It is also necessary to observe occasionally the way the parkers handle the cars and to make sure the club has adequate insurance coverage in the event that cars are damaged.

UNIONS

American unions have not made a great deal of progress in unionizing clubs in the past, for the following reasons:

1. Club employees enjoy good working conditions.
2. Club employees receive higher pay than the industry average.
3. Unions that control hospitality industry workers are very solvent and are not hungry for new members.
4. Only small numbers of employees staff the individual clubs.
5. Club personnel constitutes a very stable work force.

This trend, however, is rapidly changing. There are now over ten club chains nationwide owning from five to over two hundred clubs, and the number is rapidly growing.

The nineties will see a lot of union activity in the club business. Because they will expend more effort to attract new members, management must be prepared to deal with unions in a constructive, law-abiding manner.

Any union has the right by law to talk to any club employee. Therefore nothing is gained by putting stumbling blocks in its way—this only gives the opposition selling points. On the contrary, the manager should volunteer to announce to all employees that there will be a meeting with union representatives before or after work, it being the employees' option whether or not to attend. Management has the right to request a copy of the union's constitution and bylaws, a roster of its officers, and its objectives. This is as far as management can go without professional advice, which will be needed when the union files "exclusive representation." A labor management specialist should be hired and his or her advice followed. This will save the club countless hours and many headaches.

REVIEW QUESTIONS

1. What resources do the managers have at their disposal and to what purposes?
2. Why is time so important to the club manager?
3. List the steps a manager may suggest to the board of directors/governors when the club is experiencing financial difficulties.
4. What is the value of having new employees serve a probationary period?
5. What is the difference in management structure between a military club and an equity club?
6. What are the various types of tests management can administer to new employees to evaluate their worth?
7. What steps are necessary in delegating a job to an employee?
8. What three categories of persons are barred from employment by the Equal Opportunity Employment Act?
9. Why is it a dangerous practice for a club to allow someone to work for tips only?
10. What hazards are posed by working in the kitchen? List some safety measures that would help prevent them.

CASE STUDY

Carrie Gomez, a 38-year-old Hispanic woman, was hired by the personnel director of a club for a position in the housekeeping department. The director, José Rodriguez, also a Hispanic, conducted the entire interviewing and hiring process in Spanish without ever finding out that the woman did not speak English. She was a legal employable alien.

A crisis occurred when a member asked the woman, who was dusting the furniture in the foyer, a very simple question and received as an answer a shake of her head. The member immediately complained to the manager and accused him of using very bad judgment in employing the woman as a housekeeper.

Other facts in the case are:

1. The woman is a good worker.
2. As she and her supervisor both speak Spanish, there is adequate communication between them.
3. The woman has been on the job for 5 months.

Outline the steps the manager must take to resolve this situation.

4 Managing the Clubhouse

STAFF

The lifeblood of a club is its membership. The manager provides the members with the services they pay for through direction of the club's staff. Largely because of good salaries and employee benefits, the club business as a whole has attracted high-caliber, steadfast workers and ranks as the most stable of employers in the hospitality industry. The successful operation of a club depends greatly on the organization and management of the staff.

The organization of the club's personnel is very simple if management can start from scratch, as in the case of the formation of a new club or the reopening of one. However, very few managers encounter this kind of situation. More typically, the manager "inherits" an existing organization and, with it, the problems. Poor internal organization may be one such problem. Others are poor food, poor service, poor maintenance, and discontented employees. These sometimes can be caused by:

1. Departments and divisions not being clearly defined. Employees must have a clear idea who their supervisor is to function effectively.
2. Salary scales based on longevity. An example of this would be an employee in a menial job making more money than a skilled cook only because she has been on the job for over 20 years.
3. Unfair pay raises. For example, an employee who is a good worker with a cheerful, outgoing personality who has no ambition to be promoted but who, because of his personality and good work, has been given raises indiscriminately. Now his salary is far higher than is usually paid for the job.
4. Favoritism and/or nepotism. Employees hired because of their relation to someone or because of someone's partiality have an unfair advantage over their peers.
5. Inadequate or unenforced job descriptions. Employees may not understand what their duties are or what is the proper chain of command.

Essentially, a club's organization is based on economic factors. Members must be adequately assessed and staff must be properly remunerated. Behind the successful functioning of a club, in effect, lies its budget.

BUDGETING

In its simplest terms, a budget is a plan indicating how management can expect a club's business to perform during a specified period of time. A budget forecasts the amount of money coming in during that period; it determines how some of that money will be disbursed; and it states how much money should be available at the end of that period. Budgeting also allows the manager to make plans for expansion, repairs, replacement, or improvement of facilities. More important, perhaps, is the fact that a budget, when properly used, becomes a control device. Basically, there are four ways in which a budget assists in achieving such control. These are:

1. A budget forces a careful study of the club's operations. Such an analysis, if conscientiously applied, can reveal possible problems and allow management to take steps to prevent their occurrence.
2. A budget provides management and club personnel with an overall plan and goal. Establishing an obvious and reasonable goal tends to increase efficiency.
3. A budget provides a standard and a guide for evaluating the actual performance of individuals and activities.
4. A budget provides controls over expenditures.

Budgets take time to prepare and it may take the manager and some of the administrative personnel away from things that might seem more pertinent to immediate operations. Information is needed to prepare an efficient budget, a task the manager cannot do alone. Nor can a manager be absolutely sure that the forecasts made are realistic. In addition, to be effective, a budget must have the cooperation of the entire organization. Making a budget work means using it throughout every department in the club. To do this, the manager must make known the plans and goals of that budget to key personnel throughout the operation.

Types of Budgets

There are five types of budgets required for sound business management. Each of these is listed below with a brief description.

1. A *pro forma budget* expresses the manager's financial goals as percentages. With sales representing 100 percent, each budget item is a percentage of sales. Prepared separately or as another column in the "Monthly Operating Budget" (see below), the pro forma budget can easily be compared to the actual financial statements each month.

2. An *annual operating budget* forecasts the income and expenses of the succeeding fiscal year.
3. A *capital expenditure budget* provides a program for the expansion, repairs, replacement, or improvement of capital assets within the capability of the club.
4. A *monthly operating budget* forecasts the income and expenses of the succeeding month, using actual income and expenses of past months as a basis for the forecast, as well as the manager's own projections of future events.
5. A *cash flow budget* shows the flow, in and out, of funds and the amount of cash on hand at any given time.

    To provide additional detail in key areas, appendixes may be included with the above budgets. Examples include, but are not limited to, the following:

- A *renovation and maintenance budget* states when to repair and when to remodel.
- A *sales budget*, based on previous experience, tells what numbers of people will be served and what dollar volume may be anticipated.
- A *labor budget* projects the number of employees needed to serve members, how many man-hours or days will be expended, and how many dollars it will take to meet the projection in terms of an average wage.

Budget Considerations

The budget is designed as a plan, but more often than is admitted, poor planning and preparation enter the budget picture. A manager could sit down with figures from a previous period and manipulate a few of them here and there to come up with projections that are not accurate. It could be that no consideration has been given to changes that have taken place since the previous period, or the manager may not have looked at any of the outside factors influencing management decisions in the future.

Useful steps in preparing the budget include the following:

1. Discuss in advance, with the board and the committee involved, any new items that management wishes to include in the budget.
2. Ascertain the general level of income of the operation (usually by department) and establish appropriate costs for this level. Along with past budgets, the manager may utilize statistical data from other clubs or refer to national averages for the industry as a whole. If the budget is departmentalized and categorized first, it is easier to put the whole package together in a form which is both realistic and informative. This also allows the manager to set specific deadlines for various projects within the budget, name project leaders, and coordinate activities.
3. See that activity budgets are prepared at the lowest possible level. First-line supervisors, such as the bar manager and the chef, should prepare the budgets for their respective activities, as these individuals have the greatest knowledge

about their activities and their future outlook. In addition, if their performances are to be compared with the budget, they should have something to say about what goals are established. It is not the club manager's job to write the budget for the activities, but rather to review the budgets to enable the club to meet its established goals.

4. Involve employees in the master plan. Management seldom thinks to include the dishwasher in the budget picture, but if a manager projects a 5 percent decrease in breakage to cover the purchase of a new dishwashing machine, management certainly is going to have to involve the dishwasher to achieve that goal. The prospect of a new glass washer will perhaps serve to motivate the dishwasher.

5. Do not consider the budget to be written in stone. Budgets can be changed. If food prices climb rapidly, the budget must be adjusted accordingly. If labor costs skyrocket in the club's locality, this may necessitate a rise in menu prices and the whole budget may have to be recalculated.

Useful knowledge to collect when preparing the budget includes:

1. The department's actual operating and budget variance figures from previous periods.
2. The goals set by management and the goals set by others such as the board and the committees.
3. Experience, reports, and statistics concerning the sales potential of the separate departments.
4. Past and future operating policies.
5. National and local economic conditions.
6. Trends of national sales and expenses.
7. Menu prices, popularity of menu items, portion sizes, and costs per portion.
8. Labor statistics within the club by department.
9. Merchandising information.
10. Past population data.

Forecasting Sales

Probably one of the most difficult jobs in preparing a budget is the forecasting of sales, a task made even more difficult because of the inefficient methods of record keeping often used. The estimated sales figure is important not only because it is the largest of the figures projected but also because most of the other budget calculations are based on it. Obviously, if the sales figures are off, the total budget picture will be distorted.

The manager who has at his disposal information on total sales, number of members, average check by department, average sales per employee, and so forth, is in a much better position to forecast future sales than is the one who begins with last year's sales and hopes for a certain percentage of increase in volume. The first manager is in a position to do something about his or her situation, whereas the second manager would do just as well depending entirely on astrological forecasts. As in preparing the rest of the budget, the forecasting of an accurate sales picture depends on the amount of involvement and cooperation the successful manager can generate from within the organization itself and on the proper use of the employees' talents.

The per capita method of forecasting sales consists of computing the average per capita sales for the past 3 months; adjusting this figure based on historical trends, large seasonal parties, and so forth; and multiplying by the estimated membership for the period under consideration. Clubs with radical seasonal changes might have to research the per capita information from the previous year.

Budgetary Controls

Adherence to the following six steps will enable the manager to prepare more accurate budgets, thereby enhancing the control of club operations:

1. To prepare and implement a good budget, engage the cooperation of the entire staff.
2. To ensure cooperation, make known the goals and the future plans for the budget to all key personnel.
3. Budget by components first, then prepare the overall budget. Remember that budgets for the components should be prepared at the lowest possible level by first-line supervisors and activity managers.
4. Adjust the budget to existing costs and sales conditions.
5. Keep the budget close at hand at all times; the budget is a tool to be used.
6. The more people are involved in the implementation of the budget, the greater are the chances of its eventual success in terms of dollars and cents earned and saved.

The day has passed when a budget could be prepared successfully by the manager in conjunction with the bookkeeper. The key to efficient budget making and usage are employee involvement and cooperation. A manager's success depends largely on the degree to which he or she can inspire these qualities.

MANAGING THE FOOD DEPARTMENT

Managing the food department is probably the most difficult of the manager's tasks and the most challenging. Operation of this department differs from that of a restaurant for two reasons: (1) The same persons are using the club day after day, and (2) the members pay both dues and normal restaurant charges. The food department may be subsidized by a portion of the dues money so that the club dining room can display an elegance the average restaurant cannot match at comparable prices. Club luxuries could include but not be limited to:

- A master chef
- A pastry chef (sometimes called a master baker)
- A maitre d' and dining room captains
- Fresh seafood and the finest meat products
- Unusual specialty items such as fresh Norwegian salmon, fresh Maine lobsters, Beluga caviar, etc.
- Fresh flowers on the dining room tables
- Show plates
- Matched, high-quality china, glassware, and silverware
- Linen tablecloths and napery
- More-than-adequate service
- Frequent live music and entertainment

Assisted by the clubhouse manager, the food and beverage manager, the chef, and the maitre d', the manager must be involved in all of the planning. A professional manager must always be one step ahead of the board and the house committee in spotting potential problem areas and finding solutions for them.

That the club food business is undergoing a radical change does not make the manager's job any easier. Several factors account for this change:

1. Demand has increased for family dining with special menus for children. In many clubs it is going to become necessary to have a "family dining room," where members with children can dine in a less formal atmosphere.
2. A much more varied menu must be offered than in the past, following the lead of the free-standing, medium-priced, table-service restaurants.
3. Members will have more time to spend at the club creating the potential for increased food revenue.

Setting Standards and Costs

The first standard to be established pertains to the food budget. A certain percentage of the cost of goods sold determines food prices:

$$\frac{\text{Actual cost}}{\text{Percent of cost}} = \text{Selling price}$$

The percent of cost is fixed by the pro forma budget. Subtracting the flexible and fixed expenses and net bottom-line percentages from sales (100 percent) gives the percent of cost. The flexible expenses are those that are closely tied to sales, such as labor. Fixed expenses are those that occur regardless of sales, such as insurance. The lower the percentage of cost, the higher the selling price:

$$\frac{\text{Actual cost: \$2}}{\text{Percent of cost: 40\%}} = \text{Selling price: \$5}$$

In the event that the flexible and fixed expenses are too high to meet other club and restaurant competition, the general manager can use certain strategies to lower the selling prices with minimal cost to club members.

- Analyze all of the expense items. Each of the accounting firms specializing in hospitality accounting publish the average expense percentages for establishments similar to the club.
- Suggest to the board that some of the dues money be used to subsidize the food department.
- Study the possibility of lowering the prices called for by the budget but getting the right percentage through a sales mix. Feature items with lower costs, such as pasta or chicken dishes.
- Adjust the à la carte menu. Analyze the items included in the entree and remove one or two of these to reduce the food cost. For example, if the menu calls for a salad with the entree, price the salad separately.

Food Production Labor

The next standard to be established in the food department is labor. For purposes of control, the cost of preparing food is separated from the cost of serving it.

Developing a labor standard for the staff in the kitchen can be done by using the "factor method" (Table 4.1), which proposes that all food-preparation employees be paid by the hour. These include the executive chef or other employees who might be paid an annual wage.

The standard is based on the kitchen payroll divided by the number of factors produced. Every entree that is served has a factor value based on the amount of time it takes to prepare it.

To implement this standard the following steps are necessary:

Table 4.1   A Menu with the Preparation Factors

Menu Item	Factor Number	Total Sold	Total Factors Produced
Rib-eye steak	1	335	335
New York 10-oz. strip steak	1.5	390	585
6-oz. filet mignon	1	310	310
Blackened roast chicken	3	150	450
Half a fried chicken	2.5	100	250
Filets of grouper	2	30	60
Red snapper	2	190	380
Shrimp scampi	4	85	340
Fried shrimp	2.5	130	325
Total		1720	3035

1. The general manager will arrange to meet with the food and beverage director and the chef to analyze the menu. They will decide on the entree item that takes the least time to prepare and give this item a factor value of one. Then they will determine if any other item takes about the same time to prepare.
2. A factor number will be selected for the rest of the entrees, using both whole and half factors. For example, another menu item might take twice as long to prepare as the item that has a 1 factor. This then would have a factor of 2. Menu items might take a half factor more than another, which would be represented by 1.5, 2.5, etc.
3. The total number of each entree sold is determined from the scatter sheet (a record of the menu items sold during any one period of time).
4. Multiply the factor (which indicates preparation time) by the total number of entree items sold.

For example, if the weekly kitchen payroll is set at $1500 (= the gross wages plus the fringe benefits required by law, i.e., employer's share of Social Security, Worker's Compensation and federal and state unemployment insurance), then, using the figures in Table 4.1:

$$\frac{\$1500}{3035} = \$.49, \text{ the value of each factor}$$

The accounting department can prepare such calculations on a weekly or monthly basis. Usually factor charts will provide sufficient information to get started. When the factor value is at its lowest, this becomes the kitchen standard. This means that kitchen production is at its highest and this figure can be used to establish a bonus system. This method can also be used to obtain a very close figure for the labor cost of the individual menu items. This can then assist in determining menu items that are popular and profitable, as management will now have both a food and labor cost (this is called the prime cost). Knowing the prime cost, the selling price, and the profit contribution, each menu item can be placed in one of five categories, called the:

1. *Trumps*. The most popular and profitable items on the menu.
2. *Spades*. Very popular items on the menu but not as popular or as profitable as the Trumps.
3. *Hearts*. Very profitable items on the menu but not as popular as the Trumps or Spades.
4. *Diamonds*. Items not as profitable or as popular as the Trumps, Spades, or Hearts; consideration should be given to some substitutions.
5. *Clubs*. Items neither popular nor profitable—must be changed.

MANAGING THE DINING ROOM

Labor costs in the dining room are always difficult to determine. The amount of service must be gauged by the members' wants. No managers have ever been relieved of their duties for providing too much service. In the club business, there are no set standards because boards differ in their perceptions. The manager's responsibility is to see that the service personnel are well trained and effectively utilized. Part of their training must teach them to sell.

Clubs have a choice in developing their menus or having an à la carte menu (where every item is priced separately), table d'hôte menu (where one price includes a complete dinner), or a combination of the two. The cocktails and wine (either by the glass or bottle) are priced separately for the regular dinners. If the member is ordering from the à la carte section, the server has an opportunity to sell the following items in the order given:

1. A cocktail or a glass of wine
2. The daily specials
3. An appetizer (then the order for the entree is taken; if a salad is not part of the entree order, then a salad might be sold)
4. A dessert
5. Coffee, tea, milk, or a fancy drink such as an Irish coffee. (If only coffee is ordered, then a cordial such as Drambuie, brandy, or Bailey's Irish Cream could be suggested.)

These suggestions are important because such items can increase the dollar sales and the check average. The check average is determined by dividing the dollar amount of sales by the number of diners.

$$\frac{\text{Dollar amount of sales}}{\text{Number of diners}} = \text{Check average}$$

This calculation should be made for every meal the club serves.

Guest Check Control

Management may permit tips or exact a voluntary or involuntary service charge. If the service charge is shared with the servers, it increases their compensation. If the club has a system allowing the server to be identified, then the server with the highest check average could be rewarded monthly. This procedure would also keep the entire body of servers informed of their check average.

Identifying the server can be done in many ways, some of which are:

1. Have the servers write their names or assigned numbers on each duplicate check. If this is combined with the "chef's receipt and issue system" (explained later in this chapter), it will not only identify the server for check-averaging purposes but is a food control measure.
2. Have a food checker/cashier located between the kitchen and the dining room. The server gives the original of the duplicate check to the checker, who records the name or number of the server on it. Having a food checker also assures that

every item served is on the check, as the server must pass the checker on the way to serve the member.

3. Have the host or hostess control checks by putting the servers' numbers on them.

MENUS

The dictionary defines a menu as "a list of dishes served" or "a bill of fare." The menu, however, is much more than a list to the modern club manager. Indeed, if the only reason for having a menu were to list a number of items, its value to the club industry would diminish as members became more familiar with the items offered. Instead, the industry spends thousands of dollars annually on the designing and printing of menus, activities which, in themselves, have become career fields.

When a new club menu is being considered or an old one revised, management could have a planning session with the food and beverage director, the chef, and the service personnel. At this time a thorough briefing could be given on three important aspects of menu dynamics:

- How members look at and respond to the menu
- How the menu can assist members in making their selections
- How the menu can sell members what the club wants them to buy

This should enable the service personnel, in particular, to anticipate the members' acceptance or rejection of menu items.

How the Member Reads the Menu

When someone first opens a menu, experience has shown that the eyes rest immediately on the center of the page (Fig. 4.1). This is done with no conscious effort but, rather, is an unconscious optical reflex. This area then becomes the prime target and hence the prime space on the menu. The "law of primacy" states that the first thing a person sees is the thing that will be remembered. This center space should therefore contain information regarding an item or items above average in profitability and popularity.

Next the member's gaze rises to the upper left-hand side of the page (Fig. 4.2). This space could be gainfully employed in promoting profitable items such as appetizers, soups, or chef's specialities.

The eyes of the member then travel across the top of the menu page in a normal left-to-right reading pattern (Fig. 4.3). Consequently, the upper right-hand corner is where to begin listing the bill of fare. The items are not listed by price but according to member preferences and house profits. Items could also be listed by category—some seafood items together, for example—but not all. Interest, not arrangement, is the issue. Also, items should be priced so figures end in odd numbers of 25, 75, and 95, never in zero or double zeros: it has been proved that shoppers would find a number like $4.95 more attractive than $5.00.

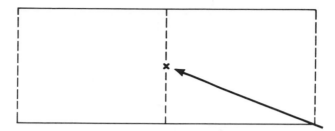

FIGURE 4.1 *Menu, left to center.*

The eyes now follow the items toward the bottom of the right-hand page (Fig. 4.4). This area should be reserved for the not-so-profitable or less-popular items. Low-cost popular items should be high on the listing where the chances of selling them is increased.

The menu reader's eyes now travel across the bottom of the menu page (Fig. 4.5). Even though this is the least marketable space, it might be used to explain the goals of management or to explain particular refinements of the food production and/or service. Or this would be where to spotlight a single item which the member can get no place else, i.e., "Mom's Homemade Apple Pie with Crowley Cheese." Desserts may be profitably merchandised on the back of the menu or on a separate dessert menu list.

From this knowledge of how a member sees the menu, management can decide where the offerings on the menu should be placed. Because each dining room is different, as is each bill of fare, it is up to the manager to decide where each item will appear on the menu and to fully inform the employees why it is so placed.

Use of "Color" Words on the Menu

Linguists say that the average English-speaking American has an active vocabulary of less than six hundred words, which should say something about the wording of menus. *"Pot-au-feu"* may impress a few people with the manager's knowledge of French (and chefs trained in European cookery are often prone to use these kinds of

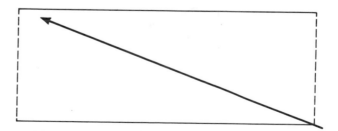

FIGURE 4.2 *Menu, center to left.*

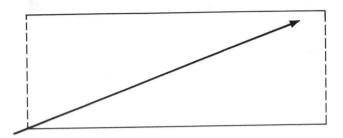

FIGURE 4.3   *Menu, top left to right.*

terms), but "Homemade Beef Broth with Chunks of Beef and Assorted Vegetables" will sell more soup to Mr. and Mrs. Average American. Likewise, why confuse with *au jus* when the words *natural gravy* will convey the meaning so much more accurately to both the member and the server?

There are, however, certain "color" words that serve to enhance the menu by calling to the reader's mind visions not only of what the menu item will look like but even what it is going to taste like. For example, use popular words that describe the regions from which items come:

Virginia Ham	Hungarian Goulash
Canadian Bacon	Smithfield Ham
Southern Fried Chicken	Yankee Pot Roast

Regional labels often tell how dishes are prepared and how they will taste. Other good menu "color" words are:

sizzling	broiled
spiced	glazed
imported	candied
special	honey-cured
roasted	oven-baked

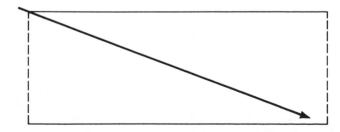

FIGURE 4.4   *Menu, top right to lower right-hand corner.*

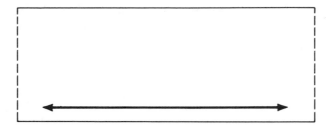

Figure 4.5 *Menu, bottom.*

sugar-cured	peanut-fed
hickory-smoked	barbecued
genuine	maple-cured

Words that denote quality are also salesworthy, for example:

Imported Russian Caviar
Genuine Maple Syrup
Roast Boneless Sirloin of Beef
Ripe Hothouse Strawberries
Broiled Live Maine Lobster
Prime Filet of Gaspé Salmon

Judicious word combinations call forth pictures that will tempt club diners to choose certain items. Pot roast with vegetables can be more evocatively expressed, for instance, as:

Tender Dutch Oven Roast of Beef
with
Fresh Garden Vegetables

On the other hand, "Oven-baked Filet Mignon" would not do! At an employee meeting, it may be advantageous to solicit suggestions from the employees about how menu wording might be improved. This enables management to get them involved.

A word of warning: The word *fresh* is a sure winner on all menus—as is the phrase *All our bakery products are baked here,*—but care must be taken to be honest, as most people can tell the difference between fresh and frozen foods and between commercial bakery and homemade goods. In general, care should be taken to prepare foods as advertised.

Menu Monotony

For the club manager, as well as the chef and his kitchen personnel, the advice "beware of menu monotony" represents good, solid thinking. The same members will be returning again and again and have a right to expect new items at least monthly.

It is true baked potatoes "go with" roast beef, but so do whipped potatoes, Dutchess potatoes, oven roast potatoes, even home-fried potatoes. Also, Yorkshire pudding, fresh horseradish slivers, and/or hot buttermilk biscuits "go with" roast beef. Club members will appreciate small changes such as these for the variety they lend to the menu.

Menus should not be repeated on the same day of every week either. Systematizing and standardizing menu items may be efficient, but too much of a good thing, repeated too often, can be very monotonous. It may be standard practice as well as a good promotion to publicize a "Beef and Burgundy Night," but to have it on the same night of every week, to the exclusion of other menu specials, could discourage members who might otherwise partake of the fare.

A serious problem for servers is trying to describe a new dish to members. The difficulty lies in their never having tasted it. It would serve two purposes if a new menu item were served to the employees at dinner: First, they could sample the dish and if they like it, could sell it to club members. Second, the kitchen gets an opportunity to practice preparing an item before it is served to members.

Menu clip-ons are an excellent way of advertising specials that may be new menu items or new recipes for old ones. One restaurateur listed broiled blackened red snapper on the regular menu and stuffed red snapper, a new item, on a menu clip-on. Sales of both items were about equal, but together they represented an increase in the variety of his seafood entree sales without another item having to be added to the inventory. Servers should be instructed to "push" particular items each meal, using phrases such as "the fresh swordfish is delicious today." Some chefs use a chalkboard in the kitchen on which are prominently posted "Items to Push" and "86 Items" (the slang term for items that are sold out).

Finally, constant communication among management, food preparation staff, and service personnel regarding menu items is a "must" if clubs are to avoid the doldrums of the monotonous menu.

Menu Anticipation

As soon as the club member peruses the menu, he/she should know:

The type of cuisine the club serves
The number of choices or options the menu offers
Approximately what the cost will be for the meal

The manner in which the above information is imparted is most important and the menu is the chief vehicle for this task. Every person in the organization who deals with members should understand fully what is meant by "menu anticipation." This term does not only apply to the physical structure of the menu but the manner in which the items are arranged and presented. It also means placing the proper items together in the proper places and under the proper headings so the member can identify them with the least amount of time and trouble.

Menu anticipation also means variety. Many clubs featuring typical American cuisine have added pasta and other Italian dishes, others a New England boiled dinner and a barbecued item. This type of menu planning answers the members desire for something different. Also, no one wants to sit at a table and read a menu offering five kinds of chicken when their mind is set on seafood. Nor does the beef eater appreciate the menu offering nothing but seafood. This principle applies to the selection of food accompaniments and desserts as well. *Variety is important.*

Groupings of menu items can also be varied. Steaks, chops, roasts, seafood, appetizers, soups, salads, and desserts are traditional categories. Categorizing in terms of how the food is prepared is a new and interesting approach that makes the same menu look very different. "From the Broiler or Grill," "Chafing Dishes," "Cold Plates," etc.: Every category or mode of presentation tells the member something. A well-conceived menu makes the server's task easier, too. There are fewer questions to answer, hence time is saved.

Principles of Menu Planning

The descriptive words used on the menu would mean very little to club members, however, if the following considerations were ignored:

1. *Eye-appeal and Color.* All plates should be arranged with some thought as to how they are going to appear to the member. This is even more important when clip-ons or color photographs are used to promote food sales. If the members do not get on the plate what they have seen in the photo, they may be very unhappy.
2. *Quality.* The condition of and the manner in which the menu reads implies the quality of the foods that will be presented. If this quality is less than diners assume after seeing the menu, they will be unhappy.
3. *Menu Balance.* A certain amount of balance is projected to the member by what is on the menu. Balance is upset when:
   • The order arrives without the specified vegetable.
   • The food is arranged haphazardly on the plate.
   • The food is over- or undercooked.
4. *Standardization.* Members do not appreciate too much food on the plate any more than too little. They do expect to receive an adequate serving of whatever is ordered. "Portion control" means serving the right amount, neither too much nor too little, to satisfy the expectations of the member.
5. *Flavor.* The use of "color" words on the menu may suggest to the member the way the item actually tastes, or should taste. If food flavors are flat and bland, the members will feel cheated and the time, effort, and money expended on the menu—not to mention the food—will have gone for nothing.

In summary, menu planning must be based on a sound relationship between the menu itself and the products it sells. Without continuous application of the five aforementioned principles, the menu becomes fiction, not fact, in the mind of the club member.

Production Facilities and the Menu

Far too much menu planning is done before any consideration is given to the facilities to be used in preparing the items presented. Management must realize that once the investment is made to print a menu, it is too late to think about whether its offerings can in fact be produced. Because an item cannot be prepared in sufficient quantity due to a lack of, or the condition of, production equipment or facilities, the kitchen is forced to take short cuts, which result in failed menu offerings and dissatisfaction on the part of kitchen staff and club members alike.

Adjusting the Menu to Fluctuating Costs

One of the industry's problems is that prices may rise high enough after a menu has been printed to seriously affect the profit that was predicted. The following suggestions may assist management in altering the menu without changing standard menu prices. (The principles applied to meat may be applied to all menu items.)

1. Have the chef reduce the amount of meat in a meat dish. For example, a Filet Mignon Shish Kebab could be prepared using only 5 ounces of filet mignon instead of 6.
2. Check out all low-cost, high-volume items on the menu and instruct servers to mention them first if a member asks, "What's good tonight?"
3. Offer, at infrequent intervals, a table d'hôte "Filet Special Dinner." The price can be adjusted according to the cost of meat in a complete "soup-to-nuts" dinner.
4. Offer "extras" in combination with certain low-cost dinner items. For example, a menu clip-on special may feature a cup of soup.
5. Run a beef item for which both portions and selling price can be adjusted— another kind of steak not printed on the menu, such as a rib eye, T-bone, or sirloin strip.

Note: It is not recommended that an item be removed from the menu. Pushing substitutions reduces loss.

MENU-PRICING STRATEGIES

In these days of ever-fluctuating food costs and spiralling operating costs, it is virtually impossible for the manager to say, "I'll make a set profit on each and every item on my menu." What is true today will not necessarily be true tomorrow. Profits depend on current and accurate cost data, and must be adjusted to conform with existing conditions if profits are to be maintained.

A problem arises from the mistaken belief that an unprofitable operation can be reversed merely by increasing menu prices. Too frequently prices are raised without investigating the real cause of the problem, which could be inability to control costs.

In this case not only does a price increase fail to solve the problem; it also has an unfavorable impact on the membership.

The first step in menu strategy is a thorough analysis of the menus presently in use at the club. The analysis starts by gathering cost data on every item appearing on the menu. A "scatter sheet" is used to determine sales trends and the popularity rating of each food item listed (Fig. 4.6). Management can then study guest checks to understand the relationship of one menu item to another and to gauge food sale trends during the course of the meal. Institute within the club dining room a "Customer Comments Card" (Fig. 4.7).

Once a month, at both lunch and dinner, Member Comment Cards could be placed on each table as it is set. After the meal the cards would be collected by the busperson and given to the dining room manager. The cards would then be forwarded to management for study. Experience has shown that the cards are not of as much value if used more frequently. Knowing the items sold and members' preferences is the first step in arriving at a fair profit percentage.

Menu Item	Number Sold Daily							Weekly	Month to Date
	S	M	T	W	T	F	S		
Appetizers									
Salads									
Entrees									
Desserts									

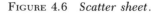

FIGURE 4.6 *Scatter sheet.*

Dear Member:
Your comments on the meal and service would be appreciated. The item ordered was
_____

THE MEAL: Excellent__ Good__ Fair__ Poor__
THE SERVICE: Excellent__ Good__ Fair__ Poor__

Please check to express your opinion

FIGURE 4.7 *Membership comment card.*

Using the Sales Matrix

To make the menu-pricing strategy work, it is necessary to establish a reasonable range of profit. This must be consistent with the membership's objective of getting an excellent meal for a fair price.

Leaders in the hospitality industry have determined certain average menu item food costs for the industry as a whole. These may not suit every club but could be useful as a guide. These are:

Menu Categories	Average Food Cost Percent
Desserts	35
Appetizers	20–50
Fast-selling entrees	35–45
Slow-selling entrees	30
High-priced entrees	45–55

Using these figures as guides, it is possible to break the menu into categories and arrive at viable profit percentages:

Menu Categories	Profit Percentage
Appetizers	20–50
Salads	10–20
Entrees	30–55
Vegetables	15–25
Beverages	10–20
Desserts	15–35

Note: If a table d'hôte menu is used rather than an à la carte menu, the profit percentage will have to be averaged out. This is accomplished by adding the total percentages and dividing them by the number of items.

Once profit objectives have been categorized, there are three factors to be considered in pricing the menu item:

- The raw cost of the food used in preparing the item
- The potential market for the product
- The risk involved in carrying the item on the menu

After careful consideration of all of these factors, each item on the menu should fit into one of the following sales categories:

High Volume–Low Cost
Low Volume–Low Cost
High Volume–High Cost
Low Volume–High Cost

(*Note:* This is a different approach from the profit and popularity analysis explained previously.) Such an analysis is referred to as the menu sales matrix.

Considering, in turn, each item on the menu that requires pricing, assign it to one of the above categories. Using the profit percentages list, it should be possible to determine individual profit percentages as follows:

Item	Category	Desired Profit Percentage
Soups	High Volume–Low Cost	80

The inclusion on the sales matrix of a specific menu item has to be made in terms of the sales potential. What is true of the menu in one club may not be so in another. Besides the market potential, there is the question of the risk factor involved in carrying the item. One club may be perfectly capable of carrying and handling fresh live lobsters; for another, the market may be lacking and a high risk factor may be involved. In essence, the categorization of each menu item on the sales matrix becomes a management decision.

Costing the Menu

Of necessity, in analyzing the menu and in utilizing the sales matrix, much has to be left to the good judgment of management. In arriving at a true raw food cost, the opposite is the case. True food cost depends wholly on the reliability of cost figures and usable weights. The manager may establish food cost objectives in advance of the procurement of food items, but in the final analysis, the cost of the goods sold and the yield from preportioned servings will determine whether cost objectives have been met.

A good commercial cookbook will yield figures on all recipes. These figures must be used to calculate portion costs. For example, pasta dishes (gaining in popularity each year) have retained their profitability through the years and can be prepared in any quantity desired.

Factoring Tight Food Costs

A second method of arriving at a reliable portion cost is as follows: Determine that portion of the original weight that will actually be used (original weight less waste, shrinkage, etc.). For example, if there was a 1-pound loss in cooking a 5-pound roasting chicken costing $.50 per pound, the usable weight would be 4 pounds. Calculate the cost per pound by dividing the cost price of $2.50 by 4 pounds, which is $.63. Then boning the chicken and dividing the weight of the meat into $2.50 gives the real cost of the main ingredient in a chicken salad.

Once the cost of the chicken meat is known, the cost of all the other ingredients would be added to arrive at the total cost. When all the ingredients have been costed and added, the salad is again weighed and found to be 3 pounds. Say the cost of the meat and other ingredients is $3. The cost per pound is then $1, or $.062 per ounce. The portion size is 6 ounces for a cost of $.37 per serving.

Finally, by using the method described previously of determining the selling price by dividing the actual cost by the percentage of cost desired, the selling price is determined.

Profit Objective

Once the menu has been researched, the food items categorized, and the menu selections costed on a per-portion basis, profit can be planned through the use of the techniques outlined below.

The entire concept of profit planning rests on the identification of three items: sales, fixed and variable expenses, and net results. Fixed costs are those which remain constant regardless of the level of sales volume. Variable costs will vary with the number of meals produced.

Using the financial statement, the manager will start by determining what profit contribution, if any, the food department must make. This is then expressed in a percentage of sales. Using sales as 100 percent, each expense item is converted to percentages. The percentages, without sales or cost of goods sold, are totaled and subtracted from 100. If this figure is the same or less than the cost of goods sold, the food department is in great shape as long as club members like the food and service. For example, if the calculated percentage of the cost of goods was 43 percent and the actual percentage was 40 percent, management has 3 percent of sales yet to spend.

In the event the calculated cost is more than the actual cost, then the club cannot achieve its management objectives. The difference in percentage points between the two costs is the amount of reduction that must be made. The corrective steps are as follows:

1. The pro forma budget would be checked to see if there was any variation in expenses. For example, if the labor cost was set at 35 percent and the actual cost was 39 percent, then 4 percent of the variance has been identified. Then labor controls could be reviewed, starting with scheduling. If the controls are adequate and 39 percent of sales is needed, then the pro forma budget must be adjusted.
2. If the variance is not found through the comparison with the pro forma budget, then the cost of food must be lowered or sales increased. A checklist to review the cost of sales can then be used:
   • Checking the purveyors' invoices. Has there been a price increase large enough to affect the menu price?
   • Are good receiving procedures in effect?
   • Is there any loss by improper storage methods?
   • Are recipes being followed and correct portions being served?
   • Are employees' meals controlled?
   • Are all used guest checks accounted for?

If the checklist does not explain the variance, then the menu itself must be examined. There are many ways to reduce food costs without raising prices. Some of these are:

1. Reduce portion sizes. Some person in management should periodically check the food on plates that are picked up after the meal. If there is a substantial quantity of food left on the plate, the reasons for this could be that the portion was too large, or that the food was not prepared properly. If, after investigation, portion sizes can be reduced, the food cost will follow.
   Also, study the advertised portions to determine if they can be reduced. Could the New York prime sirloin steak be reduced from 12 to 10 ounces for the same price, or could the New Orleans battered fried shrimp be reduced from 6 to 5 ounces?
2. Study the à la carte portion of the menu. Can any item that is now included be separately priced or reduced in cost? For example, could a salad, if included with the steak, be eliminated or decreased in size?
3. Increase sales by pushing items that are not included in the à la carte servings. This could include cocktails, appetizers, salads, desserts, beverages, and after-dinner cordials.

FOOD AND THE MEMBER

Four details assist in giving the member a dining experience that will be remembered: presentation, temperature, taste, and service. Management must ensure through supervision and training that these basic factors bring pleasure to the members.

The first step is to place the prepared food on the properly prepared plate. The one thing necessary to prepare the plate is to control its temperature while empty. Heat the plate if hot food is to be placed on it; chill the plate if it is to be used for salads or other cold foods.

Modern equipment makes it easy to preheat plates. A cart containing a heating element is filled at the dishwashing machine's clean-dish side, wheeled to the cook's plate-preparation line, and plugged in to an electrical outlet. The cook can remove one plate at a time at any desired temperature.

When prepared, the plate should be absolutely clean of grease or vegetable shreds. Each item should have a separate and distinct place on the plate. Any item that may run into another should be served on a separate side dish.

Garnishing

The appeal of any dish can be greatly enhanced by garnishes. There are an infinite number of ways that a plate can be made more attractive. Some garnishing ideas for appetizers are:

1. If the item to be garnished is clear, such as soup, use a thin slice of lemon sprinkled with parsley, a few slices of stuffed olives, slivers of cucumber pickle, a few tiny slivers of carrot for a color-contrasting orange, or a few pieces of slivered, salted almonds, to name just a few ideas.
2. If the item is jellied, use chopped olives, watercress, mint, parsley, slivers of pickle, sliced hard-boiled eggs, or slices of lemon.
3. If the item is lightly creamed, use croutons, egg dumplings, diced cooked vegetables, pimento strips, grated cheese, a floating center island of salted whipped cream 2 inches in diameter, crisp bacon, or shredded, salted almonds.
4. If the item is heavily creamed, use buttered popcorn, slices of smoked sausage or franks, or diced crisp bacon.
5. If garnishing fruit cups, use a sprig of mint, a green or red cherry, a whole strawberry, or a small dip of ice cream or sherbert.

Some garnishing ideas for main-course plates include:

- If the item is seafood, use lemon slices or wedges; parsley; paprika; pimento strips; strips of green pepper; radish slices; rolled anchovy fillets; capers; a tomato slice topped with slice of lemon; celery and carrot strips; stuffed, ripe, or green olives; or watercress.
- If the items are meat and poultry, use parsley, apple slices, lettuce and tomato, sliced pears, cucumber and celery strips, ripe and green olives, or green pepper rings.
- If the items are salads, use carrot or celery curls, cheese balls, cherry poinsettias, cucumber curls, green pepper rings, onion rings, pickle fans, radishes (plain and rosettes), slices of fruit, or melon.

The person who prepares the plate should place a cover over the plate when it is finished. This allows for some lag time between the finishing of the plate and the server picking it up. Most plates if left uncovered for 5 or more minutes will return to room temperature. It is the dining room supervisor's responsibility to ensure that when the plates are ready they are picked up by the server and delivered to the member.

Serving the Member

In any club the most important person is the member. Regardless of the attractiveness of the dining room or the quality of the food, unless the service satisfies, the dining room cannot be successful. The maitre d', the captains, the hostess, and the servers have more personal contact with the members each day than the general manager has each week.

The serving of food is the broad title used to describe the entire dining room operation and includes all factors of person-to-person membership relations. This relationship can be divided into three parts: reception, sale of the menu, and service to the member.

Preparation for the reception of the members starts well before their actual arrival. Each night after the dining room is closed, every table should be cleared. If there is an after-hours cleaning crew, they could wipe and clean the tables and chairs, or this can be done the next morning. The setting up of the room is determined by the type and variety of the menu for that particular meal.

Each table in the room should be set up with tablecloths, the proper silverware, glassware, chinaware, and linen. A room should never contain extra tables that are left bare. If the room is too large, use room dividers or lounge furniture to decrease its size. This establishes an image of efficiency, whereby the member senses that management knows how many persons will be served (using the same forecasting principles governing food preparation) and that their club is prepared for them. A good measure to use is to set up 10 percent over the forecast.

Seating should be varied to suit the needs of the members, with singles and deuces spaced along the perimeter and the fours, sixes, and eights in the middle of the room. Most fine clubs have switched to round tables for the sixes and eights. Round tables promote conversation between guests and enhance the gregariousness of a club atmosphere.

The dining room manager should mentally divide the room into server's stations and check for the service setups at each. The size of the club will dictate the number of stations. Each station should be equipped to handle the members in that section of the room. The station could have condiments, coffee, cream, ice and tongs, glasses, ice water and pitchers, silverware, linen, butter in iced trays, a coffee warmer, and serving pots. In addition, the section should have sufficient tray racks to meet the server's needs.

The next check for the dining room manager is the lighting. It must be checked to be sure that the club has the right atmosphere for the meal. If there are candles on the tables, they should all be lit just before the room is opened.

Ventilation and temperature are the next items to be checked for member comfort. Then the entrance should be inspected for any loose gear. Finally, the host/hostess station should be set up with menus and reservation forms.

DINING ROOM SERVICE

There are basically six types of dining room service a club can offer: French, English, Russian, American Club, buffet, and cafeteria.

French service is the most elaborate form of table service. The food is brought into the dining room on a cart (called a "gueridon") and displayed to the members. For example, if the entree were crown roast of lamb, the server would parade the roast around the table for all the members to see.

The server would then slice the roast and attractively arrange the lamb and the vegetables on the plates and serve them to the members. The food on the cart could also be in a bowl or a chaffing dish. Food also can be arranged on serving dishes, supplied with serving spoons, tongs, or forks and presented to the members so that they may help themselves. This is called a "variation of French service." A single dish or the main course may be served in this fashion. French pastries and other desserts are often offered to the members from a tray.

Another version of French service is the salad cart. The salad ingredients are placed on the gueridon and wheeled to the table. Then the salad is mixed at the table. This is a particularly spectacular way to serve Caesar salad. Still other variations are to serve flaming desserts, called flambés, such as cherries jubilee, flambéd at the table, or have prepared salads and desserts on a cart that is presented to the members so they can have a wider visible choice.

English service is sometimes called "host service." In this style of service, the food, the plates, and the serving spoon, carving knife, and cook's fork are placed in front of the host or hostess, who carves the turkey and apportions it with the vegetables. The server stands to the right of the host or hostess, receives the plates and serves them to the guests. This service is used for holidays such as Thanksgiving, when a member can order a whole turkey. (The club suggests a weight based on the number of persons in the party.) The member can handle the dinner as if at home without the labor and cleanup. This form of service can also be used for private parties and should be available to the members.

Russian service is the most popular form of service in clubs. In this service the entree, vegetables, and garnishing are placed on the plate in the kitchen, carried into the dining room, and served. This type of service was originated for formal dinners by Czar Alexander of Russia in the nineteenth century as a direct slap at the French court for their "pièces motées." These were great mountains of food wheeled into the banquet chamber, where the guests were served.

American club service is also very popular. This service is a combination of the traditional forms. The entree may be placed with the vegetable on a plate in the kitchen, the salad and the dessert prepared at the table or served from a cart. In short, the best parts of the traditional services are used to satisfy the members' needs.

Buffet service enables the members to serve themselves from an array of displayed dishes called the "buffet line." The food table or tables (many clubs use a separate table for salads and desserts) are usually beautifully decorated with ice and other carvings and flowers. The buffet line can consist of the entire meal or just salads (sometimes called a "salad bar"). Other single items may be appetizers (such as a "raw bar," where oysters are shucked, for example) and desserts. In most buffet-service meals, a single price includes the complete meal.

The guests, either served or serving themselves, should have the choice of a salad plate and a large dinner plate. Usually at a buffet dinner the soup, drinks, and bread and butter are served at the table, as it is very hazardous for members to walk around with these types of items. Trays are not used, for diners are encouraged to make as many trips to the buffet table as they desire. When hot foods are presented on the buffet table, a server should be available to slice the meats and serve the vegetables. Another very nice touch, if the club can afford the additional labor cost, is to have a server at the end of the line to carry the club members' plates to their tables.

A "smorgasbord" is the name given buffet-style service of Swedish origin, which offers a great variety of items. A large selection of typically Swedish foods are featured: open-faced sandwiches, seafood in many different styles, salads, meats, and vegetables. This kind of buffet usually uses separate tables for desserts.

Cafeteria service is sometimes used by the clubs at a snack shack for breakfast or a very informal luncheon. In this type of service, the food items are placed on a table with the hot items such as scrambled eggs served in a chafing dish. The items are paid for separately.

Proper Service of Food

The general rules for food servers are:

1. Check the plates at the kitchen pickup counter to observe that they have been garnished and the food neatly arranged.
2. Place a plate cover over every plate.
3. Bring all food from the kitchen on a tray.
4. Check to see that the table is properly set.
5. Serve food on the left side of the member and remove from the right. Serve and remove all beverages, including water, from the right of the member.
6. Use the left hand when placing or removing dishes from the left side of the member, and the right hand when working on the right side. This avoids bumping the member's arm.
7. Present serving dishes from the left side when the members serve themselves. Place the serving silver on the right side of the dish, with the handle turned toward the member so that the handle can be reached easily.
8. Never reach in front of a member or across a member to serve another.
9. Place each dish on the table with four fingers under the plate and the thumb on the upper edge.
10. Hold silverware by the handles when laying it on the table.

11. Do not lift glasses from the table in order to fill them. They can be moved, however, to a more convenient location.
12. Use underliner dishes for juice and cocktail glasses, soup bowls, and dessert dishes. They should be placed in the center of the cover in front of the member.
13. Place the salad plate, when it accompanies the main course, to the left of the member and about 2 inches from the edge of the table. When the salad is served as a separate course, place the plate directly in front of the member.
14. Individual trays containing bread or rolls are placed in different places on the cover depending on the number of persons at the table. For one to four persons, place one tray in the center of the table; for six to eight persons, use two, one on each side of the table.
15. Place the cup and the saucer to the right of the knives and about six inches above the edge of the table.
16. Set tea and coffee pots on small plates and place them above and slightly to the right of the coffee cup. Set iced beverages on small plates or coasters.
17. Serve all items such as butter chips, cheese, and so forth, with a fork or a spoon.
18. Place milk in a glass to the right of and below the water glass.
19. Always remove the soiled dishes of one course before serving the next, and crumb the table as needed.
20. When serving members in a booth, stand at the end of the table and serve each item to the left or right.
21. Serve everything with the hand farthest from the member: use the right hand to serve a member at the left and left hand to serve a member on the right.
22. Remove soiled dishes with the hand nearest the member while substituting the next course with the hand farthest from the member.

MANAGING THE BAR AND COCKTAIL LOUNGE

Management, with the board and the committees involved (probably the budget and house committees), would decide on brands of alcoholic beverages the bar would carry and which of the measuring and pouring methods would be used.

Measuring and Pouring Methods

The most costly and important ingredient in the majority of drinks is the alcoholic beverage it contains. Therefore, if the recipe calls for an ounce and a half (4.44 ml) of scotch in a scotch and soda, the bartender must be able to measure this amount quickly and accurately and pour it from the liquor bottle into a glass.

The equipment available for the manager's selection in measuring devices runs from a small measuring glass, called a "jigger," to pouring spouts attached to the bottle (one type is called a "budget pourer" and may be purchased to pour any size drink), to very sophisticated electronic devices.

Other than the jigger, the mechanical devices are of two types, called "gravity flow" and "pumping" devices. Yet a third way to pour drinks is called "free pouring."

Free pouring (pouring directly from the bottle into the glass) is the recommended method for all clubs, as it creates a charismatic and friendly atmosphere that is one of management's objectives. This method, however, requires two things, a "dicing tray" in the ice machine and training sessions for all bartenders. The reason for having the dicing tray is to produce small ice cubes that will pack more uniformly.

To train the bartenders, fill a bottle (use any bottle except one that has contained alcoholic beverages, IRS regulations ban their reuse) with water. Color the water with a few drops of food dye and get a measuring cup from the kitchen. Next fill six glasses with ice and, using the colored water, measure the drink that will be served and have the bartenders pour this into each glass. It will only take a few sessions until they can pour accurately by sight. Use a jigger for drinks served in other glasses. Other measuring methods are as follows:

1. *Jigger.* The jigger method is slow and not completely accurate because of the bartender's having to hurry, but it does add some glamour to the bar. The bartender can be taught to hold the jigger on a slant, pour its contents into the glass, then add a splash from the liquor bottle without overpouring.

2. *Gravity Flow.* There are two types of gravity flow methods, one whereby the bartender actually handles the bottle with a measuring pourer attached to it; the other has the bottles locked in a rack, called the "Stoner system." The Stoner systems are very expensive and are labor-intensive. Some pourers are faster than the jiggers, some slower. All have one advantage and that is that every drink poured is recorded. The type attached to the bottle makes some brands (because of bottle shape) top-heavy and awkward to handle.

3. *Electronic Systems.* There are two basic types of electronic measuring systems available. One type pumps the beverage from the bottles, the other type uses suction. Either system can be located at the bar or in another room. The bottles can be hooked in tandem so that replacement is no problem. They are very fast in shooting the right measurement into the glass and make for easy accountability. However, these systems represent a major investment and their cost must be equated with the volume of sales and any risk factors involved. A portable bar can be equipped with this type of device and adds to an intimate atmosphere of a party, as the guests can serve themselves. New machines have cash registers and inventory attachments so that a bartender can record a sale and have the product poured in one operation. The last advantage of the suction type is that it overcomes the natural capillary attraction of the bottle and completely empties it. This cannot be accomplished by any other method.

4. *Draft Beer.* There are two kinds of draft beer systems and machines. The first uses the "economy box," a refrigerator and tap that is placed behind the bar. The barrel of beer is cooled and dispensed with the aid of a tank of carbon dioxide gas. It is a dependable, very economical system, but it has limitations. The refrigerator can only hold one to three barrels of beer and when these are emptied, service is interrupted, as the box must be serviced from behind the bar. The keg must be transported behind the bar, put in the box, and con-

nected. In some clubs this may necessitate bringing the beer through the cocktail lounge.

A better draft beer system is to hold the beer in a refrigerated walk-in box, readily accessible to the delivery area. This "remote draw" system delivers the beer to the bar through refrigerated lines. The beer and the tap can be 100 feet apart without affecting the quality of the product. The barrels can be hooked in series.

5. *Beer Coolers*. If bottle or canned beer is to be sold in the bar, coolers will be needed. Many types are available but all require the same supervision. The boxes must be kept clean and the beer stock must be continually rotated. Each time the cooler is stocked, all the beer should be removed, the box cleaned, and the fresh beer put in first. Then the beer that was taken from the box is put back in on top.

Other equipment needed in the bar and cocktail lounge include:

A blender, to be used for some exotic mixed drinks and all frozen drinks
A hot plate for a pot of coffee
Fruit pans
Cash register, optional when the club has inhouse credit
Double sinks
Cold-water glass washer
Speed rail
Glassware, including shot glasses
Ashtrays
Paper goods, napkins, coasters, straws, toothpicks
Paring knives

Standard Drink Portions

The portions of alcoholic beverages served in each drink is set by management. The size is determined by:

• The desires of the membership and their willingness to pay.
• The size of the glassware used. A 1-ounce drink in a 10-ounce glass may be too light, whereas 1½ ounces in a 4-ounce glass may be too strong. Clubs generally pour 1¼ or 1½ ounces in a 6-ounce highball glass. If the member desires a lighter drink, then an 8-ounce glass is used. The member would order a "scotch and water tall" to get the larger glass for a lighter drink.

Brands and Recipes

In the liquor trade, alcoholic beverage brands are divided into three classes. The first class is the "well" brands, which are usually kept in a metal rectangular box that hangs from the bar sink. These brands are usually purchased at a set price and many times are the cheapest brands the purveyor has in stock. These are the brands the members will receive when ordering a "scotch and soda" or a "rum and coke." The second class is the "call" brands, which the members specify in ordering such drinks as a "J and B and soda" or a "Bacardi and coke." The third class is the "super call" brands. Top-of-the-line and imported, with the exception of bourbon, these include: Irish whiskey from Ireland, rye whiskey from Canada, scotch from Scotland, vodka from Finland and Russia, rum from the Caribbean, and tequila from Mexico.

The manager, with the board and the house committee, should determine the class that the bar will serve when the member orders a scotch and soda. A "best-sellers' list" of the call brands sold in America is available from any purveyor. Some clubs have found it very rewarding to have call brands in the well. It adds prestige to the club; the members make sure that, when a guest orders a drink, he or she is told about the club policy. Two other advantages for serving the better brands is that it speeds up service and reduces the inventory of the brands carried. It is also a good idea to display the "super" brands on the back bar.

Recipes must be standardized for every bar and every bartender. This is the only way management can be sure that a member will always get the same drink, in the same proportions, and mixed the same way.

The manager soon learns that there is no "right way" to mix any drink, unless it is an invention of the club. Therefore, a good book of alcoholic recipes must be purchased so that the drinks the club serves will be uniform. Then these recipes can be compiled into a handbook for every bartender. It is necessary to be selective in preparing the handbook, and bartenders should be asked for input so that not only are all the standard drinks covered but any and all exotic drinks the members may want are included.

Bartenders

It is virtually impossible to teach experienced bartenders, who find it hard to do their bartending the "club's way" if they have always done it differently. Habits that are hard to break are:

Drinking behind the bar
Not using tongs or a scoop to pick up ice
Not using a pick to place garnishing in a glass
Not closing the cash drawer after each sale
Not using a measuring device, unless they have been taught to free-pour
Not smiling or being pleasant to members
Eating behind the bar
Sloppy mixing and serving
Not using a coaster or a cocktail napkin when serving drinks at the bar
Not keeping hands and fingernails clean
Being unkempt in their personal appearance
Smoking behind the bar

A good rule of thumb is to hire inexperienced bartenders and give them sound training in the club's methods.

MANAGING THE CLUB'S WINES

Every club, with the proper licenses, must have a supply of wine on hand to sell by the glass or bottle. It is management's responsibility to develop a wine list in keeping with the members' desires. There is rarely a ceiling on the price of fine wines, and it is always an excellent idea in composing a wine list to get a committee involved. Fine American wines from California, the Midwest, and New York should be on the list as well as wines from France, Germany, Portugal, Spain, Italy, and Chile. In addition to the formal wine list, some clubs have a manager's wine selection under various entree items on the regular menu. The holding of the wine for sale is very critical. If the club has a basement where the temperature is fairly uniform year round (50 to 70 degrees F), the club could use this as its wine cellar.

The temperature of the wine contributes immeasurably to its enjoyment. Though everyone thinks to chill champagne and the appetizer and white wines, sometimes the red, dessert, and other wines are served too warm. The rule established in Europe centuries ago, that these wines be served at room temperature, was simply due to unheated wine cellars.

The alcoholic content of wine is measured by volume. The wine, when fermented, can range from 10 to 14 percent by volume. To raise the alcoholic content the wine is "fortified" with brandy.

One of the major deterrents to selling wine by the bottle is the server's timidity in trying to get the cork out. As uncorking the wine bottle at the table adds to the member's pleasure, it is important that this be done. Two ways to overcome this fear of uncorking are through training and servers having their own corkscrew. Most major wineries have training departments that can be contacted through the local distributor and that will conduct courses at the club.

A very fine way to handle the sale and the serving of wine is through a sommelier, or wine steward. This person's primary duty is to sell and serve wines. Tradition has it that the sommelier has the only key to the wine cellar, which is worn around the neck, and a small silver pan to allow the wine to be tasted before being poured.

There are other niceties of wine service that perhaps would please club members:

1. Before the cork is removed from the bottle, the label is displayed to the member who ordered the wine.
2. After the cork is removed, it is placed before the member who ordered the wine so that the wine aroma may be sampled. In addition, many fine wineries stamp their logo on the bottom of the cork.
3. The sommelier now pours a small amount of wine into the host's glass for sampling and waits for a nod of approval.
4. Next the women, then the men are served, the host last.
5. If the wine is chilled, it is then returned to the iced wine bucket.
6. If the wine is served at room temperature, it is placed on the table in a pouring basket.
7. The sommelier frequently observes the table so that if more wine needs to be poured, it can be served. It is a mark of bad service if the member has to pour the wine.

The service of champagne and other sparkling wines is slightly different. The bottle is displayed to the host so that the label can be identified. The bottle is turned away from the table, pointed upward, and the metal foil covering, the "hood," is removed. The hood is a twisted wire holding a small metal disk, which keeps the cork in the neck of the sparkling wine bottle. This fixture is necessary, as the secondary fermentation has built up a high pressure within the bottle. In serving sparkling wines, the server must satisfy two conflicting wishes on the part of the host: first, to hear a loud pop when the bottle is opened and, second, not to spill any of the high-priced libation. The best way to serve these wines is to hold the bottle by the neck with the left hand, the thumb firmly on top of the cork. With the right hand, remove the metal foil and the hood by untwisting the wire and easing them out from under the thumb. If the bottle is kept on a slant with the wine covering the cork, the cork can be eased out. There will be a small pop and the wine, if properly chilled and handled gently, will not overflow.

Types and Classes of Wines

All wines are divided into two types, generic and varietal. The term "generic" denotes the area where a wine is produced. Generic wines are Burgundy, Chablis, Sauterne, Rhine, and Chianti.

Even though many American generic wines may not completely resemble, in flavor, the European counterparts which give them their names, the quality of most brands is excellent. One wonderful thing California has that is rare in Europe is the weather. The weather in Europe is the primary factor in determining whether or not a year's harvest is of vintage quality. The term "vintage year" is rarely used for American wines, as the weather allows all American wines, of the right quality, to be vintage wines.

Varietal wines receive their name from the grapes that are pressed to make them. Usually the varietal wines found on a club's wine list are Chenin Blanc, Pinot Chardonnay, Gray Riesling, Traminer, Pinot Noir, Cabernet Sauvignon, Gamay Beaujolais, Zinfandel, and Chardonnay.

American wineries produce a complete line of generic and varietal wines. The American government permits its wineries to label varietal wines with the name of the grape if 51 percent of the wine in the bottle or more was made from that particular grape. There also exist some very popular wines that are neither named after the district where they were produced nor the name of the grape used. Some of these are Lancers and Mateus Rosé from Portugal, Nectar Rosé from France, and some fine rosés made in California.

Wines are also divided into five classes:

1. Appetizer wines, such as Sherry, Vermouth, and Dubonnet
2. Red wines, such as Burgundy and Chianti
3. White wines, such as Sauterne and Chablis
4. Dessert wines, such as Port and Madeira
5. Sparkling wines, such as Champagne and Sparkling Burgundy

In describing the taste of the various types of wines, the vintners have developed their own vocabulary. They use the word *dry* to indicate the tartness of the wine: It might be very dry, dry, or semi-dry. *Full-bodied* and *generous* mean it is rich, smooth on the palate and has a strong taste; *light-bodied* means it tastes less strong. *Full-flavored* means that the taste of the grapes from which the wine was pressed is readily apparent. The "aroma," bouquet, or "nose" indicates a wine is pleasant-smelling.

Appetizer Wines

Appetizer wines are so called because they are favored before meals or for cocktail use. The Vermouths are sweet and dry. The dry (French) is the most popular to drink. Sweet Vermouth (Italian) is the type used to mix martinis. The Sherries are also both sweet and dry. The drier appetizers are preferred because they tend to sharpen diners' appreciation for the food to come.

Vermouth is a wine made with herbs and other aromatic substances. The dry is a pale amber, the sweet a dark amber. A light dry Vermouth also exists. Sherry is often made from the Palomino grape and has the taste of dry Vermouth but is so pale it is almost colorless. In producing Vermouth, natural white wines are selected and aged. Then they are flavored by steeping the herbs in the wine or by adding the herbs to the wine (infusion). Vermouth ranges from 15 to 20 percent alcohol.

Sherry, the most popular of all of the appetizer wines, is characterized by its nutty flavor, obtained by its being aged at warm temperatures. It ranges in color from pale to dark amber, and is made extra dry, medium dry, dry, or sweet. The sweeter "cream" or "golden" Sherry is sometimes used as a dessert wine. The alcoholic content of Sherry is usually about 20 percent.

Red Dinner Wines

Burgundy is a generous, full-bodied dry red wine, traditionally heavier in body, flavor, and bouquet and of a deeper red color than the clarets. California Burgundy is made from one or a number of grape varieties, including Gamay, Petite Sirah, Pinot Noir, and Refosco. Burgundy and claret are often made from the same grapes. A blend producing a lighter-bodied wine is called a claret.

Claret is the name of a red wine that is dry, pleasantly tart, light- or medium-bodied, and ruby red in color. Wines of this type are the most widely used wines at meals. This is true in every wine-drinking country in the world. California wines marketed under the name of claret are made from one or more grape varieties such as Cabernet Sauvignon, Ruby Cabernet, Carignane, Mataro, Mondeuse, and Zinfandel. It is not unusual to have a claret made from the same type of grape used for Burgundy.

Zinfandel is a claret made from the Zinfandel grape. It has a distinctive fruity taste and is only produced in California.

Cabernet Sauvignon is a claret that has been pressed from and has the distinctive fruity flavor and aroma of the Cabernet Sauvignon grape. It is stronger in flavor and bouquet than other clarets. In California it is fuller-bodied and deeper in color than Burgundy. Cabernet may be made from any cabernet grape but it cannot be labeled "Cabernet Sauvignon" unless made from Cabernet Sauvignon grapes.

Grignolino is a claret, which is named for the grape from which it is made and which has the distinctive flavor and aroma of that grape. Grignolinos are orange-red in color and sometimes the lighter wines are sold as rosés.

Rosé wine is a pink dinner wine sometimes called a "luncheon" wine. It has also been called an "all-purpose wine" because of its versatility. Rosé wines range from dry to slightly sweet, are fruity-flavored, light-bodied, and made from the cabernet, gamay, grenache, and/or the grignolino grapes.

"Vino rosso" (mellow red) is a generalized term given to Italian red wines. They will usually bear family names and are in a class by themselves. They are slightly sweet to semi-sweet, medium- to heavy-bodied, ruby red in color, and blander and softer than traditional red wines. Their alcoholic content is 10 to 14 percent by volume, the same as other red wines.

Red Chianti is usually dry, slightly tart, fruity, and ruby red. Traditional Chianti is made from the Sangiovese grape. Other grapes however, are used at some vineyards and labeled "Chiantis."

Concord, Ives, and Norton are red dinner wines with the characteristic flavor, aroma, and tartness of the corresponding grapes grown in the eastern United States. Concord ranges from semi-sweet to very sweet. Both Ives and Norton are slightly drier.

White Dinner Wines

White dinner wines vary from extremely dry and tart to sweet and full-bodied. Traditionally, the white wines, with their delicate flavor that blends best with white meat, seafood, and fowl, were the only wines served with these entrees. This tradition has long since been broken, and today white wines are served with any dish. They are also very popular as cocktails and appetizers.

White wines range in color from pale straw to deep gold and in alcoholic content from 10 to 14 percent. The most popular white dinner wines are Chablis, Rhine, and Sauterne.

Chablis is very dry with a fruity flavor and a delicate gold color. It is slightly fuller-bodied and less tart than Rhine wine. Traditionally it is made from a number of Burgundy grape varieties, notably from the aristocratic Pinot Blanc and Chardonnay. True Chablis is made in the United States from these grapes but also from Burger, Golden Chasselas, Green Hungarian, and many other varieties.

Chardonnay, Pinot Blanc, Folle Blanche, and Chenin Blanc are all Chablis-type wines named for the grapes from which they are produced and receive their distinctive flavors and aromas. Chardonnay is sometimes referred to as Pinot Chardonnay. Chenin Blanc is made from the Chenin Blanc grape. This grape is also used for wines labeled "White Pinot," which vary from dry to very sweet.

Rhine wine is the generic name (from the Rhine valley in Germany) given to any white wine that is thoroughly dry, pleasantly tart, light-bodied, pale golden, or slightly green-golden. The original Rhine wines were made from only a few special varieties of grapes, notably the Riesling varieties, but wines from many other grapes are classified as Rhine wines in the United States. They are usually bottled in a tall tapering bottle.

Riesling is a white Rhine wine made from one of the varieties of the Riesling grapes and having its particular flavor and aroma. The best California Riesling is produced from the Johannesburg Riesling grape, sometimes labeled "White Riesling." There also are Gray Riesling and Franken Riesling (sometimes labeled "Sylvaner") made from the corresponding grapes.

Traminer and Sylvaner are Rhine wines named for and having the distinctive flavors and aromas of the grapes from which they are made.

Hock and Moselle are other names given to Rhine wines. They have separate geographical significance in European wines but none in the United States. *Hock* is used in some English-speaking countries as a synonym for Rhine wine.

Sauterne is a golden-hued, fragrant, full-bodied white wine ranging from dry to sweet. There are three kinds of sauternes marketed in the United States: Sauterne, dry Sauterne, and sweet Sauterne, sometimes called Haut, or Chateau, Sauterne. The wide variations are explained by the fact that the sweetness of the Sauternes is not regulated. California Sauternes, however, are generally drier than those of France. Traditionally, Sauterne is a blend of three varieties of grapes—Sémillon, Sauvignon Blanc, and Muscadelle du Bordelais, but a wide assortment of other white grapes are used in the United States.

Sauvignon Blanc and Sémillon Blanc are Sauterne-type wines named after the grapes from which they are made with the flavors and aromas of the respective grapes. Both are usually dry but are sometimes marketed sweet or semi-sweet.

White Chianti sometimes resembles Rhine wine or Chablis, but it is usually typically Italian and very robust, which is unusual for a white. It is dry, somewhat fruity, slightly tart, and medium-bodied. Customarily it is made from Trebbiano and Muscat grapes.

Light Muscat wine is made from Muscat grapes with the characteristic Muscat flavor and aroma. This wine has steadily gained in popularity. Sometimes the white is labeled "sweet white wine." Although the flavor is unmistakable, Muscats can vary from completely dry to very sweet. When this wine is made from a special variety of Muscat grapes, it can be labeled Muscat Canelli or Muscat Frontignan.

Catawba, Delaware, Elvira, and Scuppernong are white dinner wines grown in the eastern and the midwestern United States. They have the particular flavors, aromas, and tartness of the grapes from which they are named. Catawba is produced both dry and semi-sweet like Sauterne, while Delaware and Elvira have more Rhine wine characteristics. Scuppernong is a light amber color and usually is a sweet, light Sauterne. Delaware is closer to a Rhine wine.

Dessert Wines

These are sweet, full-bodied wines served with or as dessert. Their alcoholic content is usually around 20 percent. They range from medium-sweet to sweet and from pale gold to red in color.

The three most popular types of dessert wines are Port, Muscatel, and Tokay.

Port wine, originally developed in Portugal, is a rich, heavy-bodied, fruity, sweet wine that is usually a deep red. There is a lighter-bodied port called "Tawny Port," usually made from grapes not as rich in color as those used in making the red port. White Port, which is straw-colored, is said to have been specifically developed as a sacramental wine. Port can be made from one or more of a dozen varieties of grapes, including Carignane; Petite Sirah, Tinta Cão, Tinta Madeira, Trousseau, and Zinfandel.

Muscatel is a rich, flavorful, sweet dessert wine made from Muscatel grapes and having an unmistakable flavor and aroma. Its color ranges from dark amber to red. While most Muscatel is made from the Muscat of Alexandria grape and is golden, at least seven other varieties of Muscat grape varieties are used in California to make Muscatel in different flavors.

Red and Black Muscatel are wines made from the Muscat Hamburg grape and are red and a very dark red.

Muscat Frontignan and Muscat Canelli are made from a special variety of Muscat grape; both names refer to the same grape.

Tokay has an important place among dessert wines because its sweetness is midway between sherry and port. It is amber-colored and has a slightly nutty taste like sherry. It is made by blending Angelica, Port, and Sherry. California Tokay is not to be confused with the Tokay made in Hungary, to which it has no similarity except in sweetness, nor with the Flame Tokay grape that may or may not be used in its production.

Angelica wine is a white dessert wine resembling White Port. Traditionally the sweetest of the dessert wines, it is fruity like a cordial and straw or light amber in color and very mild. Angelica originated in California and is produced from a number of grapes, including Grenache and Mission.

Kosher Wines

The term "kosher" can be applied to any wine certified by a rabbi. Thus, any type of wine, red or white and of varying alcoholic content and sweetness, can be termed "kosher." Kosher wines are produced wherever wine is pressed, but the bulk of these red sweet wines are produced in the East and Midwest where cane and/or beet sugar may be added to the wine.

Sparkling Wines

Sparkling wines are dinner wines which are also enjoyed as with an appetizer, as a dessert, or as a festive drink on any occasion. These wines have been made naturally effervescent by a secondary fermentation in either a bottle or a vat. They can be white, red, or pink and have a wide range of flavors. The alcoholic content of sparkling wines usually ranges from 10 to 14 percent by volume as does that of most red, pink, and white dinner wines.

The most popular types are Champagne and Sparkling Burgundy.

Champagne is generally pale gold or straw colored. Champagne is made in four different degrees of dryness:

1. *Nature* is the driest.
2. *Brut* is very dry.
3. *Sec* is semi-dry.
4. *Doux* is sweet.

Champagne is made from one or more grape varieties. By tradition, however, it should be made from Chardonnay, Pinot Blanc, or Pinot Noir, the latter a black grape. Many other grapes are used, however, depending on the market price. These are Burger, Emerald Riesling, Folle Blanche, French Colombard, Green Hungarian, Saint Emilion, Sauvignon Vert, Catawba, Elvira, and Delaware. The sparkle is put into the wine by a secondary fermentation.

Pinot Noir or one or more of the dark-skinned Champagne grapes is used to make the wine base for Pink Champagne. The Pink Champagne color results from letting the grape skins remain with the wine during fermentation until the desired hue is obtained.

Sparkling Burgundy is a red wine made sparkling by the same method used to make Champagne. It is usually semi-sweet or sweet. Barbera, Carignane, Mondeuse, Petite Sirah, and Pinot Noir are the grapes favored for the production of this wine.

Sparkling Muscat is a Champagne-like wine with a Muscat flavor. It is made from light Muscat wines from Muscat Canelli grapes. This wine is also called "Moscato Spumante."

Sparkling Rosé is very similar to Pink Champagne but uses the same grapes as are used to make Pink Rosé wine.

Crackling Wines

These wines are less effervescent than the sparkling wines. They are known as crackling, petillant, or fizzante. In the United States they must be fermented in the bottle or in a closed cantainer.

Carbonated Wines

White and red wines are occasionally made effervescent by artificial carbonation. Taxed at a lower rate, they are less expensive than sparkling wines.

A wine drink that has been around for a long time is Sangria. Low in alcoholic content, Sangria originated in Spain and is gaining in popularity worldwide.

Another wine drink that is gaining popularity in America is the "wine spritzer," made with any kind of wine and seltzer water. These are also called "wine coolers." These drinks of moderation have become so popular that innovative bartenders are making up their own recipes.

MANAGING THE CATERING DEPARTMENT

The word *catering* is used specifically to describe a club function ordered by a club member or a group of members, planned with club personnel, paid for by the member or members, and not open to the public. (The Internal Revenue Service has ruled that non-profit clubs may be allowed to have 10 percent of their total gross business from nonclub members.) Catering can be very profitable and an excellent promotional device for a new club.

A catered affair may be a banquet, just food, or just beverages, and may be held on the club's premises or in a member's residence.

The management must plan a place for the selling of a catered affair. This can be in the catering manager's office or at some quiet place within the club. It is important that the person booking the party has the undivided attention of the club's employee. The "red carpet" should be rolled out with coffee, sweet rolls, or cookies served in the morning and a cold drink in the afternoon.

In the club business it is sometimes necessary to plan on room service, if the club has guest rooms, as part of the catering division.

Catering is a very important function of every club, for it is a service that is not always available in the local community. The catering division usually consists of one person, the catering manager (sometimes called the "catering director" or "social secretary"), who works with the chef, the head bartender, and the housekeeping departments to provide the catering service.

Catering is a place for the entire staff to show their professionalism. It gives management an opportunity to show off and dress up the club and sometimes to put the employees themselves in costume. It gives the club a chance also to serve unusual, more exotic, or more expensive dishes than the members desire on a regular basis. A club in Alameda, California, has a complete gold service it offers its members for catered affairs. Another club in Miami, Florida, has four costume changes available for its employees to wear for private parties—Mexican, Japanese, Italian, or Western. Catering also gives the chef and the kitchen staff a chance to be creative in setting up menus, laying buffet tables, and making ice, sugar, and tallow carvings. It provides a change of pace for the entire staff.

The club employee planning the menu should have a diagram of the club rooms available for private parties. Many of the party details could be drawn on the diagram, including seating arrangements, the location of the musicians' setup (if a band is used), and whether or not there will be dancing.

Off-premise catering can be a source of additional business while providing a very nice service to the members. Whether or not the club can or will provide this service must be decided by the board. They must also decide if there is to be a rental charge for the use of the club's property when no food or drink is sold. The club may be called upon to furnish any or all of the following equipment and/or services for many different types of parties:

- China, glassware, silverware, and linen
- Chairs and tables
- Personnel such as cooks, servers, and bartenders
- Food to be prepared at the club or at the member's home
- Beverages of all kinds

The key to successful food catering is to be able to serve a large number of persons a breakfast, luncheon, dinner, or late supper at the right temperature and within a reasonable time. The variety of items that can be served is limitless. One method of organization is to divide the presentation into categories. For example, hors d'oeuvres could be arranged as follows:

- Light
    Chips and dip
    Pretzels
    Stuffed celery
    Peanuts
    Popcorn
- Medium
    All of the light hors d'oeuvres plus raised puffs of chicken and tuna
    Deep-fat-fried, breaded vegetables, such as zucchini, broccoli, etc.
    Barbecued meatballs
    An assorted cheese and cracker tray
- Heavy
    All of the light and medium hors d'oeuvres, plus a
    Watermelon fruit boat
    A cut of beef (the cut depends on the host) carved at the table with rolls,
        butter, mustard, horseradish, catsup, and mayonnaise

The trays of hors d'oeuvres might hold up to 100 pieces. The number of persons one tray will feed is usually estimated according to the substance of the item it carries. For example, a deep-fried vegetable tray would feed forty persons, whereas a shrimp tray might only feed thirty. Hors d'oeuvres should be divided into hot and cold items:

- Hot items
    Mini drumsticks of chicken
    Teriyaki beef pieces and shrimp puffs
    Pizza rolls, cocktail franks, and fried shrimp
    Stuffed mushrooms, rumaki, and cheese sticks
    Miniature tacos
- Cold items
    Cold cut platters to include pastrami, roast beef, ham, corned beef, sliced
        turkey, and assorted cheeses
    Tuna, chicken, shrimp, gelatin, and potato salads
    Bagels, smoked salmon, and cream cheese
    Pickles, olives, etc.

In presenting full meals, the club has all of its menu items and some special dishes to offer. These may be too expensive or too complicated to have on the regular menu. Whatever the types of items served, a party menu must be prepared that takes into account the labor costs, including those of setting up and tearing down the room.

In pricing the alcoholic beverages for parties, members have a choice among three methods:

1. Pricing by the person and by the hour, Usually there is a price for the first hour based on an estimated consummation of 2.5 drinks. The hourly price thereafter could be based on 2 drinks. For example, if the club normally charged $2.50 per drink, one hour of cocktails would cost the host $6.25 per person. A two-hour party would be priced at $11.25. This is not always the best buy for the host if there are going to be children, nondrinkers, beer, or wine drinkers at the party.

2. Pricing alcoholic beverages by the bottle (the host takes home all opened bottles), wine and soft drinks by the glass. Cost is determined by multiplying the number of drinks the club gets from a bottle for a particular beverage by the price the club charges for it.
3. Pricing individual drinks. If the club has a cash register, it can offer to ring up each drink at the club's regular price; the host pays the total on the cash register tape.

A private party contract must always be executed that gives the details of the party. These might include:

flower arrangements	cloakroom attendant
special equipment	candelabra
overhead projector	blackboard and chalk
cassette tape player	imprinted matches
video setup system, microphone	ice carving
wedding or other special cake	cigars, cigarettes
piano	cordials after dinner
podium	music
special lights	special time to serve cham-
guest book	pagne and/or cut cake
spot or flood lights	doorman and valet parking
flags	

Three matters of club policy should also be included in the contract:

1. Payment Arrangements: if the host is a member, the club usually does not require a deposit and the party totals appear on the member's next month's bill. If the bill exceeds a certain amount and the club must expend a great deal of money for a band, flowers, and so forth, some clubs may require a deposit. Other, more affluent clubs allow a member 3 months to pay if the party is over a certain dollar amount, customarily $5000. Usually the club will require a nonmember who books a party to provide a substantial deposit, in many clubs as much as 50 percent of the total, then the balance is paid the night of the party.
2. The amount of gratuity to be paid to the staff.
3. A guaranteed minimum and maximum number of guests and the last date this number can be changed. The rationale for the maximum number is that some special items might be required that may have to be prepared in advance.

MANAGING THE HOUSEKEEPING AND MAINTENANCE DEPARTMENT

Management's objective in the housekeeping and maintenance department is to create and maintain a clean, wholesome, and beautiful environment for the membership. This includes the total property of the club.

This department will be organized and have five or more supervisors. For some this supervisory responsibility will be a part of the regular job. For the individual in charge of housekeeping and maintenance of the clubhouse, the responsibility will be full-time.

Starting with golf, the golf pro will be responsible for keeping the pro shop, the driving range, the practice putting green, the starting area, and the golf carts neat and clean. The golf superintendent must keep the course in playable condition, clean the roughs, and keep all tees free of trash. The golf superintendent will also supervise a mechanic to keep all of the golf course maintenance equipment in good repair. The tennis pro will be responsible for the neatness and cleanliness of the pro shop, the area surrounding the check-in area, the courts, the wind screens, fences, and walkways. The aquatic director has complete responsibility for the pool or pools. This includes the cleanliness and neatness of the bathhouse, the pool, the pool apron, the outdoor furniture, and the surrounding area.

The club may have many other outdoor facilities such as stables, riding trails, jogging paths, and so forth. If there is no one in charge of these areas, the general manager must take the responsibility for their neatness and cleanliness and delegate the chores to someone. If the areas are closely adjacent to the golf course, the golf superintendent may be given the responsibility for them. The health club and/or spa is usually part of the clubhouse so its cleanup is part of the housekeeping department's responsibility. The physical fitness director, however, must work with the head of housekeeping to see that this is accomplished.

The housekeeping and maintenance of the clubhouse must be the responsibility of a very competent supervisor, holding special qualifications. Keeping the clubhouse and the surrounding area neat and clean is the major part of the job, but this person should have sufficient knowledge to deal with any maintenance problem. This would include assisting management with maintenance contracts on the air conditioning, heating plants, refrigeration, and other equipment such as cash registers, computers, and office equipment, and being the contractor's contact at the club.

Some of the cleaning and maintenance can be done by outside contract, even some of the routine daily maintenance. For example, if the club served breakfast or when a special party called for a breakfast to be served, it might make good sense to have a contractor clean the club after closing the night before so that the regular staff could walk into a clean club the next morning.

Other areas where contractors may be of practical assistance would be in major projects like drapery, venetian blind, and other window treatment cleaning, carpet and vitreous tile cleaning, hard-to-wash windows, and upholstery cleaning.

MANAGING THE HEALTH CLUB

Management of a health club within a club is not a simple matter. As discussed in Chapter 2, many clubs hire a physical fitness director and have him or her supervise the purchase of the equipment and establish the opening programs.

Financial Structure

Establishing a health club is a very expensive undertaking. The cost of preparing the space, purchasing or renting the equipment, and hiring a qualified physical fitness director could deplete the club's operating capital. Serious consideration should be given to charging for its use. If the club is unbundled, charging separately for many of its facilities, then there is very little problem. Charging a fee for the use of the health and fitness amenity could even serve as a trial balloon for the unbundling of services.

Planning the Facility

The ideal location for the health club would be between or readily accessible to the men's and women's lockers or changing rooms. The club must have a dress code so that both male and female club members may use the facilities at the same time. Amenities the health club might offer include:

1. *A Sauna.* This is a room in which the temperature is high enough to make the occupants, who sit on benches, freely and profusely perspire. The former name for a sauna was a "Finnish steam bath."
2. *Jacuzzi Pools.* These are large tubs of heated water with continuous jets of water shooting outward from its sides. If the club has only one pool in a separate room with a shower, it could be reserved for couples or males or females at specified times.
3. *Aerobic Dancing.* Requiring a separate room in the health club, this activity is especially popular with females aged six to sixty. A qualified assistant could be hired by the director to conduct and supervise the classes.

Employee Fitness

One important purpose of the health club is to keep club employee healthy and fit. The health and fitness of the employees should be of continual concern to the management of all clubs both large and small. The reasons are:

- A fit employee is more productive.
- An ill employee who is dedicated and loyal to the club may continue to work while ill and infect members or fellow employees.
- An employee who cannot report to work because of illness could disrupt the entire club.
- Excessive claims to health care insurance companies often raise rates.

Hundreds of companies have set up exercise centers with physical fitness programs for their employees and have amortized the cost through increases in productivity and man-hours worked. The establishment of a fitness program in the club could be implemented as follows:

1. The hours of employee use must not interfere with members. The employees' program could be scheduled in the early morning, 1 hour before the room is opened to members.
2. The program must be strictly voluntary and on the employees' own time. Management must have each employee sign a statement that they are physically able to participate in the program.
3. The general manager should do everything possible to encourage the management staff to participate in the program.
4. The ideal program for persons not regularly exercising is to start with a 30-minute session 3 days a week, for example, Sunday, Tuesday, Thursday, or Monday, Wednesday, Friday.
5. Each employee must have a personal interview with the physical fitness director before starting an exercise program.

MANAGING COIN-OPERATED MACHINES

The vending machine not only offers an additional service to club members but can be profitable as well. This service need not be limited to the club's operating hours, as in many temperate zones machines can be placed in a sheltered outdoor area. For many clubs, vending may represent the only cash sales.

The vending machine is not new, as there were machines in use in the nineteenth century. The vending machine as big business, however, is new. Every club, regardless of size and location, has vending machine service available for its use.

Use of vending machines is only limited by the general manager's imagination and good taste. In planning for both vending and coin-operated recreation machines, management should first consider the club's property as a whole, visualizing where the machines would of the greatest service to the members, then consider the product line available. Questions that could be asked are:

1. Are there unobtrusive places in the clubhouse for one or more cigarette machines?
2. What machines could be in the locker rooms?
3. Would female members like to have free sanitary napkin dispensing machines in the locker rooms and bathrooms?
4. Would the golf committee like to have an automatic golf ball dispensing machine outside the pro shop to furnish balls for the driving range? The machine could be either free or operated by tokens sold in the pro shop.
5. Where are the best places to put the cold drink machines? There are rest areas on the golf course—should machines be put there? Of course, they can only be placed where there is electricity.
6. Would a coffee, tea, and hot chocolate machine outside or inside the pro shop provide a needed service for the early golfers and tennis players?
7. Where could the recreation machines be placed? The computerized race, sports, and air games are very popular with both children and adults. They create a terrible racket, however, so the board would have to confer on their placement and whether or not they should be coin-operated or free.

Management might first consider a change (dollar bills to coins) machine. Items to be considered for vending could include:

- Aspirin and other nonprescription drugs, in addition to those kept in the club's first aid kit
- Toothbrushes and toothpaste
- Combs
- Sanitary napkins
- Cigarettes
- Hot coffee, tea, and chocolate
- Hot soup
- Cold drinks, either by the can, bottle, or cup
- Cold beer by the can
- Ice cream
- Sandwiches
- Cookies and candies
- Potato and other types of chips
- Mints and chewing gum
- Milk—white, whole or skim, and chocolate.
- Fruit juices

The manager has three choices in the marketing of these products.

1. Take a contract with a vending machine company and/or a soft drink bottling company to furnish the machines, the products, and the necessary repairs for a percentage of the gross receipts. If this option is selected, the club should use the sealed bid purchasing method, as the company's percentage of the "harvest" (the trade word for collecting the coins) could range from a high of 80 percent to a low of 25 percent. Such contracts are usually 1 to 2 years in length and are sometimes renegotiated if the service and quality the company provides are not satisfactory or a new sealed bid procedure is established. This option has, by far, proved to be the best for the club since companies have installed meters and locked boxes on the machines.
2. Rent the machines, buy the products at wholesale, and have club personnel stock them and harvest the coins. In most instances, it has been found that the time spent in not only servicing the machines but getting them repaired (*Note*: A club employee must be with the repair person at *all* times) was not as economical as having a company provide the machines and be responsible for their maintenance.
3. Purchase the machines and the products. In addition to the expenses in option 2, this option requires the club to make a substantial investment and when the warranty runs out, to bear the cost of all repairs.

INTERNAL SECURITY

Many clubs have problems with internal security, the most common is larceny. Larceny is defined as "the unlawful taking and carrying of personal property with the intent to deprive the rightful owner of it permanently." Larcenies occur frequently as the cost of living rises. The temptation to "help oneself" becomes sometimes irresistible. The following are a few of the types of larcenies that plague club operations:

Cash stolen from an unlocked safe
Forced removal of locks
Removal of property with no sign of forced entry
Theft of bank deposits by messengers or persons unknown
Bad checks cashed by employees
Bad checks cashed by members
More coupons redeemed than sold
Stealing by falsification of documents
Cash left unsecured and/or unattended
Merchandise, goods, or equipment removed by employees or others without
   authorized access

It is a primary responsibility of management to remove or regulate *opportunity* for employees who might be tempted, for one reason or another, to steal. As yet there has been no effective yardstick devised to measure the predisposition to steal, but regulation of opportunity minimizes the chances of someone giving in to temptation. The manager must make it clear to all employees that it is to their own benefit to cooperate in keeping themselves and their fellow employees honest. Such intramural effort is termed "internal security."

Sample Problems

The text proposes to demonstrate, by use of two hypothetical examples, important areas in which internal security measures were found wanting and to make recommendations for ensuring that the strongest possible deterrents are established in these areas. It may be that the primary reason for laxity in internal security is that employees are not properly informed as to why certain security measures must be taken and about the possible consequences of their complacency in these matters.

Cash Receipts and Disbursements

Helena Haphazard has been hired as club cashier. On her job application she states that she has an interest in mathematics and is good at counting money. She has a high school education and has done some secretarial work. She also understands the mechanics of operating a cash register but has had no bookkeeping or accounting experience.

Helena is hired as the head cashier and given a crash course in the front office. She is given a copy of the regulations governing membership and told not to make any exceptions to these rules. Beyond this, Helena is given a couple of forms on which to account for her transactions over the course of her working day. She is now in charge of the club's transactions involving the cash flow of nearly $3000 a day. The club manager is satisfied. Helena has been checked out and her references all pronounce her to be "honest."

The club was audited 3 months after Helena was hired with the following auditor's statement of conditions:

1. Four bank deposits totaling more than $6000 were unaccounted for and, under the existing procedures, it was not possible to establish exact responsibility for these losses.
2. Cash receipts were not deposited on a daily basis.
3. Payee lines on checks received from members were not always promptly filled in and checks were frequently not endorsed "for deposit only."
4. The cashier was not adequately fidelity-bonded relative to the amount of cash on hand.
5. Signed receipts were not available to determine whether the funds in question had been sent to the bank.
6. Funds were turned over to another employee, who presumably had no knowledge of the amounts contained in the bag and was not required to sign for the bag's contents before taking it to the bank.
7. When counting cash and preparing deposits, the cashier was in a location to which many people had access. She was constantly interrupted by waitresses wanting to make change and by members cashing checks.
8. The safe containing large sums of money was left open during business hours. Helena admitted she had been given no specific instructions on what to do if she left the office during office hours. Several employees including the manager had access to the room while Helena was away.
9. A number of returned checks from members and employees were found in the safe, and Helena admitted that no attempt had been made to make them good other than to notify the member or employee by mail about the returned checks.

Merchandise

Cornelius Complacent has been working around clubs for a long time. His personnel record shows him to be a hard worker, willing to put in long hours. Previously he has held positions calling for minor responsibility, and he has performed so well that he has finally been elevated to a position where he is in charge of the club's storerooms.

Cornelius' duties consist of receiving, stocking, and inventorying all merchandise used in the food and beverage departments of the club. In his previous job he became thoroughly familiar with the day-to-day operation of the club, he also is in demand for the setting up of special functions that require some knowledge of precedent. He is available to go out and procure "emergency" supplies on a moment's notice and, is a favorite of the membership, and does "favors" for them. Of course, this necessitates his being away from the storeroom from time to time, but he is usually able to cover himself by leaving his keys with the chef or by delegating the responsibility for checking in merchandise to one of the kitchen maintenance people.

Despite Cornelius' devotion to duty, this club also receives a negative report from the auditors. Here are a few of the conditions listed:

1. Prenumbered receiving reports and stock transfer documents were not in use.
2. Monthly inventories were usually prepared by Cornelius with the aid of a cook and/or a bartender.
3. Stock was not kept in the order listed on the inventory, nor had it been rotated.
4. Adjustments to stock record cards totaled more than $2000 in shortages and apparently no attempt had been made to investigate.
5. Receiving, stocking, and inventorying were the responsibility of one person.
6. The person in charge of the storeroom had access to perpetual inventory records.
7. Unauthorized personnel had access to the storeroom. Cooks selected their own merchandise and sometimes, when busy, did not fill out forms or sign them. Forms that were filled out often were not dated. Cleanup people helped themselves to supplies as they were needed.
8. A spot check showed over 200 pounds of chicken unaccounted for. (Cornelius tried to explain this, saying the chicken may have been used for a special function that was not recorded.)
9. Storeroom doors were left unlocked during the day.
10. Locks on food and beverage storerooms were not of sufficient strength and quality to ensure safety in relation to the amount of stock on hand.
11. Incoming merchandise was left unattended before being put into stock for long periods of time.
12. There was no system for security in the storeroom area, where outside access could be gained by merely forcing a window. The manager said that security patrol officers were "good" about checking the building at night and had reported to him one night when the window in the storeroom had been left open.
13. Forced entry and removal of property had been reported once, but no attempt had been made to report this crime to the police, to file an insurance claim, or to determine the amount of merchandise removed.

Control of Employees

A comparison of the auditors' reports with the list of larcenies reported should indicate the importance to the club manager of the implementation and enforcement of good internal security measures. On assessment it would be difficult, in the two examples cited, to prove the dishonesty of any of the employees involved. Yet thousands of dollars of the club's money and property were lost and no specific areas of responsibility for these losses could be established. *Opportunity* was present in each case. *Temptation* was the catalyst, and people with a predisposition to steal were given a "green light." Losses from the outside were invited because of shoddy security precautions. Consequently, employees who were basically "honest" may have become involved in larcenous incidents. Starting with the clubhouse manager, internal security must be maintained from top to bottom!

Besides strict adherence to regulations set up for the control of cash and merchandise, the manager can insist upon certain precautions. These will help to maintain an active security check on incoming and outgoing employees. It may not be economically feasible to employ inside security guards, but there are certain measures which can be taken to minimize potential losses, even in the area of petty pilferage.

One good rule is never to allow employees to carry in or out of the building large packages or bags. The employee who carries in a bag containing a clean uniform may be carrying out a steak wrapped inside his soiled one. The waitress who has gone shopping prior to coming to work and comes in loaded with packages which she deposits inside to "keep them safe while she works" may, in reality, be using this as a means to supplement her shopping list by taking a few choice items from the club and secreting them away with her own. The unfortunate thing is that too many employees consider this kind of act as merely "borrowing": The club can "afford" a bar of soap or a carton of salt and she doesn't have to buy it that week. Besides, doesn't she give extra time to the club every once in a while?

A good rule is to rotate employees who are in a position to carry away items in quantity from the premises. A good many times, in cases of pilferage, the losses are collusive; that is, thefts are carried out by the person with access to the merchandise in collusion with someone on the outside. The means of getting the merchandise out to that person are many and devious. For instance, if Joe knows he is making a regular trip to the dump with refuse every Tuesday and Thursday, and it becomes routine, the opportunity to steal is there. He has now only to succumb to the temptation.

Making all employees aware that there are periodic and unscheduled checks on their activities while on the job is an effective deterrent to larceny. If these same people believe that there is an ongoing program of security within the club, they will think twice before succumbing to temptations that invariably arise when they come into contact with things of value in the performance of their duties.

Any insurance company will warn of the risk involved in depending upon the "loyalty" of older employees. Statistics indicate no correlation between longevity of employment and the propensity to steal. Again, older employees should be made aware that security checks are universal, even up to the manager, and they should be encouraged to pass this information along to the newer people as they are hired.

Management must take a positive, not a negative, approach to the subject of internal security. Make checks and balances a daily function of everyone who is in a position of trust or responsibility within the club. Employees should understand that thefts by any one of them affect all of them.

Controlling the flow of data from bottom to top in the hierarchy of the manager-employee relationship serves to help minimize potential losses of the club's assets and the resulting break in routines which follow the discovery of such losses. In many cases, the amount of time lost in investigating losses, plus the necessity of involving employees who are totally honest can be as devastating to the operation as is the actual loss itself.

Training Suggestions

It is suggested that internal security be taught to the first-line supervisors then to line employees. The first group should be indoctrinated in individual job responsibility in their particular areas, including cash receipts and disbursements, merchandise controls, and/or the control of employees.

The training session with regular-line employees should be concerned with stating overall policies of management and emphasizing that all employees are expected to cooperate fully with supervisors in eliminating the opportunities for larcenies on the premises. Unfortunately, many managers find it very difficult and some think it is degrading to discuss larceny openly. There are other ways to handle this, but open discussion is best.

Once all employees have been fully informed of internal security procedures, it is necessary for the clubhouse manager to periodically spot-check for "leaks" in procedures. It is necessary to approach internal security impartially so that all employees are treated equally.

The following lists of rules, principles, and standard procedures governing cash, merchandise, and inventory illustrate the vast number of activities that require constant management attention.

Cash and Other Assets

1. Individual responsibility in the handling of cash is fixed.
2. Accounting and other business functions must be separated and performed by different individuals.
3. Spot checks should be made to assure correctness of operations and accounting.
4. No one person is in total control of a business transaction.
5. Employees handling cash or securities must be properly bonded.
6. Announced cash counts should be performed periodically by persons other than those assigned the daily duties.
7. Periodic reviews of the internal control system should be made.
8. Operating instructions for each position and the prescribed procedures must be in writing.
9. A sufficient number of cash registers should be available, in good working order, and controls utilized. Cash registers should be read and cleared as per regulations.
10. Receipt-to-deposit procedures must be reviewed and deposits made daily.
11. Transfers of cash must be accompanied by signed receipts.
12. Prenumbered receipt vouchers for cash not recorded on register should be in use and copies retained to support journal entries.
13. No more cash should be on hand than is actually needed.
14. Sales slips and guest checks must be prenumbered and accounted for, then reconciled with register tapes. Overages and shortages must be documented.
15. Vouchers and supporting documents are stamped "Paid."
16. Checks received in payment are promptly stamped "For Deposit Only."
17. A record of individual shortages and overages should be maintained and used as a basis for investigation or disciplinary action.
18. The cash maintained in the checking account should be the minimum amount required for efficient operation.
19. Appropriate security measures must be enforced in the areas where cash is kept. Safes are opened only to remove and receive cash and are promptly closed and locked.
20. Periodic follow-up should be made on delinquent accounts.

Merchandise and Inventory

1. All inventories must be spot-checked by disinterested personnel and amounts on hand verified against stock record cards.
2. Monthly inventories of food, beverages, supplies, and all shops should be taken monthly, inventories of renewal and replacement items taken every 6 months.
3. Book values of fixed assets must be determined accurately and recorded in specified records.
4. Fixed assets are permanently marked with name and inventory number.
5. All inventory shortages are promptly noted and investigated.
6. Depreciation of assets are controlled by IRS regulations.
7. Accountability for merchandise must be maintained at all times. Individual responsibility is maintained through use of requisitions.
8. Accountability procedures should be departmentalized.
9. Costs of foods and beverages are computed to determine gross profit.
10. Sensitive and expensive items are accounted for in terms of expected sales.
11. Portion yield, waste, and scrap must be accounted for and documented.
12. Access to storerooms should be restricted to accountable personnel.
13. No one person has full control of all functions of inventory, procurement, and dispensing.
14. Guest checks should be utilized in bars, checked for accuracy, and variances investigated.
15. Guest checks are checked against inventory used.
16. Private party charges must be controlled, signed by sponsors, and all payments recorded as soon as possible after transactions.
17. All incoming merchandise must be accounted for, weighed and counted, and invoices checked against original purchase orders. Merchandise should be stored in a predetermined place as soon as is practical after delivery.
18. Unauthorized personnel, such as salespeople, drivers, and trash disposal workers, should not have access to storeroom.
19. Locks and other forms of physical security must be maintained in perfect condition.
20. Responsibility for physical internal security is delegated to the person in charge of a department or section. Windows, doors, and alarm systems must be checked at the close of each business day.

REVIEW QUESTIONS

1. What is the relationship of job grading to skill levels?
2. How is the responsibility and reimbursement chart used?
3. What are the six steps management can take to realize effective budgetary controls?
4. What is meant by "menu anticipation"?

5. What must menu designers keep in mind when preparing a new menu?
6. What are the contract details necessary to adequately control a catering function?
7. What are the various options that a member would have in ordering drinks for a catered function?
8. What are the manager's options in placing vending machines in the club? Which option has proved to be the most successful and why?
9. With what reasons could a manager convince the board to let employees use the health club?
10. What is meant by the term "internal security" and why is it necessary?

CASE STUDY

Edith Hunt, General Manager of the Devious Golf and Country Club, is having serious problems with James Con, her chef. Edith is the new general manager brought in 2 months ago to try and cut the losses in the club's food department.

James, who has been at the club for the past 2 years, is a master chef and the food at the club is outstanding; however:

1. He insists on doing both the purchasing and receiving. His argument against a basic control procedure of separating the two is that only he knows the quality and the quantity of the items needed.
2. He will not disclose the recipes for at least a dozen items he prepares frequently. James reasons that they are his personal recipes and he will not share them.
3. James will not implement a chef's duplicate receipt system. He says that it takes too much time and that he has to feed many persons who do not have a guest check, such as the persons delivering bread and milk. His rationale for doing this is that it is the only way he can get the quality and service the club needs.
4. James does no competitive shopping and has been buying all of the club's produce, groceries, and meats from just three local purveyors.
5. He will not practice any principles of portion control or even study the plates coming back from the dining room with items half-eaten. The average age of the membership is 63.5 years. James says that he knows the portions are large but that is what he is building the club's food reputation upon! His slogan is, "You will never leave the table hungry in my club."
6. James insists on coming out to the dining room after dinner and soliciting accolades for his efforts. There is nothing wrong in doing this, however, James refuses to wear a clean jacket because, he says, the members don't care, they appreciate that someone in the club is working.

James' methods cause the club in some months to have a food cost as high as 82 percent. The 6-month food cost average is 74.6 percent. On food business of $125,000 per month, the club loses from $18,000 to $25,000.

The chef's popularity with the members is so high that the board felt their only out was to fire the manager, who had informed them of some of the things that were going wrong, and to hire Edith Hunt. After reading Edith's first report, however, which detailed the chef's deficiencies, the board agreed that something had to be done. She was asked to explain in writing how she would approach each of these problems.

Prepare Ms. Edith Hunt's report.

5 Managing the Club's Support Department

ORGANIZATION AND RESPONSIBILITIES

The head of the support department is frequently called the controller, other titles for this position are office manager and head bookkeeper. Under the supervision of the general manager, the controller directs the employees responsible for purchasing, cashiering, storekeeping, and record keeping.

The purchasing agent is responsible for making all of the club's purchases by both open and sealed bid. In a small club, however, purchasing may be the responsibility of the manager or assistant manager. The purchasing agent works with the department heads and the general manager to establish the specifications needed for all items and processes all the purchase orders. Although a great amount of attention is required to organize this function, the dollars saved by purchasing properly are the easiest dollars the club will save.

Purchasing is not only important from a profit standpoint, but the quality of many of the things that the club needs depends upon the specifications (hereafter called specs) that have been established. This is particularly true of food. Management, with guidance from the chef, must determine the quality of the food the members require and will support. For example, it might be a good food promotion idea to serve U.S. Prime grade meat, but if the members won't pay the price for the club to meet its profit standards, then the specs must call for a lesser grade.

Purchasing is a complex business. Quite often the least expensive item purchased might be the most expensive in the long run. For example, in purchasing produce, when a case of lettuce (twenty-four heads) graded fancy, is priced at $12, it may be more economical than a case at $10 if three or more heads are not usable. Thus, the purchasing must be judged by its overall effectiveness and not only by the price of the individual items.

To purchase effectively and economically, all of the following must be considered:

The purchaser
Purchasing ethics

Purchasing methods
Purchasing sources
What to purchase
Using purchase orders

The Purchaser

The person responsible for expending club funds occupies an increasingly important position as the costs of material and labor continue to rise. This key individual must, even though the specific items and their specs will be written on the purchase orders, have some knowledge of food, beverages, and other miscellaneous materials and purchasing factors. The purchaser must have the personality to make agreements easily with other persons, in particular, purveyors, with whom he or she is the club's principal contact. Good relationships with purveyors can mean important leads on food prices, for instance, and reduced tension when problems arise. The purchasing agent must have the poise to meet or talk to purveyors and other company representatives in a friendly but strictly businesslike way.

The agent's next important qualification is that he or she be loyal and honest. The integrity of this person will be put to the test occasionally as certain unscrupulous salespeople attempt to "buy the business" or attempt to influence the purchaser's judgment with personal favors or gifts, a practice that is growing. The Internal Revenue Service will not allow a tax deduction for such things as a company yacht or a box at the stadium for the National Football League games. Giving away television sets is also nondeductible except as a promotion device.

Management must insist that a marketing spreadsheet be prepared for all competitive food items (Fig. 5.1). These sheets should be forwarded to top club management each week so that they can be analyzed.

If used properly, the market spreadsheet can assist in buying competitively but it is not the total answer to effective purchasing. The club should attempt to budget the expense of sending the purchasing agent to the National Restaurant Show in Chicago, a regional restaurant show, or the National Hotel/Motel Show in New York. These shows can help keep the purchasing agent abreast of the new products and trends of the industry.

Purchasing Ethics

The successful agent must understand and abide by the recognized ethical practices of purchasing. It is quite proper to shop the market and discuss trends with purveyors as long as they are not chiseled. "Chiseling" is the term used for beating a purveyor down by disclosing prices offered by competitors or suggesting to the purveyor that the price quoted is too high. If a purveyor lowers a price, there is no way of knowing what the right price is or how low it will go. Also, if the club buyer has a reputation for chiseling, the purveyor will quote high, knowing the price will be reduced before the sale is final. Purveyors must be encouraged, therefore, to quote only one price, the lowest that can be offered, by turning down any offer higher than the competition's and not allowing reductions in price. One manager had an irate

Date _____					
Needed	Quantity	Details	Co. #1	Co. #2	Co. #3
Tomatoes	5 lugs	#1 fancy			
Lettuce	6 cartons	fancy			
Endive	5 baskets				
Radishes	5 bunches				
Cucumber	1 crate				

FIGURE 5.1 *Marketing spreadsheet.*

purveyor visit her after his company had been cut out for being too high. She had just implemented the spreadsheet system and his prices proved to be higher than his competition. He was furious when he learned that the club checked prices. His comment was, "Why didn't someone tell me? I could have sold it to you cheaper but all they asked me on the phone was my price."

The following summarizes the purchaser's code of ethics:

1. I will not disclose the price quoted to me by a purveyor to any other purveyor.
2. I will not ask the purveyor to reduce the price to meet my needs. However, I can tell the purveyor my menu needs and ask if the company has the products to meet them.
3. I will give every purveyor who asks an opportunity to quote the prices of their products to me.
4. I will be loyal to my employer.
5. I will exhibit the highest degree of honesty toward my employers and to all purveyors.
6. I will accept no personal favors or gifts from any purveyor.

Purchasing Methods

There are many purchasing methods used by clubs, three of which are outlined below.

APPROVED PURVEYORS   Management control of purveyors doing business with the club can be handled through an Approved Purveyors List, registering purveyors who have a good reputation in the community. That is, they are known for their professionalism, quality of their products, and adherence to ethical standards. The information for the list is compiled from the manager's past contacts and from references given by other club managers in the area and by managers at CMAA meetings. This list may also be expanded by solicitng suggestions from department heads and other club employees. It is given to the purchasing agent with instructions that these are the only purveyors authorized to sell to the club.

All new purveyors who wish to get on the list must have a personal interview with the manager. The first question asked by the manager, after the purveyor's sales pitch should be, "Who in this area is presently buying your products?" Managers should never buy a product without first calling the customers who are using it and should never be the door opener for a purveyor unless they are personally familiar with the product being sold or feel that its exceptional quality demands that a decsion be made immediately.

OPEN PURCHASING Open purchasing is buying on the open market from a purveyor who can supply the club with the best quality products at the lowest price. The usual method is to decide on the items needed using the purchase order forwarded by the chef and then to list them on the market spreadsheet. A separate sheet is used for each class of items. The purchasing agent then contacts the approved purveyors and fills in the prices quoted by them on the sheets. A study is then made to determine the best overall price, which is determined by multiplying the quantity of each item by its price and then totaling the results. It has been the experience of most managers that if quality and service are important to the club, an order should not be split. The purveyors' expense in providing delivery service is rising so rapidly that soon they will have to follow the pattern of major chains of department stores and charge for delivering their wares to the club. Thus, as long as the purveyor is providing a free delivery service, it is in the club's best interest not to split an order.

SEALED BIDS According to sealed-bid purchasing, the needs of the club are determined at least a month in advance. The purchasing agent can find companies using sealed bids by telephoning and asking companies if they would be interested in bidding on the monthly or quarterly requirements for the club. Companies that have been known to bid at a reduction in their regular prices are dairies, bakeries, meat markets, draft beer distributors, and ice cream companies. The agent should check as many companies as possible, for businesses are often interested in guaranteed production and sales for a specific period of time.

To start sealed bidding, a letter is sent to the company interested in bidding, listing the following information:

1. The items the club wishes to purchase and the specs for these items.
2. Delivery information, including estimated delivery requirements. These could be daily, weekly or monthly.
3. The estimated quantity of the items the club expects to use during the bidding period.
4. The date on which to submit the bid.
5. The date when the bids will be opened.
6. Whether or not the company should send a representative to the bid opening.

Purchasing Sources

In purchasing meat and meat products, many clubs use four primary sources of supply:

1. The meat packers, who slaughter and butcher the animals. The meat packer is the best source for the larger cuts of beef, such as rounds, ribs loins, and chucks, and for lamb, veal, pork, and pork products. Lamb and veal may be purchased in three ways from most packers—by the carcass, the side, and the quarter. Some also cut steaks and chops, which are sold by the carton.
2. The meat processors, who buy the large sides or carcasses of animals and turn them into cuts, steaks, and chops.
3. The meat jobber (sometimes called the meat wholesaler). This company does no butchering except perhaps to grind some meats. It purchases selected cuts and cutup steaks and chops already boxed.
4. The local supermarket. These are retail companies, however, some clubs have found it advantageous to have an account with retail companies, from which they sometimes receive a small discount.

Note: The four sources are listed in the order of least cost, with the packer almost always being the most economical source. To assist the agent in buying meat, the National Association of Hotel and Restaurant Meat Purveyors, Suite 1728, 120 S. Riverside Plaza, Chicago, Illinois 60606, has published a booklet entitled "The Standardized Meat Cuts." The booklet has been endorsed be the U.S. Department of Agriculture.

What to Purchase

The food section in the local newspaper is recommended reading for every person engaged in purchasing food, as supply and demand causes the produce market to fluctuate more frequently than any other. The newspaper will keep the purchaser informed of the produce items in heavy supply. Also, the U.S. Agriculture Department publishes a monthly bulletin, "Plentiful Foods."

In purchasing groceries, the prices of the national purveyors like Sexton and Monnark should be checked against the local purveyor brands and recorded on the marketing spreadsheet. In purchasing produce, groceries, and seafood, most purchasing agents will need some professional advice to grade their quality and freshness.

The purchasing agent will also be buying equipment, furniture, furnishings, alcoholic beverages, china, glassware, silverware, linen, kitchen equipment, and miscellaneous supplies for all departments. The board could establish a policy that any purchase over $500 that is not a line item in the budget must be approved by the general manager. Also, the board must approve any item costing over $1000 not specified in the budget. In some clubs this authority has been delegated to the chairperson of the Finance Committee. Or a policy could be established by the board that any single piece of equipment costing $500 dollars or more must be purchased using sealed bids.

Before any large purchase is made, a master plan should be developed by the board, the general manager, and the appropriate committee. Then this plan, with appropriate implementation dates, should be transmitted to the agent.

The Purchase Order

Good management requires that, whenever possible, all purchases be recorded on purchase order forms (Fig. 5.2). These forms become an integral part of the internal control system and can accomplish the following:

1. Establish both a contractual and cliental relationship between the club and the purveyor.
2. Provide a means of establishing receiving procedures.
3. Provide a ready reference for price requisitions, brackets, and inventories.
4. Provide a control document for the paying of accounts.
5. Provide a record of the contingent liabilities and the accounts payable of the club.
6. Encourage the purchasing agent to check prices, as the price of the item must be entered to complete the document. In a small operation, a two-part form would be enough to supply the club with a record of the price, quantity ordered, the promised delivery date, and a receiving document.

In addition to the instructions on the form, an arbitration clause may be included so that any disagreement between the club and the purveyor can be arbitrated.

Cashiers

The support department hires the cashiers, the food checker/cashier, and the store-keepers for the club. In the event the club has a receptionist/cashier position or a central cashier, this person should report to the controller. Centralization is important, allowng the persons who handle the club's cash and inventories to be responsible to only one person. The controller's office is, or should be, a separate space where access is limited to authorized employees. As this is the place for a drop safe, with a slot and a chute through the wall, this office is kept locked at all times with a buzzer control usually at one of the clerk's desks.

Department Cashiers

Each cashier at the end of a shift must prepare a daily activity report (Fig. 5.3). This report is used as the transmittal document for the club to move cash from the activity level to the safe. This report along with the daily activity cash register receipts and charge slips are deposited in the drop safe. The report takes into consideration whether or not the cashier has a permanent change fund. In the remarks space on the report, the cashier, bartender, etc., must record any unusual happening in the club during their shifts, an accident, for example.

	Date	Purchase Order No.

From　　　　　　To　　　　　　Deliver to

Being governed by the instructions herein, please enter our order for the following:

Quantity　Item　Description　　　　　　　　　Unit　Price　Amount

Date Required　　Discount %　　via　　　　　　Purchaser's Signature

Billing Instructions

a. Separate invoices must be rendered for each order.
b. Do not pack invoice with order, send by mail.
c. Transportation charges, when applicable, must be added to the invoice.
d. The name of the club and the P.O.# must appear on all invoices and statements.
Notice: Noncompliance with these instructions will delay payment while the documents are returned for correction.

NOTIFY US IMMEDIATELY IF YOU ARE SHORT OF ANY ITEM OR CANNOT MEET THE DELIVERY DATE.

Part 1	Purveyor Copy
Part 2	Office Copy
Part 3	Receiving Copy—Forwarded to Office
Part 4	Receiving Copy—Retained by Receiver
Part 5	Purchaser's Copy

FIGURE 5.2　*Daily purchase order form.*

	Item No.	Item		Amount
Lines 1 thru 6 to be filled in by cashier	1.	Cash Turned in (Detail Below Item 20)		$
	2.	Change Fund (−)(When Turned In With Receipts)		
	3.	Refunds (+)		
	4.	Cash Sales		
	5.	Charge Sales		
	6.	Total Sales		$
Person verifying cash and charges will verify lines 1, 2, and 5 and fill in lines 7 thru 11	7.	Change Fund		
	8.	Cash Receipts		
	9.	Total Cash Verified (Line 7 + 8 = 9)		
	10.	Charge Sales		
	11.	Total Verified (Line 9 + 10 = 11)		$
Person reading the register will fill in lines 13 thru 18	12.	Closing Register Reading		
	13.	Opening Register Reading		
	14.	Register Amount (Line 12 − 13 = 14)		
	15.	Over-Rings (−) and Under-Rings (+)		
	16.	Refunds (+) (To Be Used When Refunds Are Reflected in Regular Register Readings)		
	17.	Adjusted Register Reading (Line 14 ± 15 + 16 = 17)		
	18.	Cash Overages or Shortages (Circle: Overage or Shortage)		$

Register No.

Name of Department   **Signature of Cashier**   **Date**

19. Breakdown of Revenue
(To Be Filled In By Bookkeeper)

Name of Account	Account No.	Debit Amount	Credit Amount
Total		$	$

Signed Refund Vouchers Will Be Attached
REMARKS: (Use reverse side if necessary)

20. Detail of Cash Turned In
(To Be Filled In By Cashier)

Coins	Cents $	
	Nickels	
	Quarters	
	Half-Dollars	
	Total Coins	$
Currency	Ones	
	Fives	
	Tens	
	Twentys	
	Total Currency	
	U.S. Checks	
Checks/ M.O.'S	Other Checks	
	Money Orders	
	Total Checks/M.O.	$
	Grand Total Cash Turned In	$

Signature of Person Designated to Read Register   Signature of Person Designated to Verify Cash and Charges

Note: To Make Corrections: Line through error. Write correct amount above error. Initial and date. Corrections are made only by person making error. *No corrections will be made to lines 1 through 6.*

FIGURE 5.3 *Daily activity report.*

Food Checkers/Cashiers

There are many advantages in combining the positions of food checker and food cashier that most progressive clubs are doing so whether on a strictly charge basis or not. The ideal spot for the checker is between or in the pantry-holding section, if it is located next to the dining room. Servers hand the checker the guest check on the way into the kitchen. The advantages of this procedure are:

1. The server's number can be written on the check. This only takes seconds and must be done so the server's number appears on both the original and the duplicate. The checker keeps the original and returns the duplicate copy to the server. This is then given to the chef, who keeps it as a record of the food served (the chef's duplicate guest check receipt system is fully discussed later in this chapter). With this procedure guest checks do not have to be given out to the servers by number and balanced after each shift.
2. The checker can assist the server in seeing that additional items ordered by the member after the original order is taken are recorded. These items could be desserts, after-dinner drinks, or just late orders of items not on the original check. This helps to keep the servers honest. Servers, as well as bartenders, sometimes give the club's goods away for an extra tip.
3. If a member leaves without signing the guest check, the server is known and can be asked who the member was.
4. This system places the burden on the server to protect the club against a walk-out, if the club accepts cash. It is very difficult to distinguish between a walk-out and the server pocketing the money. In some states the server is held responsible for the value of the items appearing on the chef's duplicate.
5. By being able to identify the server, management can balance the overall check average for any meal against the server's average. Servers with high averages can be complemented and the one with the highest given a cash award. This may increase sales even though the member count remains the same. For management purposes, this knowledge separates the "order taker" from the interested, enthusiastic salesperson. Rewarding the top achiever of the month with a cash bonus is one method of getting everyone's attention.

The Central Cashier

The central cashier is the only person who should have the combination to the drop safe because most insurance companies will not cover the club for loss of money, securities, or inventory unless there are signs of breaking and entering. Other losses of cash or inventory are called "mysterious disappearances."

The duties of the central cashier are:

1. To remove club envelopes from the safe, open them one at a time, and check the receipts against the daily activity report. If they balance, the cash and checks, if any (many clubs will give the bartender a change fund to cash members' personal checks even though the bartender cannot accept cash for drinks) are accumulated. The charge slips and the daily activity report are then passed to the bookkeeper.

2. To receive all of the club's mail and open all mail that has the club logo on it. (This works very well, as management always knows that checks for payment of bills go to one place.)
3. To cash personal checks for members.
4. To act as a departmental cashier as needed.
5. To prepare and make the bank deposits and give the deposit receipt to the bookkeeper. This method fulfills one of the basic control objectives of separating cash and record keeping.
6. To handle and distribute the petty cash fund.
7. To issue cash to any department needing a change fund either for operations or to cash members' checks. The way to keep errors at a minimum is to issue a permanent change fund.

The Bookkeeper

Given there is truth to the old adage that "history is prologue," the club's books as historical prologue are useful in many ways. Along with the club's monthly bulletin they serve as sales and activity forecasts. Knowing whether or not a party was a success both artistically and financially can assist management in planning similar events in the future.

The bookkeeping section of the support department can be completely or partially computerized. Computerization of the various club activities from the dining room and bar to the sports departments will be discussed later in this chapter.

The club bookkeeper can handle many tasks. Some of the more routine tasks are:

1. Reading the cash register, checking the daily activity reports against the cash register tapes, and preparing a cashier's over and short report (Fig. 5.4). This report is an excellent management tool, as it pinpoints areas of carelessness or dishonesty on the part of cashiers. When a cashier is consistently over (cash exceeds the cash register tape), one of three actions have caused this and all are equally disreputable:

   a. Money is put into the cash drawer without being rung. One of the bar scams that management must watch is the cash drawer being left open between sales; a bartender could be keeping track of the funds placed in the cash drawer by placing peanuts or stirrers in a glass beside the register.
   b. A member being shortchanged. Overages and shortages are both errors and the cashiers must be taught to be very careful in any transaction with the members.
   c. The bank given the bartender to begin the shift could have been short or over.

2. Checking the bank deposit slip against the total of the daily activity reports.
3. Supervising the person or persons who handle accounts receivable, accounts payable, payroll, and cost controls.

Day	Month _____			
	Cashier	Cashier	Cashier	Cashier
	Over Short	Over Short	Over Short	Over Short
1				
2				
3				
4				
5				
6				
7				
8				
9				
10				
11				
12				
13				
14				
15				
30				
31				

FIGURE 5.4   *Cashier's over and short report.*

Bookkeeping tasks may be done in different ways:

1. Have a computer at the club, prepare, post, and produce the required data.
2. Rent time on a computer. This is done by having a computer terminal in the club with a dedicated telephone line (a private line used for no other purpose) that connects the club to a "mainframe" (a computer with the capacity to handle many terminals).
3. Contract with a computer company to massage and reproduce the data. Many clubs have been doing this for years by having a contract with a bank to do their payroll.
4. Use a bookkeeping machine.
5. Post by hand.

The Storekeeper, or Steward

The storekeeper, or steward, is responsible for all of the inventories of the club. If a purchase order system is in effect, each time merchandise is delivered, the storekeeper has a signed copy of the sales record to keep and a signed copy to send to the accounts payable clerk.

COMPUTERS

A major task of the controller is to supervise the computer systems in the club. The controller and the assistant controller, who could be the bookkeeper, should be the only people who have been trained to troubleshoot when there is a computer problem. This is necessary because computers will not only be used in the accounting office but in the dining room, in the bar, in the pro shop for sales (if point-of-sale registers are used), and for computing handicaps, and in the golf superintendent's office.

The programs designed to do the club record keeping and other calculations are called the "software." There are at the present time over twenty companies making programs specifically for the club industry, and many other companies that will customize a series of programs to meet any club's special needs.

Whether developing a new computerized system, or upgrading or evaluating an old one, a great deal of research must be done if the club is to have the system best suited to it. The research should include the following:

1. Will the installation or upgrading save labor? If it will, what positions can be eliminated and how many hours of labor can be saved by doing the job more quickly with computerized programming?
2. If it will not save any labor, will the speed and efficiency with which reports, billings, and financial statements are generated be worth the investment? With the proper system, the speed at which transactions can be recorded and billings prepared is truly amazing. Many of the cruise ships have done away with cash and allow the passengers to charge all items not included in the cruise package, for example, beauty and barber shops, boutiques, massage parlors, wine, bar bills, ship-to-shore telephone calls, and other services. Ships carry from 600 to 2500 passengers on the 7-day cruises, they dock on Saturday morning, having only closed the bar and cocktail lounge at 2 A.M., and slip the week's bill, containing the last bar and cocktail lounge charges, under the passenger's door by 6 A.M. They do this in less than 3½ hours, week after week. Serious consideration must be given by management to the use of computers if an increase in cash flow results from this earlier posting and mailing of member charges.
3. Never be the "first kid on the block" to have a system like no other club. The first question to ask the computer company is, "What clubs are using your software?" The club's investment in time and money is large and a personal visit to a club to check out its software would be a very worthwhile expense.
4. Will using a computer make the staff more accurate? The answer is no. The computer will only accept data that is given to it. The trade has an expression for this: "GIGO" (garbage in–garbage out).
5. In the event the club is partially computerized, the question is, "Is the new software compatible to the hardware (the computer) that the club already has?"

The last precaution that management must deal with is members' interference. Members who are part of the business community will all have had some experiences with computers both good and bad and will freely offer advice. It is wise to very discreetly check their credentials before following their advice. The club computer system must be very versatile, requiring expert advice.

A blueprint should be drawn of the clubhouse, the pro shop or shops, and of the golf superintendent's office, showing the location of each piece of equipment. Then decisions must be made as to what information is needed and where. A mainframe computer can be established in the clubhouse with terminals for input of data from locations within the clubhouse and modems with dedicated telephone lines for areas not in the clubhouse. This is the ultimate use of a computer system, as all data is immediately available for study at one location. For example, all heavy equipment used in maintaining the golf course would be on the computer. The date of purchase, the original cost, the dollars and labor hours spent to maintain the equipment, and its depreciation factor and life expectancy can be used for budgeting and other purposes. It may be determined that individual computers in remote areas would be more cost-effective.

These are the types of decisions that only management working with a computer expert can make. To find an expert who would only be concerned with the club's best interests and not in selling hardware and software, it is recommended that the nearest college or university be contacted.

Membership Accounting Systems

Computers may be used to serve any or all of the following functions:

1. Membership billing.
2. Activity tracking. This can be used if the club has, for example, a minimum spending policy in the dining room. Under this policy the club would need to know not only how much money a member spent but what it was for. For example, if the club had a $50-per-month minimum in the dining room, the computer could be programmed to track this. If the member spent only $35, the program would automatically bill an additional $15.
3. Accounts receivable with complete membership information and member proofing system.
4. Complete financial reporting. The approved detailed budget could be printed with the financial statement and each variation noted with the percentage of difference.
5. Accounts payable. Separates vendor individual accounts and can total the expenditures from each purveyor and print the checks.
6. Payroll. The system could include all details of deductions and print the checks and the state and federal employee monthly or quarterly tax returns.
7. Inventory control. Monthly inventory sheets are set up by holding areas (storerooms, refrigerators, and freezers) with all items recorded that could possibly be in that area. The item names are entered with the last price in for the accounting period and changed as necessary. By this method the sheets are always ready for the monthly inventory or more frequently if necessary.

8. Word processing.
9. Desktop publishing. This has many uses, including the monthly bulletin and all types of promotional printing.
10. Fixed asset accounting. This will set the value and the allowable depreciation on fixed assets.
11. Database manager and report generator. A database is a collection of interrelated data. In the computer world, "database management" describes the manipulation of a collection of data by electronic means. For example, instead of analyzing the scatter sheet manually to find the percentage of any item sold to the total menu, have the computer do it. The computer is fast and, if fed the right data, is very accurate.
12. Event scheduling.
13. Spreadsheets. These would be used for very detailed and comprehensive reports.

Pro Shop Accounting Systems

The computer can provide information for the members as well as for the club. The following are some of the programs available:

- *Membership Change Post Capture.* This information can be captured on a computer in the shop, on a terminal, or on the main computer.
- *Member's Name, Class, Dependents, and Validation.* This information is needed to identify members and, if the club has unbundled its activities, to verify their eligibility to use them.
- *Various Search Features.* These, including alpha, can be used to rapidly retrieve information on members and their eligibility.
- *Member Guest Validation Watchdog.* Many clubs whose golf courses are crowded set a limit on the number of guests a member can invite to play golf in any given period. This program keeps track of guests.
- *Member Handicaps.* A record of handicaps may be necessary if members register their scores after every round of golf. As their scores change so do their handicaps.
- *Delinquent Balance Evaluation.* This is necessary to know whether or not a member is eligible to use the club's facilities.
- *Issuing and Tracking of Rain Checks, Gift Certificates, Special Orders, and Layaway Plans.* If the club charges its members either a greens fee (to play the course) or a golf cart rental fee, and play is interrupted by inclement weather, a policy must be established for refunds. Pro shop merchandise can be very profitable. Therefore, many clubs use promotional ideas such a gift certificates, special orders, and layaways.

Inventory Control
Inventory control is handled with a point-of-sale cash register and will work in any sales department. The register can be connected to the computer to increase the variety of the things it can do. The following information can be stored and retrieved.

- *Multiple Pricing Levels.* This program will change the prices automatically by classification both up or down. For example, the pro shop manager is overstocked on an item that only sells in the summer and now it is October. To have a quick sale it is decided to reduce the item by 25 percent. The program will print the new price tags and change the prices in the register.
- *Inventory Tracking.* The beginning inventory and all purchases can be recorded and stored and then each sale is deducted so that a "book value" inventory total on every item is available at all times.

Food and Beverage Point-of-Sale Systems

Food and beverage point-of-sale machines have two types of keyboards: reed and micromotion. The reed type has raised keys and cannot be waterproofed. This means that the entire operation can be put out of commission if any type of liquid is spilled on it. The micromotion machines are operated by touching the screen and are usually waterproof. It may be necessary in ordering one to obtain a warranty on its waterproof capacity (Fig. 5.5). The machine should have the capacity to display more than one menu so that the pre-entered inventory can be reduced with each sale, thus providing a book-value inventory.

Some very special features that can be provided by this machine are:

1. Members' charges can be posted directly to their accounts in the accounting office.
2. Point-of-sale registers can also be used as precheck machines; that is, they can be connected to a recorder in the kitchen and orders for food sent to stations there electronically.
3. The machines can print guest checks that will identify servers and bartenders. Optical scanning allows identification of guest checks so that additional items can be added to them. This is particularly important in bar operations so that members can run a tab.

Precheck Machines

There are different types of precheck machines on the market. Which the club decides to use depends on the number of functions the machine is to perform. Precheck machines can simply be used for transmittal of information from the dining room to stations in the kitchen, or computerized, they can serve as storehouses of very detailed, analytical information.

Computerized machines will, depending on the hardware purchased, perform the following:

- Prenumber a guest check and identify the server by name or number.
- Have a keyboard that communicates with records in the kitchen, and be programmed to send the items to the proper stations in the kitchen or pantry.
- Optically scan the checks and identify any check so that additional items can be added.

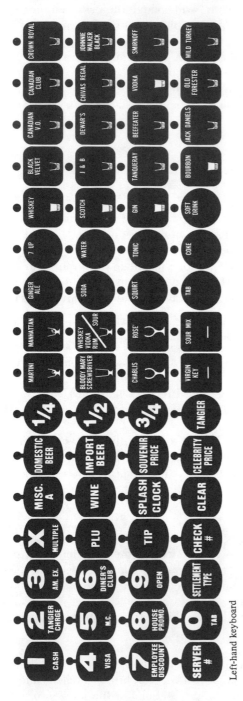

Left-hand keyboard

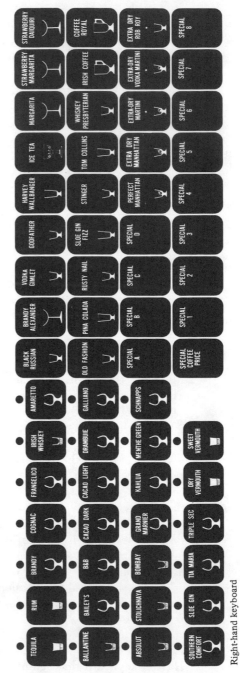

Right-hand keyboard

FIGURE 5.5 Micromotion keyboards (courtesy of American Business Computers, Akron, Ohio).

- Accumulate totals of items ordered and act as a computerized scatter sheet in the same way as a point-of-sale cash register.
- Total the sales of each individual server and print a detailed summary of the items sold, allowing management to evaluate the server's sales ability.

Inventory Control

It is necessary to plan the inventory in every department or there will be too little or too much of many items. Inventory planning is composed of two categories of information: what to purchase and in what quantity. In the food department, for example, the first category is controlled by the menu the club is going to serve. Inventoried items would include:

1. The items printed on the menu.
2. The special items for each meal the club is going to offer.
3. Food for special functions.
4. The items it takes to prepare, season, and serve the food, such as cooking oil, flour, sugar, condiments, and fruit and vegetables for garnishing.

The second category, how much to purchase, is controlled by usage, by members and employees, and by the pipeline. The bin tally card can also be used for the delivery date of perishable items so that the oldest item is always used first.

The taking of inventory in the bar is slightly different as the bar and cocktail lounge inventory may be located in four or more places:

1. Soft drinks and beer in cans or bottles, if the club must purchase them in large quantities, may be kept in a secure area at the rear of the club.
2. Draft beer will have its own refrigerated holding area.
3. Alcoholic beverages may be kept in a separate locked holding area.
4. A supply of beverages must be maintained at the bar or bars.

If canned or bottled beer is sold at the bar, the cans and bottles must be counted and recorded. Soft drinks may be sold by the bottle, by the can, or through a dispensing system. The bottles of alcoholic beverages can be inventoried in different ways, but experiments have shown that the most efficient way is to call each opened bottle half full.

Inventory control is the responsibility of the purchasing agent under the direct supervision of the controller or general manager.

Inventories are planned with high and low stock levels. For example, a pale yellow men's golf shirt, size 15 with short sleeves, is the best seller in the golf pro shop. The purchasing agent has set the high at fifteen shirts and the low at three. This means that when the stock level reaches three, a dozen shirts are ordered. A great deal of research must be done to accumulate the data on stock levels. A database can be created to handle this in connection with a point-of-sale cash register.

Following are some ideas that may help expedite inventory control in the food department and at the same time ensure the accuracy of inventory records.

1. Identify every holding area the club uses by a letter or a number and prepare an individual sheet for each area. If a separate chest is used for ice cream or if the cook's work box is inventoried, then even these items would have a letter or a number. The numbers or letters of the type used to identify boats are the kind to use, because they resist moisture. By using this identification system, items that should be inventoried are rarely overlooked.

2. Set up the holding areas so that every item has a designated place. Some clubs place items according to their usage. For example, items that are used most frequently are placed closest to the door regardless of their class. In the dry holding area, for instance, a type of canned fruit may be used at every meal as a garnish and may be the only fruit kept at the front of the holding area. In a holding area with shelves the inventory goes much more quickly if taken horizontally, top to bottom, then left to right.

3. Prepare the inventory sheets on the computer. The first time a computer is used, type in the page number and sheet number (example: page 1 of 20), the area designated, the item, and the current price. This should be updated the last week of the month so that when the quantity of the items is entered, the computer will automatically do the calculating.

   There are three ways to price an inventory: by the actual price paid, by the average price paid, or by the last price paid. The last is the pricing method many clubs use because this is the true value of the item and the gain or loss by inventory can be handled automatically in the general ledger section of the computer. If the actual price paid is used and items are carried over from 1 month to the next, then the inventory sheets must carry two lines for each item. Also, when received, every item must be tagged or marked with a grease pencil so that the same items that are priced differently can be listed. If the price of the inventory items is averaged, the club must maintain a "perpetual inventory card system" and "a daily requisition system." These systems will be detailed later in this chapter.

   Note: Experience has shown that neither the actual-price nor the average-price method is worth the additional time each takes.

4. In the taking of the inventory, two people should be involved, one to do the counting and the other the recording. If the club employs a storekeeper, or steward, this person should be one of the two. If every item is tagged and has a "bin tally card" (Fig. 5.6), or is marked with a grease pencil, then a numbering system can be used to speed up the taking of the inventory. A bin tally card designates the place for each item, gives the number assigned to each item, and can indicate the "high" and the "low" inventory level.

COST ACCOUNTING

The support department is responsible for accumulating all of the documents necessary to do the cost accounting for the club. It is management's responsibility to establish procedures so that these documents are properly prepared and forwarded. The objectives of cost accounting are:

```
┌──────────────────────────────────────────────┐
│                                                │
│               BIN TALLY CARD                   │
│                                                │
│  ────────────────────────────────────────────  │
│                                                │
│    Holding Area          Bin Number            │
│                                                │
│  ────────────────────────────────────────────  │
│                                                │
│    High                  Low                   │
│                                                │
│  ────────────────────────────────────────────  │
│                                                │
│    Delivery Date                               │
│                                                │
└──────────────────────────────────────────────┘
```

FIGURE 5.6 *Bin tally card.*

1. To safeguard the merchandise of the club.
2. To safeguard the cash of the club.
3. To curb payroll abuses and to pay only for the work performed.
4. To give management detailed and accurate information on financial problems in the club (if there are any) so that fast corrective action can be taken.
5. To give management detailed and accurate information so that accurate decisions affecting selling price, services, recreation, and entertainment can be made.

Cost-control Systems

Cost-control systems must be established to protect the assets of the club. These controls should be used for inventories, cash, and property. The systems have four common elements.

1. They must be practical and accurate. As a system is developed, it should be evaluated against actual club figures. A good system for all food and beverages, for example, should supply two facts: the dollar value of the ending inventory, and the dollar value of the product used or missing. The total of these should be the value of the beginning inventory plus the value of the purchases. Management would then compare the cost control figures with the figures on the financial statement. A variance over or under 2 percent or an excessive dollar amount should be investigated. For example, if the standard for the club was a 40 percent food cost and the financial statement showed 43 percent, then the dollar value of the sales in the food department must be considered. If in a club

with a $100,000 monthly food business and a food cost of $43,000, a loss of $3000 should be investigated. The same percentage and dollar values also apply to the bar department. Investigation, when necessary, should be carried out as follows:

a. Check the invoices for the month. Have there been any price increases that have not been reflected in the club's pricing policies?

b. Check the receiving procedures the club is using. Are all items weighed and counted? Has a receiving area been set aside so that delivery people do not have access to other areas of the club?

c. Check the holding areas. Are perishable foods being kept at the proper temperatures? Is management informed if food is old or spoiled and must be thrown away?

d. Check the preparation of food and drinks and the portions being served. Does the club use batch cards to indicate the proper preparation of the items and the portions being served? (For example, if the club's policy is to pour 1 ounce of alcoholic beverage in a drink and the bartender is pouring a larger portion, then the cost percentage will rise.) Also, if food and drink are returned because of errors, are these being recorded?

e. Check guest checks or the chef's duplicate copies compared against the actual dollar sales.

f. Take inventories, if necessary, more than once a month.

2. They must give detailed information. The system must be so detailed that discrepancies can be revealed and responsibility pinpointed.

3. They must save money. The cost of the system in labor and materials must not exceed its value.

4. They must not interfere with the work routine. Personnel who prepare food and drink must not have their work interrupted to keep records. Clubs that have tried to have the chef record all items removed from the holding areas have not obtained accurate results.

Every transaction in the club must be exactly defined and leave an "audit trail." This means that in the event of a problem, "footprints" will clearly show where an employee strayed from the path. Items composing the "audit trail" include:

- Beginning inventory
- Purchase orders
- Requisitions
- Guest checks
- Ending inventory

For example, the club maintains a book-value inventory by adding all purchases to the beginning inventory and subtracting all items on the requisitions. In 1 month this figure was 1200 pounds, the physical inventory 700. In checking the beginning inventory, it was found that the club had 1500 pounds of choice ribs of beef on hand;

7800 pounds was purchased during this accounting period for a total of 9300 pounds. Ribs on the requisitions totaled 8100 pounds, while the ending inventory showed 700 pounds in stock. This meant that 500 pounds of beef ribs were unaccounted for. Management would then have to determine whether the error was due to:

- Inventory error
- Portions being served were larger than planned
- Meat being used without filling out a requisition
- Meat being stolen

The first audit should be of the guest checks. If 8600 pounds were used, then by calculating one raw pound per serving, the requisitions were wrong or posted wrong. If the total of the guest checks, however, indicates fewer portions were sold, the club knows that it must carefully check its portions and security.

Cost-control systems are very expensive to implement and have no value whatsoever unless management acts on the information provided. Fortunately, management usually finds the club used the missing goods but the storekeeper just forgot to mark them down.

Budget-control System

The most economical cost-control system is called the "budget-control system" (BCS). This system establishes percentages that can be used to analyze finances monthly, revealing immediately if the goals for each budget item have been met. BCS treats every operating department as a separate business with its own complete overhead expenses, sometimes called the general and administrative expenses. The first step is to determine the amount of overhead that should be charged to each department by dividing the total overhead by the department sales. This figure is then used as a department expense.

To initiate BCS, management could start with the food department. This is the most difficult division to control and is the source of the largest financial losses.

Food Department Control

BCS relies on management having accurate information. The control steps that would be taken in the food department are as follows:

1. Add a percentage of the overhead expense to all of the other department expenses and subtract this total from 100 percent to establish the necessary food cost if the department is to break even. This percentage figure is adjustable. Adding one percentage point creates a 1 percent profit, subtracting one creates a 1 percent loss.
2. Price the menu.

3. Provide complete batch sheets to the kitchen, listing the ingredients, the preparation details, and the portions for each menu item.
4. Establish the storekeeper requisition control system described later in the chapter. This is only a temporary expedient, as it is very expensive, until management is satisfied that the chef is trained in the duplicate guest check system (see "chef's issue and receipt control system").
5. Establish the exact labor cost of preparing and serving food.
6. Take weekly inventories until the actual food cost is within 2 percent of the budget. Then take monthly inventories.

For example, if management developed these figures:

Sales	100%
Less	
Food cost	50%
Labor cost	35%
Laundry	3%
Supplies	3%
Renewals and replacements	2%
Overhead	12%
Total cost of goods sold and expenses	105%
Loss	5%

Note: Supplies are one-time usage items, such as paper goods, soap powder, etc. Renewals and replacements (glassware, china, silverware, table linens, and small kitchen tools) have some life expectancy.

The board of directors and the committee representatives should decide if a 5 percent loss is satisfactory. The manager will convert this to dollars. For example, on $250,000 worth of food business this represents a loss of $12,500. Can this amount be allocated to the division in terms of club dues? If not, the manager can offer the following options:

- Raise prices to eliminate loss. If it was decided to raise prices so that the food cost was reduced by 5 percent (from 50 percent to 45 percent), then this would help to reduce the losses.
- Cut service by closing the dining room during unprofitable periods.
- Consolidate the dining areas.
- Eliminate the frills—flowers on table, expensive table china, glassware, silverware, and linen.

The division would be stabilized at whatever figure was decided and by the board of directors then management would use BCS for its daily operations.

The club would now have a target to achieve and that is to stabilize food costs at 45 percent. If this figure was not reached, food cost rising to 52 percent the following month, the 2 percent "variance" would be converted to dollars to determine whether a full-scale investigation or additional controls needed to be put into effect. In the event the club's food business was $10,000 for the month, 2 percent variance would be $200. This dollar amount is directly proportionate to the amount of time and labor that should be expended to discover the reason for this variance.

Once BCS is established and working, the paperwork in the kitchen is reduced to: the chef's list of food and supplies forwarded to the purchasing agent, and the duplicate guest checks forwarded to the bookkeeper after every meal. The chef has the responsibility of insuring that all food items are received and locked in the appropriate areas. There will still have to be locked storage for supplies, renewals, and replacements and for the other divisions of the club such as the bar and pro shops. The keys, however, should be the responsibility of the department managers.

Recipes and Portions

One of the first controls a manager should implement is the use of uniform recipes and portions. Management working with the chef can develop all of the recipes used in the food department. The recipes should be typed on loose-leaf notebook sheets and placed in a binder in the kitchen for ready reference. In addition to the recipes, the sheet should also show the preparation details and the portions to be served. The notebook, of course, is to be made available to all cooks. This will be necessary if the chef becomes ill or goes on vacation. The prices charged are determined by the standards set by the club and are partially based on the desired food cost percentages and the overall relationship of one menu item to another. For example, at certain times of the year the market might be flooded with spring chickens. The club wishes to operate on an overall 40 percent food cost. If this cost breakdown were applied to the price of a fried chicken dinner, the menu price would be very low in relation to the other entrees.

The following is an example of the cost of a steak dinner, priced at $10.95.

10-ounce "Western Choice Sirloin Steak"	$3.60
1 mixed green salad with dressing	.30
1 baked potato, sour cream, chives, butter	.20
rolls and butter	.10
1 beverage	.15
Total cost	$4.35
Gross profit	$6.60
Gross profit percent	60.3%
Cost of goods sold percent	39.7%

Different menu items return different percentages of profit. Therefore, a scatter sheet is used to determine what the overall profit should be. This is computed by the same method used to compute member usage at the club. For example:

10 percent of the items sold yield 51 percent gross profit
50 percent of the items sold yield 49 percent gross profit
30 percent of the items sold yield 48 percent gross profit
10 percent of the items sold yield 45 percent gross profit

This sales mix would yield 48.5 percent gross profit, which is derived by multiplying the percentage of items sold by the gross-profit percent, adding them, and dividing by 100 percent. This procedure is necessary in order to analyze the gross-profit percentage on the financial statement, which only shows the total of all items sold. The 48.5 percent figure is a forecast that can be compared to the actual profit.

Labor cost control has three components:

1. *Approved Work Schedule.*   The composition of and need for the schedule was fully explained in Chapter 4.
2. *Employees' Time Record.*   Employees must sign in and out, using either the manual or mechanical method. A sheet of paper with the employees listed by name and a space provided for the days and the hours of work will suffice, or a time clock may be used. A permanent record of the employees' hours is a very important document.
3. *Supervisor's Certification.*   Each time sheet entry or card must be signed by the employee's supervisor to certify that the employee worked the hours specified on the work schedule. Employees are paid the scheduled time or the actual time worked, whichever is the lesser. This prevents employees from reporting in earlier or staying later than needed. All overtime must be approved in advance by the manager or his assistant and noted on the work schedule if the employee is to be paid. This advance approval can save the club many dollars and should be required no matter how small the amount of overtime.

Snack Bar Control

A club's snack bar food and beverage operation can be controlled by BCS or by what is called the "retail accountability system" (RAS). RAS establishes a retail value for every item sold, with inventories and purchases figured at both cost and retail. For example, the beginning inventory in the snack bar, added to all purchases, less the ending inventory (if figured at the selling price), should equal sales. RAS requires that every item sold be prepackaged in the club kitchen and transferred to the snack bar by requisition, which is labor costly. BCS works equally well if deliveries are arranged so that the vendor's sales slips and the club purchase orders separate the snack bar food, beverages, and supplies from those of the kitchen.

Buffet Control

The control of the cost of goods sold on buffets and the money it generates is not complicated but at the start requires a great deal of research. The control of the cost of buffet goods sold is accomplished as follows:

1. A menu for the buffet is planned. This can be supplemented by production items used from past meals, but generally these constitute only a small part of the total.
2. Every item must be weighed and priced, exactly as is done for an individual meal.

3. When the meal is over the buffet is broken down. Every item that is still saleable must be weighed and priced. This total is subtracted from the original cost to determine the actual cost price of the food used.
4. The cost of food then is divided by the total number of members served and provides the cost of each member's meal. Then the actual cost is divided by the desired percentage of cost to arrive at the sales price to be charged.
5. The gross profit is adjusted by:
   a. Increasing or decreasing the variety of items; the greater the variety the higher the cost. If there were twenty-five items weighing 100 pounds, this could feed 100 persons. However, if thirty items were used weighing 100 pounds, this also could feed 100 persons.
   b. Having less or more expensive items on the table.
   c. Raising or lowering the price charged.

If the buffet is the only choice offered, guest checks could be presold or distributed by an employee of the support department or another responsible person. The duplicate of the check would be presented to a person at the buffet line and a stub would be returned to the member for identification for a second serving. If the regular menu is offered, in addition to the buffet, the service personnel write up the guest check at the table.

In either type of meal service the member is always escorted to the table, seated, served water and invited to order cocktails or wine.

Storekeeper Requisition Control System

As explained earlier, this sytem is used to control inventories. However, to work the system needs a full-time storekeeper and a cost-control clerk. Each item received or released by the storekeeper must be posted on a stock card maintained by the clerk, and subtracted from or added to the previous total. In the food department the dollar value of the items can be the cost of the food used that day. However, in a large club there is so much paperwork involved that this system is only recommended as a temporary second step in BCS.

Management should get directly involved in the requisitioning of food for at least a 30-day period. This means that the manager and other supervisory personnel will work with the storekeeper. In some instances management may usurp the storekeeper's duties completely until the complete system is reviewed. A very careful check of all food requisitioned should be maintained. Food that is not used should go back into holding with the appropriate entry made on a form (see below). The purpose of these controls is to train the chef in food usage and to make it very clear to all personnel that management is vitally interested in the proper operation of the kitchen.

This system requires that the food and nonalcoholic beverage holding areas be manned during all operating hours. If this is not possible, breakout periods should be established (issuing the needed products prior to the meal). For example, breakfast items could be issued the night before. All food and beverages are received by the storekeeper and should be issued to the departments on a three-part, prenumbered requisition form (Fig. 5.7).

Stock Number	Description	Unit	Quantity Desired	Quantity Issued	Unit Cost	Extension	Unit Retail Price	Extension

TO: _____

FROM: _____

Stock Number	Description	Unit	Quantity Desired	Quantity Issued	Unit Cost	Extension	Unit Retail Price	Extension

REQUISITIONED BY _____ DATE _____

ISSUED BY _____ DATE _____

RECEIVED BY _____ DATE _____

PART 1   **BOOKKEEPER COPY**

REQUISITIONED BY _____ DATE _____

ISSUED BY _____ DATE _____

RECEIVED BY _____ DATE _____

PART 2   **STOREROOM COPY**

REQUISITIONED BY _____ DATE _____

ISSUED BY _____ DATE _____

RECEIVED BY _____ DATE _____

PART 3   **RECEIVING COPY**

REQUISITIONED BY _____ DATE _____

ISSUED BY _____ DATE _____

RECEIVED BY _____ DATE _____

FIGURE 5.7 *Requisition form.*

These forms are prenumbered by the bookkeeper and drawn by the storekeeper as needed. When any department needs supplies, the requisition is prepared by the storekeeper by writing the department name on the "To" line and giving it to the person authorized to draw supplies for that department. This person will complete the form by filling in the columns marked "Description" with the name of the item, unit (pound, piece, can, bottle, crate, carton, or case), and quantity desired. The form is then returned to the storekeeper, who completes the column marked "Quantity Issued." (In the event of a substitution because of a shortage of an item, the requisition is consulted and changed.) The storekeeper then notes on the "From" line at the top of the form the holding areas where the various items are, fills the order, signs the form, and delivers the ordered items. The person receiving the items signs the form and gets the third copy, the storekeeper the second, and the bookkeeper the original. The storekeeper is responsibile for the proper distribution of the forms.

Under this system, if the storekeeper has signed the beginning inventory sheets and the proper copy of the purchase order, and has a receipt for the items delivered, he or she may be held responsible for any items that are missing.

All signatures are dated. If an overissue takes place, the same form used to issue the items is used to return them to the proper holding area.

The dollar value of the food and beverages on the form, when posted to the "property and stock record cards" (Fig. 5.8), reduces the value of the food or beverage in inventory and also provides the cost of the food and beverages. Some accountants call these cards "perpetual inventory cards."

Each item in the inventory has its own property and stock record card. This card is a book-value record of the quantity of every item and the last price paid for it, created by recording each purchase and each withdrawal of merchandise. The card also indicates the holding area from which the item or items came.

In the event the total on the card is not the actual amount of the product in inventory, one or more of the following events occurred:

- Bulk goods were issued without being weighed or counted.
- Merchandise was removed from or returned to the holding area without a requisition form being prepared or corrected.
- The requisition was not changed when items were not in stock.
- Spoiled items were thrown away without being reported or a requisition filled out. Many clubs require the storekeeper to get the chef's and/or a manager's signature on the requisition form before items can be discarded.
- The inventory count was wrong.
- There were mathematical errors in either the inventory, the requisitions, and/or the stock record cards.
- Employee dishonesty.

Chef's Issue and Receipt Control System

The chef's issue and receipt control system places responsibility on the food preparation staff for control of food inventory. Usually in the food department, the person designated to be responsible would be the chef. In some clubs, the chef will delegate

Ref	Date	Quantity IN	Quantity OUT	Price	Balance	Variance

Location	Company Name	Retail Price	Stock Level	High Low

Item Name	Unit of Issue

FIGURE 5.8 *Property and stock record card.*

the task of keeping track of the food to one of the cooks. This, however, does not relieve the chef of responsibility. The system works as follows: the holding areas are kept locked when the preparation staff is not on duty. The club uses at least a two-part duplicate guest check system or a precheck recording system so that there is a record of all items ordered by the members. The duplicate of the guest check or the precheck recording serves as the receipt for all items leaving the kitchen. After each meal the duplicates are sent to the storekeeper in an envelope issued from the support department. These duplicates can serve many purposes.

- If the club is feeding its employees, whether free or for a charge, and a simplified guest check is used, a complete record of the food used can be maintained. This means that the chef can be held responsible for at least the entree items.
- This system also shows any errors the kitchen might make because there will be two checks for the same member. The server must prepare a second guest check if an entree item is returned to the kitchen and void the original check. The voided check should have the reason the food was refused and be initialed by the manager, then this information should be brought to the chef's attention.
- Finally, duplicates should be used when preparing a scatter sheet if this procedure is not being done by a cashier, a food checker, a point-of-sale register, or a precheck machine.

Purveyor's Invoice System

The purveyor's invoice system is simple, fast and accurate enough to give management a handle on the cost of food sold without taking an inventory. This system should not replace the taking of a monthly or more frequent inventories. Taking a physical inventory by counting every item is necessary in the food business but is costly in both time and labor. The invoice system is based on the assumption that the club has frequent deliveries and the purchaser desires the club to have the freshest food possible.

Management would pick one day in the week, preferably the day after the club is closed, to total all invoices of food received in the last week. For example, if the club was closed Monday, on Tuesday all invoices for food received the previous week would be totaled. This total would be the approximate cost of the food used in the last week. With the daily food sales and cost of goods sold, the gross profit can be calculated. Because there will be food in stock from the previous week, the first week of this system will lack some accuracy, however, the second week will be more accurate, and when the system is a month old the manager will have an accurate weekly food cost.

Beverage Cost Control

Besides enhancing control of the guest checks and cash, having a cashier at the bar expedites bar service. This extra help also prevents the bartender from having to handle guest checks and money.

Some clubs prepare a guest check for each transaction, and, if a cash register is used, each drink is recorded immediately after it is served. Clubs not using registers may line the checks on the back bar, but this takes the bartenders time.

The control of beverages, particularly alcoholic, offer a special challenge to the club manager. The very nature of alcohol itself seems to promote mischief and wrongdoing. It is no wonder that controlling beverages is as difficult as controlling the food department, but for different reasons. One reason is that in many clubs drinks are produced and sold by the same person. Thus the basic control rule cannot be used.

Another reason for control difficulties is that each individual drink that is prepared must be portion-controlled. For example, the club may serve a drink that contains a certain fraction over an ounce of alcohol. Such portions are difficult to prepare unless the bartender has been trained or an electronic pouring device is used.

In spite of these problems, the sale of alcoholic beverages can be controlled if management will take the following steps.

1. Accumulate the department cost data.
2. Establish standard portions, brands, and recipes.
3. Hire, if at all possible, inexperienced personnel to tend bar and train them in-house.
4. Set up separate holding area for alcoholic beverage stock.
5. Use requisitions to transfer beverages from the holding areas to the bar.
6. Establish, when possible, individual bar stations for each bartender. In many clubs not using cash registers, the only item used jointly by more than one bartender may be draft beer.
7. Install the "retail accountability control system" (discussed below) and take daily inventories until pouring cost standards are met.
8. Check the labor cost and, if it does not conform with the pro forma budget, make the necessary adjustments.
9. Take monthly inventories.

Requisition System

The same requisition procedures are followed in the bar as in the food department. Start by issuing the stock needed for the bar (this is usually done by the bar manager) and indicate where the goods are going.

Bar Stations

A bar station is a space behind the bar that is completely self-supporting. It contains all the stock the bartender needs, all the supplies, ice, and a cash register either for money or guest check imprinting or both. Through the use of bar stations, the manager can pinpoint responsibility and establish a track record for each bartender. As the bar will be controlled by "retail accountability," the only items that must be tracked are those sold from separate stations. For example, if the bar is using a "remote draw draft beer system," there will be taps at each bar station, one tap for all stations, or even taps at another bar. If the latter is the case, beer must be rung on a separate key in order to maintain control. The newest remote control systems can now be equipped with a flowmeter for each tap that will measure and calculate the retail value of the beer flowing through it. When there is product sharing of a single inventory by two or more bartenders, the best control system is to have one person in charge (with pay increase of at least $.50 an hour) who will act as a working supervisor when the head bartender is not available.

Another method of bar control is for the club to hire a "shopping service." The company hired to shop the club's bar will send in an experienced representative, usually with a temporary membership card. This person will purchase drinks and observe the bar operation, then write a detailed and comprehensive report to the manager stressing any or all of the good qualities of the staff as well as any mistakes or wrongdoing on their part and describing any notable happenings in the bar and cocktail lounge.

Labor Controls

Management must organize the labor in the bar, cocktail lounge, and dining room so that the proper amount of service is provided for club members. Management working with the head bartender and the maitre d' must decide the following:

- Which of the club's bars will be open and what will their hours of operation be?
- Will a separate cocktail server be needed in the dining rooms, the locker rooms, the card room, the television room, the pool area and, if so, from where will the service be provided?
- Will the volume of business justify one or more service bars during certain hours?
- Where in each room will party bars be set up?
- Will a bar be set up in a golf cart to service the players on the golf course?

All of these activities take personnel, so scheduling and budgets must be planned to provide maximum service to the members.

Retail Accountability

The system of retail accountability can be used in any of the club's departments where a unit of sale can be determined. This means the system can be used in the bar and cocktail lounge, all snack bars, the pro shops, and for packaged alcoholic and other beverages sold for off-premise consumption (see Figure 5.9).

The system of retail accountability in the beverage division means keeping track of all products by their retail value. For example, a fifth of bourbon (750 ml) would produce, at $.90 cents a 1½ ounce shot (45 ml), 16.5 drinks with a dollar value of $14.40 (16.5 × .90). The ½ ounce (15 ml) is lost in capillary attraction, spillage, and so forth.

The retail accountability system is designed so that management, through inventories and issues, can determine the least amount of money the bartender should have recorded. Inventories of a bar are taken in tenths with the use of a bar scale and are calculated at both cost and retail value. For example, the selling price of an item would include the cost of mixes and garnishments. A gin and tonic would be priced by establishing the price of 45 ml of gin, 120 ml of tonic water, and ¼ of a whole lime. Actual cost divided by percent of cost will equal the selling price. The gin, tonic water, and lime cost $.23; a gross profit of 75 percent in the bar would satisfy BCS requirements. The cost-of-goods sold percentage is 100 percent minus the gross-profit percentage, or 25 percent. Therefore,

Stock No.	Item	Unit	Beg Inv	Issues	Sub Total	End Inv	Amt Used	Unit Cost	Total Cost	Sell Price	Total Price
	Michelob Draft Beer	Lb.						.176		.416	
	Schlitz Draft Beer	Lb.						.146		.334	
	Michelob Beer	Btl.						.255		.56	
	Schlitz Beer	Can						.20		.33	
	Schaefer Beer	Can						.164		.31	
	Schmidts Beer	Btl.						.144		.31	
	Colt "45"	Can						.198		.38	
	Corn Chips	Pkg.						.089		.13	
	Beernuts	Pkg.						.089		.13	
	Potato Chips	Pkg.						.089		.13	
	Slim Jims	Ea.						.131		.19	
	Beef Jerky	Pkg.						.131		.19	

Retail Accountability   Cost Analysis   Responsibility

Expected Income   Sales Per Register   Bartender

Sales Per Register   Total Cost   Inv. By

Short/Over   Gross Profit   Calculated By

Gross Profit %

Remarks:_____

FIGURE 5.9 *Retail accountability form.*

$$\frac{\text{Actual cost}}{\text{Percent of cost}} = \text{Selling price}$$

$$\frac{.23}{.25} = \$.92, \text{ raised to } \$.95 \text{ or } \$1.00$$

However, in computing retail accountability, if the average selling price of 45 ml of gin is $.90, then the inventory calculation would be $.90. The system uses the lowest or most conservative price the bottle will return as the amount on which to base the bartender's responsibility.

Managers should use a standard chart, available from the brewery, to compute the number of glasses of beer that can be drawn from the barrel. Barrel is a misnomer, as the steel keg used by all breweries is not a barrel but a half barrel. It contains 58.67 liters of beer (15.5 gallons); the old beer barrel contained 117.35 liters. If the beer is drawn correctly, the number of glasses drawn cannot be determined by dividing the size of the glass into the amount of beer in the half barrel because the foam or head on the beer is 75 percent air.

Inventories should be taken daily for the first 30 days of the installation of the retail accountability system. If actual sales are within 2 percent under or 5 percent over the estimated sales, weekly inventories should be taken for the next 30 days. Then inventory in the third month should be taken in the middle and at the end, using BCS as the control yardstick. Inventories should be taken twice a month for at least 6 months before the bars are put on a once-a-month inventory because the control data must be accumulated for at least this length of time.

Happy Hours, or Reduced Prices

In some clubs it has become customary to have reduced prices in the bar at certain times as a promotion gimmick. This is simple to control if all prices are reduced approximately by the same percentage. The cash register tapes are marked at the beginning and at the end of happy hour. For example, if all drinks are reduced 50 percent from 5 P.M. to 7 P.M. for all sales during this period, for computation purposes 50 percent would be added back to check the accountability:

Regular sales	190.00	4 to 5 P.M.
Reduced sales	80.00	5 to 7 P.M.
Regular sales	300.00	7 to 11 P.M.
Total sales	570.00	
Adjusted by 50%	80.00	
Inventory check	650.00	
Product used	645.00	(less than 5% over)

This final total indicates that the bar was operating satisfactorily. If sales are reduced by any percentage, subtract this from 100 to set up the percentage of what is added to the actual sales for an inventory check. For example, all drinks are reduced 35 percent. Subtract 35 percent from 100 percent and the result is 65 percent. Then divide 35 percent by 65 percent, which gives 53.85 percent, which would be added to actual sales for an inventory check.

Regular sales	$490.00	for the evening
Reduced drink sales	80.00	
Total sales	$570.00	
Adjusted by 53.85	42.96	
Inventory check	$612.96	

Another method of control is to use a separate bar or bar stock for reduced drink prices. This method allows management to have a beginning and ending inventory and to determine the actual costs at their leisure and without disrupting normal business.

REVIEW QUESTIONS

1. What are the principle duties of the support department?
2. What are the techniques of good purchasing practices? Explain how each applies to the club.
3. What are the reasons for using a formal type of purchase order system? Describe the ways it assists in cost control.
4. List the six ethical principles by which purchasers should abide.
5. What are the basic concepts of cost control as applied to the food department?
6. What are the objectives of any cost accounting system?
7. What are the control steps necessary to control the sale of drinks at reduced prices?
8. What are the reasons for having the support department include the purchasing agent, the cashiers, and the storekeepers?
9. What is the method used to determine the types of controls the club will use?
10. What is the method used in determining allowable variances in each department?

CASE STUDY

Peggy L. was the storekeeper at the Hardy Rocky Country Club. Peggy was a fine, cheerful, pleasant, nice-looking person with qualities that were both an asset and a liability to the club. Peggy was gregarious to the extreme. She would stop work at any time to talk to anybody, leaving the holding areas unattended and unlocked to go into the kitchen, the bar, or the office to chitchat. Peggy's smile and cheerful outlook on life was contagious and had a beneficial influence on other employees in the 2 years she had been employed. Every one, including club members, knew and liked Peggy. Even though Peggy was fifty and divorced, her moral code was such that she would not date an employee or a member. She often used the expression "You can't mix work and sex." However, she would leave the holding areas frequently, allowing every employee access. The club had an efficient issue and breakout system that had worked very successfully since inception but had not worked since Peggy had been put in charge. In the past, management had checked the usage figures on the scatter sheet against the inventory shortage and they had almost balanced. Management supposed that nothing was missing but that items had been removed from the rooms when Peggy was absent. Nevertheless, the situation finally came to a head last month when the pouring cost in the bar rose 10 percent above average. Peggy held the only keys to the bar stock and many items were missing that had never been issued.

Management had discussed the unlocked rooms and the lack of signed requisitions with Peggy many times, but she had never been officially reprimanded. These discussions were gentle suggestions for her to be more careful and spend to more time in the holding areas. Now the club auditors are suggesting to the board that management take some positive action.

Which of the following options, or combination there of, would solve these problems with the least interruption to the smooth operation of the club?

1. Discharge Peggy.
2. Discipline Peggy with either a written reprimand or three days off without pay.
3. Transfer Peggy to another department and hire a new storekeeper.
4. Change the system. If management selected this option, what system or systems could be used?

6 Managing the Club's Recreation Facilities

GOLF

Golf courses usually consist of nine holes or multiples of nine holes. Each hole has a starting place (the tee); a fairway (a landing area that is closely mowed); a rough (on each side of the fairway; not as closely mowed and with trees); and a green, which contains the cup or hole, the ultimate goal for the golfer. Between the tee and green there may be sand traps, called "bunkers," and lakes or streams, called "water hazards."

The concept of the illuminated golf course has finally hit the East. The West Coast has long had illuminated courses, driving ranges, and putting greens and the extra income derived from these additions has paid for the cost of all construction and then some. Illumination will be discussed in detail in the tennis section of this chapter.

The general manager usually has two professionals to supervise the hands-on day-to-day operation of the course, the golf pro and the golf superintendent. For guidance the manager may consult with them and/or the golf committee. For a successful operation, however, the general manager must be in complete charge (Fig. 6.1).

Golf Professional

The duties of the golf professional are as follows:

- Actively works with the general manager in preparing the golf budget.
- Actively works with the golf committee in helping to satisfy the golf membership with the golf course operation.
- Sets controls for the playing of golf, i.e.:
  (1) Fixes tee-off times for the membership. Reservations, or tee times, can be controlled by a computer software system so that all members are treated on a first come–first served basis.

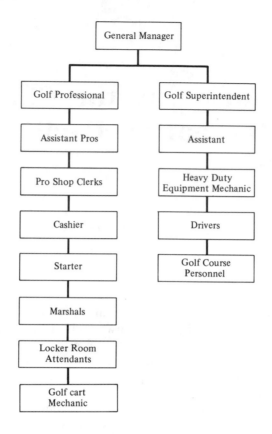

FIGURE 6.1 *Golf organization chart.*

(2) Deploys marshals to enforce the rules of play.
- Manages the operation and the personnel in the golf pro shop.
- Supervises the use and maintenance of the golf carts.
- Supervises the operation and the personnel in the golf bag storage area.
- Supervises the practice putting/chipping green and driving range.
- Gives private and group lessons on demand.
- Establishes clinics for both children and adults.
- Arranges and manages tournaments.
- With the general manager and the golf superintendent decides when the course is in playable condition. For example, the golf pro helps decide after a very heavy rainfall whether the golf carts would do serious damage to the golf course and if it should open for play.

The golf professional, in addition to performing the aforementioned duties, must be pleasant and available to the golfing membership.

Compensation

The golf professional's total income may be calculated as follows.

COMPENSATION PLAN 1

An annual salary or retainer

A percentage of the gross sales of the pro shop or, preferably, a net percentage of the profit of the pro shop. Some clubs are giving up to 5 percent of the gross sales while others give up to 25 percent of the net profit

A percentage of the golf cart rentals

All the income from private lessons and clinics

A percentage of or all of the gross income from the driving range

All the income from the rewrapping and repairing of clubs and bags

A portion of the tournament money. The pro usually receives 10 percent of the fees charged to play in a tournament, or a minimum charge of $10 per player, which is generally spent in the pro shop

Income from bag storage

COMPENSATION PLAN 2   Delete any of the items in plan 1.

COMPENSATION PLAN 3

Make the pro a concessionaire with full responsibility for stocking the pro shop with all rights to the profits realized from the sale of merchandise.

Some of the items from plan 1.

In the selection of any of the aforementioned compensation plans, the club should process all charges through its own accounting system for billing to the membership. Management should know the gross incomes of all the staff. If the pro owns the pro shop, he or she usually pays the salaries of the employees.

If the pro is a concessionaire, management should take precautions to ensure the shop is run properly and the employees are paid at least minimum wage and any overtime due. If the pro does not pay for the merchandise in the shop, the club could be held responsible. The pro can also receive certain merchandise on consignment (it will not be billed to the shop until sold). This can be a dangerous practice because the money from the sale could be spent before the invoice arrives for payment. The club should require the pro (concessionaire) to provide his own insurance or at least pay the club whatever the cost to insure his shop under its policy.

Tournaments and Group Play

Different types of tournaments can help to make the game of golf more interesting, and can provide a showcase for the more talented players. The golf handicap system allows even the most inept golfer an opportunity to win.

Tournaments have one serious drawback: they close either nine or eighteen holes to the golfers who do not wish to participate. All tournaments should be approved by the general manager, golf committee, golf professional, and the golf superintendent.

Some of the following tournaments are very popular at many clubs. Management should be aware of each of them, providing the pro a list of those they are interested in promoting.

ACE OF ACES   Once a month for 6 months or at the beginning of the season's play, a low-gross and low-net qualifier is held, with each winner competing in the Ace of Aces tournament at the end of the season or 6 months later.

APPROACH AND PUTTING CONTEST   Each contestant approaches and holes out three balls from 25, 50, and 100 yards off the green. In each case the ball should be played from a different direction. The winner is the one holing the three different balls in the fewest number of strokes.

AVERAGE SCORE (STROKE PLAY)   Partners average their gross scores for each hole and deduct half their combined handicap from their eighteen-hole total. Half strokes count as whole strokes after totaling.

HANDICAP STROKE PLAY   Players play eighteen holes at stroke play. Prizes may be awarded for best gross and net scores. Full handicaps are used.

MOST THREES, FOURS, FIVES   Players use full handicap, taking the strokes as they come on the card. Prizes are awarded to the players scoring the most net threes, the most fours, and the most fives.

BEST BALL AND AGGREGATE (LOW-BALL, LOW-TOTAL)   This is a variation of the regular four-ball match. Two points are involved on each hole, one point for the best ball and one point for the low aggregate score for the team.

BEST-BALL MATCH   A player plays his own ball. Two of the contestants are partners and play their best ball against the score of the third, who is generally a better player.

BINGLE-BANGLE-BUNGLE   Each hole counts three points. One point goes to the player whose ball first comes to rest on the surface of the green, a second point to the player whose ball is nearest the cup after all players are on the green. The third point goes to the player who first sinks a putt. In settling up, each player determines the difference between his or her total points and the total points of the other players. The winner is determined by the one with the most points. Continuous-putting rule negates the third point.

BLIND BOGEY   Before leaving the first tee, each player estimates the handicap needed to score between seventy and eighty (net). After all players have teed off, a designated party picks a "blind" figure between seventy and eighty, which remains secret until the scorecard is turned in. The player whose net score is closest to the blind bogey is declared the winner.

BLIND HOLE MATCH   Played under full handicap. The only scores that count are those that are recorded on certain unannounced holes. Selection of these certain holes are made by a designated party after the entire field has left the first tee.

BLIND LOW-NET FOURSOME   Contestants play eighteen holes with whomever they please. At the conclusion of play, a designee draws names from a hat and groups these players into foursomes; the net scores attained earlier per person are then added together to determine the winning foursome.

BLIND PARTNER EVENT   This event may be staged as an added feature of the day. After players have left the first tee, a designee makes pairings by lot. A golfer does not know with whom he has been paired until the round is over.

BOBS AND BIRDS   *Bobs* are points scored for tee shots on the green and closest to pin on par-3 holes only; *birds* are points scored for birdies on any hole.

BREAKFAST TEAM TOURNEY   All interested golfers assemble at the club for breakfast, then are split by handicap into two equal teams. The low-handicap golfer of Team A plays against the low-handicapper of Team B, and so on, until all contestants are paired. Play is in foursomes; stroke play is the rule, with no handicap. Use Nassau scoring (see "Nassau" below) to determine winners in each foursome, who get their breakfasts purchased by the losers.

CHICAGO SYSTEM   Each player is given a point quota, based on their handicap. Points are scored thus: bogey—1; par—2; birdie—4; eagle—8. The player whose point total for eighteen holes most exceeds his or her point quota (or comes closest if none exceeds) wins. The players will find their point quota opposite their handicap, as in Table 6.1.

CHOICE SCORE   The best score of the partners on each hole is used in arriving at their eighteen-hole total. Full or three-quarter handicaps are allowed, players enter their net scores to compute their round total.

CHOICE SCORE, BLIND   Same as Choice Score except only half of the holes of the course (the players do not know which ones) are used in determining the winners.

CLUB INVITATIONAL (MEN'S)   Invitations are sent out with up to 144 two-man teams accepted. Maximum difference in handicaps allowed a team is four. Teams are divided into nine flights of sixteen teams per flight. Teams are seeded numerically into flights according to their combined handicaps. Four-ball match play rules apply. Championship, First and Second flights play scratch. Flights three through eight play at 75 percent of handicap. First-round losers enter consolation flights.

CONSOLATION TOURNAMENT   This is generally held at the end of the season on any basis desired. The only players eligible to compete, however, are those who have not won a tournament prize during the season. Some clubs award a prize to every player in the tournament.

CRIER'S TOURNEY   This may be any straight match or stroke event; however, each player gets to pick out his two (or three) worst holes and revert his score on these back to par.

CROSS-COUNTRY TOURNAMENT NO. 1   Start about a mile from the course and play directly cross-country, finishing on one of the greens near the clubhouse, if possible, but designated in advance. The ball must be played from wherever it lies. If found in an unplayable position, the player is permitted to lift and tee it up with a loss of two strokes. This contest furnishes many exciting and unusual situations.

Table 6.1   Chicago System, Handicap to Point Quota

HCP	QTA	HCP	QTA	HCP	QTA	HCP	QTA	HCP	QTA
1	38	7	32	13	26	19	20	25	14
2	37	8	31	14	25	20	19	26	13
3	36	9	30	15	24	21	18	27	12
4	35	10	29	16	23	22	17	28	11
5	34	11	28	17	22	23	16	29	10
6	33	12	27	18	21	24	15	30	9

CROSS-COUNTRY NO. 2   This contest is played entirely on the golf course, skipping about, however, from one hole to another, not in the usual sequence. Play might start at the first tee and go to hole no. 6, then start at the seventh tee and go to hole no. 14, etc., until at least nine holes have been played.

CROSS-COUNTRY NO. 3.   Nine holes are enough. The course is not played in any order; instead, the tournament directions supplied each play read something like this:

First hole: From first tee to third green
Second hole: From fourth tee to tenth green
Third hole: From eleventh tee to seventh green, etc.

Played without handicap. *Note:* The tee to start each hole is the one normally following the green just played; this saves long walks between the green and the next tee.

DERBY TOURNAMENT   A fun event much like a horse race, also referred to as "Rumpsie Dumpsie." The format is simple and with proper publicity draws many players and spectators as well.

Play is over nine holes. A minimum of fifteen players are needed. Each player is given a number. Handicaps should be as close as possible. The event can be played from scratch or with full handicap.

Players draw numbers from an entry box to determine their respective tee-off positions. Each marks his or her ball with that particular number. All fifteen entries tee off in succession from the same tee and play out the hole according to the normal sequence of play. The three highest scoring players are eliminated. This same procedure is followed on the second hole: again the three highest players are eliminated. On the third and fourth holes the two players with the highest score on each of these holes are eliminated. From the fifth through the eighth hole the player scoring highest on each of these holes goes out, leaving only two players going into the final hole.

Any ties among players are broken with a "chip-off" from a point 40 to 50 yards out in the fairway. Order of play is determined by selection from a deck of cards, low card playing first. The player closest to the pin remains in the tournament. It is recommended that an official be named to make all decisions, especially in regard to who is closest to the pin during chip-offs. A tape measure settles questions quickly—this gives "duffers" a chance to win.

Prizes are awarded for the first three places, much like a horse race; i.e., if a contestant survives the seventh hole, he or she is assured of at least third place.

This event can comfortably handle three races by starting on tee nos. 1, 4, and 7. The use of nine holes leaves the rest of the course open for others to play.

DIVIDEND FLAG TOURNEY   Variations of Tombstone or Flag Event. Prize is divided among all golfers who hole out on the eighteenth green—whether they have used all their strokes or still have some to spare. This eliminates the chance that one or two players get "superhot" or take too much handicap. If no one completes the eighteenth hole, winners are all players who hole out on the seventeenth.

DRIVING CONTEST   Pick a wide-open, relatively flat fairway. Each contestant gets five drives; the best three and only shots ending in the fairway count. For quick determination of distances, erect marker flags every 25 yards from 125 yards to 300 yards. Judges stationed down the fairway can estimate yardage beyond the nearest marker. A variation of this event allows only three drives and deducts 10 percent from the drives distance for all shots ending up in the rough.

DROP-OUT EVENT   Winner is the player who can play the most holes in straight succession without losing to par. Full handicap is used. This is best played in conjunction with some other event, so players will have something to shoot for after they have slipped from par, which is likely to be fairly early in the round. In case of a tie, the lowest net score among tying players decides the winner.

FEWEST PUTTS   This event can be combined with others. Players keep track of their total putts for the round; the winner is the golfer with the fewest putts. No putts are conceded. Only shots made from the surface of the green count, even if the putter is used from off the green.

FIELD DAY   Each member brings three guests for the field day, and they usually stay for dinner. The play may be by teams of four, each member and their guests matching their best ball against that of the other groups; or it may be individual handicap stroke play. Additional prizes may be awarded for the best guest scores. The event is an excellent means of creating interest among visitors in joining the club.

FIELD DAY NO. 2   Everything is played in one day. Low gross, low net, fewest putts, match vs. par, tin whistle, and closest to pin (in classes) on par-3 hole with longest drive (in classes) on straight long hole. Ball must be in fairway. Champagne splits are given as prizes instead of golf balls with a limit of one prize to a player.

FOUR-BALL FOURSOME   There are two partners on a side, each playing his own ball. The low ball of each team counts on each hole. In other words, the side having the most low balls on the most holes wins the match. This is one of the most popular matches because it can be adapted several ways.

GET-ACQUAINTED TOURNEY   This event involves eighteen-hole stroke play with handicaps. Each entrant must play with a partner that they have never teamed with before.

HIGH AND LOW BALL   Two points are involved on each hole. One point is scored for the best ball and one for the best of the two poorest balls. For example, A and B are partners and C and D are partners. A scores 5 and B scores 3 on a hole. C and D each score 4 on the same hole. A and B win a point for the best ball and C and D win a point because their second best ball was better than A's.

JACK AND JILL TOURNEY   The mixed play lady and gentleman's better ball of partners, whereby the low ball of the women and the low ball of the men would be combined. Strokes are as they fall on the card with full handicap. The low scorer of the event is declared the winner.

KICKER'S REPLAY TOURNEY   Each player is allowed to replay any two shots in a round. The player must continue with the replayed ball once it is called. Full handicap applies.

LONG AND SHORT TOURNEY   Many golfers have good long games and poor short games, and vice-versa. This event combines the ability of these two types of golfers. One player does the driving and long work, the partner the approach work and putting. Players select their own partners.

LOW-NET FOURSOME   The total score of the four players, less handicaps, determines the winning foursome in the field of contestants.

MILLION-DOLLAR TOURNAMENT   For this event the Club has printed sufficient scrip in units of $100 and $500 each (the majority in denominations of $100). Each entrant is furnished with $10,000 in scrip at the first tee on the day of the tournament. Usually one can get a local printer to make up this scrip with a small advertisement on the back. Each entrant pays $.25, or any amount designated, for use of the scrip, with a chance at the grand prize that goes to the player finishing with the most money.

The members may make up their own foursomes or ask the pro to arrange them. Each foursome will divide itself into teams and use the following system of scoring:

2 points for low ball
1 point for low total
3 points for a birdie
5 points for an eagle

(If an eagle or birdie is scored, low ball does not count.) Each foursome will elect a captain, who will turn in the scrip after the eighteenth hole, recording the total of high player in the foursome. *Example:* Players incurring one of the following penalties must pay the sum named to each of the other players in the foursome:

$100 for playing into rough
$200 for missing ball entirely
$300 from each member of foursome to player whose ball is first on the green and first holed

Players are reminded not to borrow or to give away money to a big winner, but to play fair. Only scrip counts for the prize, which can be an article of merchandise or credit for merchandise from the pro shop.

This is another fine tournament to either start or wind up the season, also referred to as "Scrip Tourney."

MINIATURE CHAMPIONSHIP   This event is the same as a regular club championship, with a qualifying round and match-play pairings, except that matches are nine holes instead of eighteen holes. Four players play together; winners on front nine play each other on back nine.

MINIATURE TOURNEY   A thirty-six-hole event. Contestants using three-quarters of their handicaps play nine holes in the morning to qualify. Entire field is then divided into flights of eight players each, the eight low-net players forming the first flight, the next eight low-net players forming the second flight, etc. Three match-play rounds of nine holes each are then played to determine a winner and runner-up for each flight.

MIXED FOURSOMES   Partners consist of one man and one woman. The man drives from the odd-numbered tees, the woman from the even-numbered tees (or vice-versa). From tee to green, partners play every other shot. Allow half of the combined handicaps.

MIXED FOURSOMES, SELECTIVE DRIVE   Same as above, except both man and woman drive from each tee. Either ball is selected to play; the other ball is picked up.

MIXED FOURSOMES, POINT COMPETITION   With selective drive and alternate shots, one half of the combined handicaps are used just as they fall on the card. Scoring is as follows:

More than double bogey	0
Double bogey	1
Bogey	2
Par	3
Birdie	4
Eagle	5

The team scoring the greatest number of points wins.

MOST THREES (OR FOURS OR FIVES)   Net or gross scores can be used, as preferred. This event can also be used in combination with others.

MYSTERY EVENT   Players are sent out without being told what type of contest they are entering, except that it is either match or stroke play. After all the scores are in, news is released of what the event was, and the winner determined.

NASSAU (OR BEST-NINES) TOURNAMENT   This is similar to the handicap-stroke play except that prizes are awarded for the best first nine, the best second nine, and the best eighteen holes. Full handicap is used for eighteen-hole scores and half handicap for nine-hole scores. The advantage is that a person making a poor start, or tiring at the finish, may still win a prize for play on the other nine.

NO-ALIBI TOURNAMENT   Instead of deducting their handicaps at the end of the round, players are allowed to replay during the round the number of shots equaling three-quarters of their handicap. A stroke replayed must be used even if it is worse than the original. Strokes cannot be replayed a second time.

OBSTACLE TOURNEY   This event is played with or without a handicap. Each hole presents some obstacle, such as a stake off to one side of the fairway that must be played around, or a barrel just short of the green that must be played through.

ODD AND EVEN TOURNAMENT   This tournament is played in foursomes, two players making up one team. One player plays all even holes and the other all odd holes. Use one-half of the combined handicaps, no more than ten strokes difference in handicap of partners is allowed. Low net is the winner.

ONE-BALL EVENTS   Very interesting events are those in which one ball is used by the partners, the two players stroking alternately between tee and green, and driving alternately from successive tees. Such one-ball events can be just about anything listed in individual play, but the most effective novelty is secured by requiring special pairings. Among the combinations are: father and son, pro and amateur, mother and daughter, brother and brother, sister and sister, husband and wife, member and guest, and member and caddie.

ONE-CLUB EVENT   Each player carries only one club, which must be used for all shots. Club selection may be specified by club designee or selected by player. Low net wins. Variation may permit two or even three clubs.

ONE-HALF AGGREGATE SCORE   This is a variation of the to-be-described Three-Ball Match and is used when the players are of equal playing ability and one of them is not better than the other two, to justify their playing their best balls. In this case, the scores of the two partners added and one-half thereof counts against the odd player's score. For example, one of the partners takes a four and the other a three, making a total of seven; their score for the hole is 3½. The odd player must beat this in order to win.

PAR BATTLE   This event is played under full handicap. Players are advised that on the following ten holes of the course five points will be awarded if par or better is shot. On three other holes an award of ten points will be awarded if par or better is shot. On three other holes there is a five-point penalty for players who do not score par or better, and on the remaining two holes, the penalty is ten points for failing to make par. The winner is the player with the most points scored at end of round.

POINT ACCUMULATION TOURNAMENT   Scoring is handled as follows:

Any score equaling par or better, five points.
Any score from one to four strokes inclusive over par, three points.
Any score from five to seven strokes inclusive over par, one point.

The eighteenth fairway is measured off at 150 yards, 175 yards, 200 yards, and 250 yards.

A player with a handicap of twelve or less scores:

Five points for driving over 250 yards
Four points for driving over 200 yards
Three points for driving over 175 yards
One point for driving in fairway

A player with a handicap of thirteen or more scores:

Five points for driving over 200 yards
Four points for driving over 175 yards
Three points for driving over 150 yards
One point for driving in fairway

(All drives in order to score points must be in the fairway.)

The player scoring the largest number of points is naturally the winner, but second and third prizes may also be given.

POINT TOURNEY   Players are awarded three points for each birdie scored, two points for each par and one point for each hole played in one stroke over par. The event is played under full handicap; the winner is the golfer with the most points at the end of the round.

The following are some of the various types of tournaments that can be held on either a nine-hole or eighteen-hole golf course.

PRACTICE-GREEN TOURNAMENT   This is an eighteen-hole event on the practice putting green. The winner is decided by total putts. In case of ties, contestants play nine holes at "sudden death"; i.e., players are eliminated on the first hole if they fail to halve. If the club has no practice green, use the "clock" method on one of the regular greens nearest the clubhouse by marking off nine "tees" at varying distances around the edge of the green; each player putts from these nine tees to the cup.

PUTTING CONTEST The putting contest is played entirely on a putting course or green. A qualifying round is played and then the qualifiers compete on a match-play basis. The whole tournament can be run in one afternoon. An "obstacle putting contest" is one in which obstacles are placed around the putting green.

PUTTING TOURNAMENT The two players making the fewest putts in eighteen holes each wins a bag of shag balls. Entrance fee is three old balls.

RED AND BLUE TEAMS As players come to the tee, or enter the locker room, they are assigned alternately to the Red Team or the Blue Team. Play proceeds on a regular match-play basis. At the end of play when the complete field is in, the team having accumulated the most wins has their lunch purchased by the losing team.

RELAY EVENT Players select one of their scores for the first nine holes, the other score for the second nine to get their eighteen-hole total. Allow one-half or three-eighths of the combined handicap.

RELAY TOURNAMENT In this tournament a player's score for the first nine holes is added to the partner's score for the second nine holes, with an allowance of three-eighths of their combined handicaps, to arrive at a net score for eighteen holes.

REMORSEFUL GOLF In this contest players have the privilege of making their opponent replay any four shots during the round. These may be shots which players consider lucky or that they feel cannot be duplicated. For example, a player may hole out a twenty-foot sidehill putt, at which point the opponent can say, "I respectfully request that you replay that shot." The player must replay it.

REPLAYED-SHOT TOURNAMENT During this tournament each player has the option of replaying one shot on every hole. However, he or she must carry on from the replayed shot even though it may be worse than the first shot.

SCOREFEST Two teams of any size play this event. The winning team is the one that scores the most points using the following system:

Net Score	Points
over 100	2
90 to 100	5
85 to 89	10
80 to 84	15
75 to 79	25
70 to 74	40
under 70	75

SCOTCH FOURSOME (See Mixed Foursomes.)

SCOTCH TEAM TOURNAMENT Two teams are picked by the golf professional from the field of players that show up on the day of play. A captain is selected by each team. Each team numbers its players from one on upward, using cardboard signs pinned on the back of each player. Only one ball is played by each team, no. 1 player of team A shoots first, then no. 1 player of team B, no. 2 player of team A follows, then no. 2 player of team B. Then they start over again with no. 1. This keeps the entire field of both teams together, and many players meet new members that they may never have met before. This tournament can be used effectively in golf classes prior to actual play.

SCRAMBLE TOURNEY   A team consisting of four players of comparable handicaps tee off with the best ball on each series of shots being selected, including the putt. All lies (positions of the ball) may be improved except in a bunker. In the event a bunker lie is chosen as the best ball, the player who hit the ball into the trap will play first, with the usual rules in effect. The other three players will drop a ball over their left shoulders in the approximate vicinity of the first player's ball position. When the best putt is selected, each player shall putt. Should the first, second, or third putter not hole out and by force of habit tap his next putt into the hole, the remaining putters cannot putt, as the hole is considered complete. In other words, if the putt is missed, mark the ball until all have putted.

SCRATCH AND SCRAMBLE   Four-ball stroke play applies. *Example:* A and B are partners. A's handicap is ten, B's handicap is fifteen, total combined handicap is twenty-five; divided by two, this give a handicap for each player of 12½. Likewise, on each hole the scores of the two players are added and then divided by two, the result being the score of each player for the hole. For instance, A scores five and B scores four, making a total of nine. This is divided by 2, making the score of each player 4½.

The game is more interesting if the pro draws the teams without regard for the personal preferences of the members, combining a high handicap with a low handicap. This brings together players who have perhaps never played together. It gives poorer players an opportunity to play with better players and to learn more about golf and its rules.

SCRIP TOURNEY   Each player is furnished $10,000 in stage money. Each player has a partner; play moves in foursomes. The pair with the most scrip after play is over wins. Wins and losses are settled whenever they are incurred during the round. Awards can be dispensed, such as: low ball each hole, $100; low aggregate each hole, $200; birdies, $300; eagles, $500; first ball on each green, $100; first putt sunk, $200; plus anything the golf professional can devise. Penalties include: ball in rough, $100; ball in wrong fairway, $300; ball hitting tree and rebounding into fairway being played, $500; ball in water, $200; fanning, $300. This event is similar to "Million-Dollar Tournament."

SELECTED SCORE   Each contestant plays thirty-six holes. From two cards players can select their best score on each hole and apply their handicap. The player with the lowest net score for his or her eighteen holes is the winner.

SIX- OR TWELVE-HOLE ELECTIVE   Nine or eighteen holes are covered with stroke play, at the end of which players each select as their score the total scores made on their six or twelve best holes. Two-thirds of the regular club handicap is used for eighteen holes; one-third for nine holes.

SIX-POINT MATCH   Six points are at stake on each hole. In reality, two points are being fought for by each pair in the threesome A vs. B, B vs. C, and A vs. C. The low score for each hole wins four points, the middle score wins two points, and the high player wins nothing. If all tie, they are awarded two points apiece. If two players tie for low, they get three points each. If one point is low, and the other two tied, the split is 4-1-1. Generally the point allocation is obvious, but when a player gets a stroke from one opponent and not another, it is harder to figure the number of points each player wins. In such cases, merely compute results of each match (AB, BC, and AC) separately and the point split is readily determined.

SOLO-CLUB TEAM MATCH   Two teams, each with twelve players and a nonplaying captain, are chosen. The players are numbered and use only the clubs assigned to them as follows:

Player No. 1 uses driver
Player No. 2 uses no. 2 wood
Player No. 3 uses no. 3 wood
Player No. 4 uses no. 2 iron
Player No. 5 uses no. 3 iron
Player No. 6 uses no. 4 iron
Player No. 7 uses no. 5 iron
Player No. 8 uses no. 6 iron
Player No. 9 uses no. 7 iron
Player No. 10 uses no. 8 iron
Player No. 11 uses no. 9 iron or wedge
Player No. 12 uses a putter

The captain directs the team and decides which club will be used for each shot; the club specified is used only by the player assigned to it. In other words, each player carries and uses only one club. If desired, a qualifying round may be held to determine the members of the teams, or they may be selected by committee or the golf professional.

SPECK TOURNAMENT   Entry fee is one golf ball. Every entrant has a chance to win two golf balls. Players are divided into two-person teams. Scoring is as follows:

Longest ball on fairway	1 speck
First one on the green	1 speck
Closest ball to pin on approach shot	1 speck
One putt greens	1 speck
Lowest score on the hole	1 speck
Ties are split or cancelled.	

The total number of specks scored by each team are counted. The team having the greatest number of specks wins the match from the team with which it is paired. Each member of the winning team receives two golf balls.

SPLASH CONTEST   No entry fee is required, but players must contribute one new ball every time they play into a water hazard during the round. Players entering the contest but failing to turn in their score are each charged three balls. Balls are awarded to the three low-net players on a 60-30-10 split-up.

STRING CONTEST   This event is played without a handicap. Players are given a specified number of feet of string on the first tee, according to their handicaps, as follows: Players with handicaps up to eight get ten feet of string; those with handicaps between nine and fifteen get twenty feet; those with handicaps over fifteen get thirty feet. This string is used by the player to improve or shift the ball from a bad lie or rough. Low stroke score wins.

SUPER-BALL TOURNAMENT   Teams may be assigned or left to members to choose players. Play is characterized by four players to a team, stroke play, and no handicaps. Each player tees off, with a super (best) ball being determined from the shots played. Each player then hits his or her next shot from that spot, every player hitting every shot from the position of the best ball in the foursome. Another name for this event is "Scramble".

SWATFEST   The entire field starts off the first tee together. The high player and all ties drop out at each hole. Eventually there will be but one survivor. Players must be sure to mark their balls for identification. This event should not be started too late in the day, as it takes time to complete.

SWEEPSTAKES   Stroke play and full handicap apply. Each player in the tourney signs up for one new golf ball. The golfer with low net score wins half the ball; the second-best net take one-third; third place wins one-sixth.

SWITCHIES   Mixed-foursome play, with the better ball of partners counting. The husband and wife of Team A and the husband and wife of Team B change partners. In other words, husband A plays as partner of wife B, with husband B playing partners with wife A. Full handicap given with strokes as they fall.

SYNDICATE TOURNEY   Playing with full handicap, golfers post their scores, then put a ring around the score for each hole where they are entitled to another stroke. The pro looks over the scores of the entire field and picks the player whose net score is lowest for the first hole. If no one has tied the score, the player wins the hole from the entire field. If two or more players tie for low on the first hole, the pro examines the second hole, and so on, until a hole is reached where one golfer clearly has a net win. Tied scores carry over to the next hole.

SYNDICATES   A point goes to the low ball on each hole. If the low ball is tied by two or more players, no point is won, even though the remaining member or members may have taken many more strokes.

SYNDICATES CUMULATIVE   Same as Syndicates, except that points not won on tied holes carry forward and go to the first player to win a low ball. Thus, a player may not be a party to the tying on the two consecutive holes, yet on the third hole have the low ball and thus win the points for all three holes.

TARGET CONTEST   With water-soluble chalk, four circles are marked around the cup. The largest circle has a 35-foot radius, the next a 25-foot radius, the next a 15-foot radius and the smallest a 5-foot radius. Establish three tees at distances of 50, 75, and 100 yards from the cup. Contestants play one shot from each tee, using the club of their choice. Scoring: ball in 35-foot circle, one point; 25-foot circle, two points; 15-foot circle, three points; 5-foot circle, five points; hole-in-one, twenty-five points.

TEAM MATCH—NASSAU   Regular eighteen-hole matches are played by two or more teams, but the scoring is based on the Nassau System: one point for the first nine holes, one point for the second nine holes, and one point for the overall match. This method of scoring is beneficial in that it gives players a chance to salvage their game after a bad start.

THREE-BALL MATCHES   In this match three players play together. Each may play against both of the others, or if one player is better than either of the other two, that one will play against the best ball of the two poorer players.

THREESOME MATCH   One player, hitting every shot, opposes two players, who stroke alternately at a single ball. Rules for the two players are those for Scotch Play.

THROW-OUT TOURNEY   Stroke play and full handicap apply. Each player may throw out his three worst holes; i.e., only fifteen holes are counted in determining net scores.

TIN WHISTLE TOURNAMENT   This competition is on a match-play basis, with points awarded as follows: one point for each hole made in one over par, three points for par, five points for each birdie. The player having the greatest number of points at the end of the round wins. This is played on a handicap basis and strokes are taken at the hole specified on the scorecard. A par scored, less a handicap stroke, counts as a birdie.

TOMBSTONE OR FLAG EVENT   Players are supplied with small flags or sign markers in the shape of a tombstone suitably inscribed with "John Smith Died Here"; or a player composes his own epitaph, to be judged and read as part of the tournament program. As players each complete the number of strokes equaling the par of the course, plus their handicap, they leave their individual markers wherever their ball lies after the final allotted stroke. Players with strokes left after competing eighteen holes, start out again off the first tee, playing until all their strokes are used up. The player that advances his or her marker the greatest distance is declared the winner.

TWO-BALL FOURSOME   Two players constitute a team. One ball only is used by each team, the partners alternating in playing the shots. One partner drives from all the even-numbered tees and the other partner drives from all the odd-numbered tees regardless of which one made the last stroke on the previous hole. If this event is played on a handicap basis, one-half of the combined handicaps is used.

THE WHEEL   On a best-ball twosome format, each player can select as many partners as desired by contributing a stipulated fee for each partner. At the end of eighteen holes, players compare their cards with each of their partners and report the card with the lowest score using full handicap.

WHITE-ELEPHANT TOURNAMENT   Each contestant brings some useful article as an entry fee. This article is to be all wrapped up and a number attached to it starting with one and running up to as high as there are entries. Play is on a low-net basis. The winner receives package number 1, second place package number 2, etc. In this way each entrant receives a prize.

FOUR-BALL MATCH PLAY   This is the most common type of team play. It consists of partners playing their best-ball score against opposing partners and their best-ball score. The winning team is the team more holes ahead than there are holes left to play. This type competition may be played either at scratch (no handicaps) or with handicaps. The handicap differential rulings should be carefully studied and stipulated prior to the start of the tournament season.

1. *Scratch Play.*   This is golf in its purest form—no handicaps. Play is on a gross basis with the winner on each hole being the team taking the least number of strokes (best ball) on the hole. No handicap strokes are involved.
2. *Using Handicaps.*   One of the following methods may be selected:

a. *Full Difference of Strokes.* In a given foursome, the lowest-handicapper of a group gives the full difference of strokes to the other three players in the group. For example, the low-handicapper who is a three gives one stroke to the player who is a four; a five-handicap receives two strokes; a seven-handicap, four strokes. These stroke holes are so designated on the scorecard of each course played.

b. *Partial Difference of Strokes.* Some organizations allow only 70 percent to 85 percent of the full handicap differential and then proceed as above.

c. *Full Handicap.* Other organizations allow all players the full handicap stroke allotment, believing that handicaps are based on the difficulty of the holes. The lower handicap receives strokes on the harder holes and gives strokes on the easier holes, as marked on the scorecards for each course played.

d. *Simultaneous Gross and Net Play.* Still other organizations play both gross and net team-match play at the same time, thus giving the better players added incentive.

e. *Stroke Limitation.* In four-ball match play many clubs stipulate clearly that no more than one stroke per hole may be given regardless of the difference in handicaps.

EIGHTEEN-HOLE POINT SYSTEM   Each team is allowed one point for a win per hole, one-half point for a hole halved, and zero points for a hole lost. Each team reports their point total at the end of the stipulated round. A cumulative record can be kept for the season to decide the overall winner, or the team matches can be conducted on a daily play basis, the team totals added up for the day and then another match started on the next scheduled event date. In any case, the winner would be the team accumulating the most points.

NASSAU MATCH PLAY   The oldest and most often used is the Nassau format. Here, one point is scored for winning the front nine (by whatever margin), one for winning the back nine, and one for winning either nine by the largest margin. For instance: Team A wins the front side by one; Team B wins the back side by two. Each has won one side, but by virtue of Team B winning by the larger margin, Team B is the winner of the eighteen holes.

FOURSOME TEAM PLAY STROKE   Each club or company within a specified zone area designates one four-person team to represent it in team play. These teams may either be decided arbitrarily (e.g., the four low-handicap players within the club or company), or they may be decided upon by some type of scheduled competition within the organization.

Each club is permitted to enter one four-person team with play to be based on full handicap and stroke play. Two players from each team are paired with two players from another team. Both nines can be utilized. Two players from Club A are started with two players from Club B at the first tee, while two players of Club A and two from Club B are started at the tenth tee. (Method of pairing may be a blind draw; however, it is advisable to team up comparable handicaps for faster play and all-around enjoyment. The team players are then able to compare notes quickly as they pass each other at any of the nine holes.) The team score is determinmed by the total net low ball of the team on each hole. The low four teams for the season are invited to participate in a play-off and dinner dance at the end of the season.

Ties are decided by the matching of cards on a hole-by-hole basis, or if this does not work, by matching against par. If two teams end up tied for the overall prize, a sudden-death play-off is initiated.

This type of format works well for simultaneous gross and net play.

Suggested Methods for Group Play-Offs

TIES FOR GROUP WINNERS

1. Group Winners within a division will play eighteen holes, match-vs.-par, on a neutral course, using the match-play format previously decided upon to determine the divisional winners.
2. Winners during the above process will be decided by sudden-death play using the same match-vs.-par format.
3. If any game is tied, all teams from each club or company will play.
4. If more than two teams are tied within the group, then sudden-death using match-vs.-par will be used.
5. Players involved in group play-offs should not leave the course being played until the group winner has been determined.

GROUP WINNERS TO DETERMINE DIVISIONAL WINNERS

1. To determine the divisional winner, the group winners will play eighteen holes match-vs.-par. The winning team will be determined by the largest total of points/holes won from par. If teams are tied after eighteen holes, all teams of each club will play sudden-death, match-vs.-par. This means that all teams would have to have holed out the first sudden-death extra hole, which would add to the total number of points won or lost on that hole for the entire team. If still tied, play would continue in this manner until a winner was decided.
2. Teams for group play-offs will be by blind draw. The first two teams drawn are paired, then the next two teams, and so on, until all teams have been paired.

DIVISIONAL PLAY-OFFS FOR SEMI-FINALS

1. Play will be on a "home and home" basis.
2. Dates of play will be mutually agreed upon between the clubs involved.
3. Same match-play format applies. In case of a tie after thirty-six holes, sudden-death is applied.

FINALS—OVERALL TEAM WINNER

1. Dates of play will be mutually agreed upon by the two remaining divisional winners.
2. To determine the overall winner and runner-up, the two divisional winners will play each other in a thirty-six-hole "home and home" play-off.
3. The champion will be the team winning the most points/holes from the other team. In case of a tie after thirty-six holes of play, a hole-by-hole sudden-death

play-off will take place, involving all teams of each club in contention. Total wins on the first hole will determine the winner, or play will continue in like manner until a winner is determined.

INDIVIDUAL HANDICAP VS. PAR   Allow each player the full handicap. When a player has a plus handicap, par is allowed the player's full plus handicap. Strokes are taken as they come on the card. It is helpful if the card is marked at the start of play. The player then plays the full eighteen holes against par, using the handicap strokes. The winner is the player most "up" on par at the finish.

USGA Junior Championship

The United States Golf Association (USGA) has developed a junior golf program to give boys and girls an opportunity to receive proper instruction in the play of the game, its rules, and etiquette. In particular, the training helps boys and girls make prompt decisions. In team sports—such as basketball, baseball, or football—other players may provide valuable assistance, but in golf the player is alone when the ball lands in a deep bunker or behind a tree.

Golf Carts

Many country clubs are still giving their members the choice of walking all or part of the golf course. For example, Kendale Lakes Golf and Country Club in Miami has twenty-seven holes of golf. Nine holes are set aside so that members can choose to rent a cart or walk. This is a fine service to the members but can decrease a very profitable part of golf revenues. It is indeed surprising how the powered golf cart has achieved the popularity it commands today, with so little help from those most interested in promoting its use: club personnel who share in the profits derived from rental of the vehicles seem to do little to foster their use.

As a general rule, only at the well-run country club or costly resort does the golf cart receive its just due, golfers receive every encouragement in the way of courtesy and convenience when renting a cart. Too often the golfer goes into a pro shop to arrange for a round of golf and never is approached about rental of a golf cart, or the suggestion to use one is an afterthought. Also, once a golfer agrees to rent a cart, he or she leaves the shop with vague directions as to where the cart is located. This sort of shoddy treatment happens far too often and does not befit the role the golf cart plays in the golfing industry. Golf cart operations rival dues and greens fees in profit potential. Every effort should be made to give these operations the attention they deserve. In fact, golf cart operations should rank in importance with course maintenance, clubhouse, and pro shop operations.

The history of the golf cart shows that at the club level its popularity can be attributed to its innate appeal to the golfer rather than promotion on the part of club officials. Its continued success is assured with or without promotional efforts. Though many new clubs require the use of carts, many others have developed an air of complacency with respect to their use.

On the other hand, manufacturers of new and used golf carts do exceptional promotions. Their sales and rental programs cover any exigency. Along with their counseling services on maintenance and operation, they make it easy for club executives to acquire a fleet of carts and operate them efficiently.

The golf fleet operator can do much to augment the selling job started by the manufacturer and dealer. Some of the promotional methods are simple, cost little if anything, and should be automatically required at all courses. Some programs, however, may require expenditure of funds and long-range planning.

The simpler and less costly ways to increase golf cart use are those that make it easy for the member to secure a cart at the starting point of the course, and also those that ensure that the cart is clean and will last the number of holes for which it is paid. Other suggestions include:

1. Post the charges for renting a cart for nine and eighteen holes, and even more if feasible, in a prominent place. This is particularly advisable if the members are allowed to bring their friends into the club to play.
2. Maintain a set of records on each cart so that employees always know the mechanical condition and which carts are ready to go and for how many holes.
3. Post operating instructions in the pro shop and in each cart for the operator's review. General maintenance (i.e., cleaning, inspection for damage, and refueling) should be performed daily and prior to returning all carts to a convenient holding area.
4. Train all personnel handling golf carts to ensure that courteous and efficient treatment is afforded all members. If a member does not rent a cart, the employee should point out that after walking nine holes, a cart can be quickly and easily secured for the last nine.

It is a good idea to establish a golf cart rental charge for more than eighteen holes. The same principle applies here as applies to the all-day greens fee, only in this instance a reasonable additional charge should be made. Otherwise, no additional profit can be gained. For clubs with good weekend play, where all available carts can be rented for the full charge, the "second round" charge should be made available only on weekdays.

This practice is more common in clubs with a specific "need for action," such as those in isolated areas or those not having as much to offer in the way of a challenging course or playing conditions. The lowering of golf cart charges, or any other golf-related charges, might lead to a "price war" among area clubs.

A common practice in the southern areas of the country is to reduce greens fees during the off-season. This practice is being applied to golf cart rental charges also in an effort to encourage more play during the slack months. It is particularly appreciated by older persons and retirees with fixed incomes. It is certain to bring in additional income when expenses, such as maintenance, are at their highest. The same practice might be considered for slack periods on northern courses, at the tail end of the season, or after certain hours of the day.

There is a growing tendency to put together attractive "package deals" to include the amenities a golfer would want during a day of golf. For example, a new course in Florida instituted a special on weekdays for a flat $25 that included greens fees, golf cart, three quality golf balls (with the club name printed on them), and an economical lunch. Another club offered a special rate for foursomes who made advance reservations. The bargain included a 20 percent reduction on golf and cart rental fees and a 10 percent reduction on the foursome's bar and dinner bill. The volume of business generated was well worth the reduced prices. Other clubs limit special offerings to greens fees and golf carts only. The special offerings appeal to golfers and are features to consider in any club.

Another practice worth considering is offering free use of a golf cart for one round upon the purchase of a golf cart ticket for five or more rounds.

Privately owned golf carts are a nagging problem to club officials throughout the country. Profits to be derived from the rental of golf carts is revenue needed to support the operation of a golf course. Wherever privately owned carts are allowed, the lost income has to be made up in other areas. The trend throughout the United States is to phase out privately owned carts, but many development clubs still condone or actively encourage the use of such vehicles. Most of these clubs are connected with real estate projects or located in small towns where the golf club is an integral part of community activities. No promotion is as important, however, as having a planned golf cart operation that includes courteous and efficient personnel and the availability of clean, attractive, and trouble-free carts. A set of maintenance and bookkeeping records on each cart is a necessity to know how the direct relationship between the cost of the maintanence and repairs compares to the total revenue received.

Golf Superintendent

The person who occupies the position of golf superintendent is responsible for the playability of the course. The duties of this position include the following:

1. Supervising employees attached to the grounds department. At some clubs in addition to the maintenance of the golf course or courses, the golf superintendent is also responsible for the club's grounds. This could include the entrance, the grounds surrounding the clubhouse, the parking lot, and the other recreation activities.
2. Supervising the equipment barn and the mechanics responsible for equipment maintenance. Being responsible for all of the equipment necessary to maintain the course or courses and the grounds.
3. Being responsible for the proper irrigation of the golf course and possibly the entire club complex.
4. Being responsible for the proper use of herbicides and pesticides and keeping informed of federal and state regulations for their use. These regulations change according to the location of the club, how these chemicals may affect the water supply, and the time of year.
5. Working with the general manager and the golf professional in preparing the

annual budget. Being prepared to give a monthly report on the budget compared to actual expenses.
6. Being available to meet with the golf committee to discuss the condition of the course.

The following is some of the information the manager should know about the golf superintendent's duties.

Automatic Irrigation Systems

Attracting and keeping qualified, affordable labor has long been the superintendent's biggest headache. This problem alone justifies installation of an automatic irrigation system, which practically all new courses have. Automatic systems eliminate specific jobs. It has been the experience of all superintendents polled that the cost of the automatic systems can be amortized over a very short time by the labor savings.

A properly treated effluent (treated human waste) water supply has no objectionable odor or other objectionable characteristics. The use of effluent for nondrinking or cooking purposes has been a controversial subject for years and is still not settled in certain parts of the United States. More and more developers are building their own sewage treatment plants to utilize this water for irrigation and save the hassle of connecting sewage lines to already overloaded community systems. The latest figures available are over 20 years old, but the percentages still hold. The cost of city water to irrigate an eighteen-hole golf course in Colorado was $411 a day compared with the cost of effluent water at $97. This saving of $9000 a month would at that time amortize the cost of the sewage disposal plant in 3 years.

The fertilizer value of effluent water is another very controversial matter, with eminent authorities. Some contend that a variety of minerals are present; others disagree. The golf superintendent will have the water analyzed, carefully study the turf, and feed it accordingly.

Weed Control

Chemical weed control has greatly improved turfgrass management. Careless use of this procedure, however, can do serious damage to turf. Occasionally, harvesting weeds does more damage than good to the turf. Certain steps in turfgrass weed control must be taken to ensure successful results:

1. The first step is to grow good turfgrass. This reduces the necessity for frequent use of herbicides that may injure the grass.
2. Second, choose the right herbicide. This becomes more difficult as more and more herbicides and variations appear on the market. The only way a decision can be made is through trial and error, or the golf superintendent can obtain tested information from the Golf Course Superintendents Association of America.
3. Know when to use a herbicide. One aspect of determining when to use a herbicide is to gauge the benefits and risks involved. No herbicide will make the grass grow better. If the weed problem is worse than the risk of injury then treatment is justified. Application at the correct time of the year is an important

part of herbicide use. Dandelions can be treated too early, but it is important to treat seedheads as early as possible. In the case of pre-emergence herbicides, most of these are at their best when applied 2 to 3 weeks before crabgrass germination.

4. Apply the proper amount of herbicide. Too much can cause injury and waste money.

   a. The first step is determining the amount of chemical required per unit area for use by calibrating the spreader or sprayer. It is wise to check the calculations so that no mistakes are made.

   b. The second step is for the operator of the spreader to check that the spreader is laying the correct pattern.

Gaining control of the weed problem is difficult for many sites because of the hand labor involved. This is especially true in small areas with dandelions, crabgrass, and goosegrass. Once the weeds are reduced, spot treatment on a regular basis may be easier and safer than allowing a few weeds to grow into a problem that requires severe herbicide treatment.

It can be difficult to determine the exact chemical that should be used. However, management should be aware that two types of weeds must be controlled, one type taking a much heavier concentration of herbicide than the other: crabgrass and goosegrass. Also, the weeds that take the least amount of herbicide to eliminate are dandelions, buckhorn, clover, knotweed, and chickweed.

It is suggested that the general manager meet one time with the herbicide salesperson or, if no salesperson is involved, review the manufacturer's literature. Another suggestion would be for the purchasing agent of the club to prepare sealed bids for weed control materials.

Insect and Animal Control

Insects and animal pests damage golf course turf in two ways. First, they may destroy the grass by feeding on its foliage or roots—grubs, sod webworms, and chinch bugs (the most serious problem) are typical of these. Second, turf may also be affected by other insects and animals that live under the sod and seriously affect the playing qualities of the course. Earthworms, gophers, ants, mole crickets, and crayfish are examples of these.

Successful control depends on several factors. Insects vary in their tolerance to certain pesticides and to different concentrations of the same material. Their peak periods of activity also vary. To obtain adequate control before serious injury occurs, the early stages of activity must be recognized.

Just like herbicides, insecticides and pesticides undergo scrutiny by the federal government because of their polluting effect. The golf superintendent must keep abreast of regulations and use only the chemicals allowed.

Many insecticides are poisonous if taken internally and can cause skin and eye irritation after external contact. The following precautions should be observed:

• Follow the manufacturer's listed label directions and if transferring any substance to another container, label it.

- Keep all treatment products away from children and pets.
- Wash all exposed skin with soap and water after use.
- Wear goggles, dust mask, rubber gloves, and a rain suit.

Turf Nursery

An additional duty for the golf superintendent is the starting and supervision of a turf nursery. Nurseries are often discussed, often started, and often discarded, so the superintendent must be completely sold on the idea before it is ever started.

A turf nursery can be an invaluable addition to any golf course. The only drawbacks to starting one are lack of acreage and lack of money. Damage to tees and fairways is not always easy to repair, but these are the areas about which golfers are perhaps the most tolerant. Greens present a different story. Putting surfaces are critical, and even the most inexperienced hacker expects the greens to be perfect. In certain sections of the country, buying turf for greens is impossible. The sod either lacks quality or is prohibitive in price. Frequently it takes many hours of searching just to locate what is available and find the right variety.

Losing a green is never anticipated. This prospect alone makes the nursery a solid form of preventive insurance. In many instances the primary deterrent to building a nursery is the cost. There are ways, however, to cut corners and get the job done economically. The important thing is to recognize the nursery's potential value and set goals for its productive use. A good greens nursery should never be built as just a source of repair, but if greens have become contaminated, nurseries serve as an effective means of conversion.

Developing a nursery is a slow process and may take years to complete. Total costs, however, have been reduced considerably, and the satisfaction in having control over the turf that will replace a damaged green makes the expense seem worth it. In the past many nurseries have failed through lack of purpose and lack of care. Properly utilized, a turf nursery should return innumerable benefits.

Construction of the nursery should be much like the actual building of a golf green. Excavating for the open box, tiling, and using various soil mixtures is not really necessary, although using them can serve as a valuable source of information. For example, there may be doubt about the mixture of soil, sand, and peat. The nursery should be the place to try the various combinations. In constructing one, the following should be taken into consideration:

Water must be available.
Nursery should be out of the golf traffic pattern.
Nursery should be as close as possible to the maintenance barn.
Land should be level and free of trees and shrubbery.
If possible, the soil should be sterile.
Drainage must be adequate; the nursery should be built to drain naturally with a
    three-degree slope.

A nursery must be of adequate size to replace the sod on a green. On a nine-hole course it should allow for the replacement of two greens each year. Using sod to replace greens has advantages as well as disadvantages. With efficient cutting, placement, and topdressing, most re-sodded greens are quickly molded into good putting surfaces. This has the advantage of keeping the green in play with very few complaints.

A disadvantage is the rebuilding of the nursery after the sod has been stripped. The surface should be cultivated, fertilized, and replenished with either stolons (plugs of grass) or seed. It is possible to leave uncut strips which will gradually fill in the turf. However, the rate of "fill-in" is largely dependent upon the variety of grass. To assure a definite program of green reconstruction each year, the nursery needs as much attention as possible. The addition of stolons or seed, with proper fertilization, will ensure the necessary growth.

Greens nurseries can also be developed for the sole purpose of growing stolons. This type of nursery need not be exceptionally large, but it does require proper care. Mowing need not be as close as for a sod green, but it must be close enough and consistent enough to prevent the formation of seedheads. Many hybrid varieties of putting-green grasses are propagated by vegetative methods. When seeds are allowed to mature and fall to the ground, off-type grasses are very likely to infest the nursery. A tremendous advantage of the stolon nursery is its ability to perpetuate itself. With proper care, the addition of new seed or stolons is seldom required.

Establishing greens from stolons can be fairly rapid or exceptionally slow, depending upon the variety of grass used. Bentgrass, in particular, is painfully slow to mature into a good putting surface. Unless the green has been sterilized, Poa annua and other contaminants have an excellent opportunity to become competitive.

When stolons are used, the green naturally becomes unplayable. The length of "downtime" is dependent upon weather and the grass variety. Thus, proper timing for the use of stolons can be extremely critical and should be planned for the convenience of the golfer.

Whether starting a greens nursery with stolons or seed, the same preparations are required. After the area has been cultivated, sterilized, and graded, the final seedbed is readied with a rototiller or similar machine. An ideal seedbed is composed of particles that range in size from a pea to a marble. It is important that the soil not be worked into a powdery dust. When this happens, the addition of water often makes the surface much like cement. Before seeding or planting stolons, a starter fertilizer with a high phosphorus content is necessary. The presence of adequate phosphorus is essential for the quick development of seedling grasses.

Watering equipment should be placed in such a manner as to keep the soil surface continuously moist, and traffic on the nursery must be limited to eliminate the spreading of grass from the nursery to the surrounding areas.

Mowing should start whenever new growth reaches ¾ inch and then be adjusted upward or downward gradually, depending on the type of nursery. In the sod nursery, height of cut is lowered until the turf can be maintained like a putting green.

Fertilizer should be applied approximately a month after planting, preferably with a normal greens feeding. From then on the nursery is treated as an actual part of the course. Total maintenance includes fertilizers, fungicides, or any similar care that is applied to the greens. If conditions become necessary, verticutting and aerification may also be effective. Contamination, such as Poa annua, should be chemically removed long before the sod is moved to the green.

Stolon nurseries are generally mowed at about one inch. Like the sod nursery, stolons require a second fertilization about one month after planting, and monthly applications through the rest of the growing season. Regular applications of fungicides are also essential. Insecticides or other products may be used as needed. It is also advisable to keep the stolon nursery on a frequent mowing program. Because of the style of growth and the need for many stolons, it is doubtful if verticutting or aerifying will become a major part of maintenance.

In contrast to stolon nurseries, sod nurseries offer many opportunities to try certain fertilizers, programs, or chemicals, and at least a portion of the nursery can be utilized. Findings from the private tests may lead to better and more effective greens maintenance. The nursery can also serve as a place to test greens mowers, sprinkling systems, and other turf equipment. In southern areas of the United States, the greens nursery offers a perfect place to test overseeding varieties and mixtures. There may be many other ways the greens nursery can serve as a source for valuable information and improved greens care.

TENNIS

Tennis was the renaissance sport of the 1970s. For the past 20 years tennis has paled dismally on the sidelines while golf has created headlines and established folk heroes. In the seventies tennis regained its popularity, then leveled off. Golf continues its growing popularity, but tennis, in spite of the American interest in outdoor sports, has not developed in the same fashion. Tennis courts will continue as part of the construction package of the developer but will be given less and less emphasis.

Managers are not particularly concerned, as tennis players do not, as a rule, use the clubhouse after matches the way golfers do. This must be a consideration when and if the club unbundles its facilities. Maintenance of the complete tennis facility is only a small fraction of the cost of golf.

The origin of the game is not precisely known. One school of thought has it originating in ancient Persia, another in ancient Greece in the time of Homer. It is an indisputable fact, however, that tennis as it is known today surfaced in France in the thirteenth century. Using a ball made of cloth tightly wound or sewn into a hard round shape, the game was played in monasteries and courtyards of castles. In 1345 it was so popular that the Bishop of Rouen banned his priests from playing because it was taking away too much time from their duties. Some years before that King Louis X of France became the first known casualty of the game. After a marathon match he caught a cold and died. Tennis crossed the channel into England in the fourteenth century. Edward III, king of England, had a court built inside his palace in 1452.

Banned in the latter part of the fifteenth century in both France and England, the sport blossomed again in both countries but was banned again in the early seventeenth century because of the heavy gambling on the public matches. The sport returned to the domain of the rich, where it remained until the middle of the twentieth century.

In 1873 Major Walter Wingfield introduced the innovations to the game that are the foundations of tennis today. He combined elements from court tennis, racquetball, and badminton and played the game on grass. The next important step for the development of the sport came in 1874, when Mary E. Outerbridge brought balls, racquets, and a net to the Cricket and Baseball Club of Staten Island. The sport spread rapidly in the United States after its introduction and in 1881 the first U.S. Singles Tournament was held.

Tennis courts today are enclosed areas with foundations of concrete, asphalt, clay, or grass and surrounding fences at least 10 feet high. Courts may or may not provide space for spectators to watch the matches.

Hands-on day-to-day management of club courts is supervised by the tennis professional. Usually a tennis committee establishes the rules under which tennis will be played at any particular club. The tennis pro and the tennis committee assist the general manager, who is in complete charge. A typical tennis organization might include the following:

1. General manager
2. Tennis professional
3. Assistant tennis pro
4. Pro shop clerk
5. Maintenance staff person

Tennis Professional

The duties of the tennis professional include the following:

- Actively works with the general manager in preparing the tennis department's annual budget
- Actively works with the tennis committee to keep the players satisfied with the operation of the tennis courts
- Controls court use: (1) Oversees court reservations and sets the time players may use the courts, (2) enforces the court rules established by the tennis committee.
- Supervises the operation of the pro shop and tennis court personnel
- Supervises the rental of the ball machines
- Gives private lessons to members and their dependents on demand
- Establishes clinics for both children and adults
- Repairs, restrings, and rewraps tennis racquets

The tennis pro, in addition to these duties, must be pleasant and available to the players.

Compensation

The tennis professional's total income can be calculated in different ways.

COMPENSATION PLAN 1

An annual salary

A percentage of the gross sales or the net profit of the pro shop. Gross sales are from 5 to 10 percent, net sales usually around 25 percent. Or the club can give the shop to the pro to operate and manage

All income from lessons and clinics

All income from repairs, rewrapping, and restringing of racquets

All income from the rental of ball machines

A share of the tournament money. Unlike the golf pro, the tennis pro sometimes does not share in the funds from club tournaments

COMPENSATION PLAN 2   Delete any of the items in plan 1.

COMPENSATION PLAN 3   Select items from plan 1, but charge the pro court time for private lessons.

In any plan the club establishes, if the club has in-house charges, all services on any of the plans should be charged and run through the club's books.

Court Management

New Court Construction

In planning the construction of new courts, certain factors should be considered. First, it is important to decide on the kind of court to be built—cement, asphalt, grass, or clay. Some courts cost more initially to construct, but they hold up much better under constant use and are less expensive to maintain over the years. Asphalt or concrete courts generally fall into this category. Today most clubs on the West Coast are constructed of either concrete or asphalt, and in the last few years the popularity of the asphalt court has increased nationwide. Several factors have contributed to this trend, including: (1) reduced labor cost for construction, (2) new color-coating systems, and (3) a trend toward more textured surfaces.

Second, the kind of use anticipated for the court must be considered. Will the courts be used strictly for recreational play? Will there be sanctioned tournament play? These questions will help the architect or engineer to determine court size, layout, lighting requirements, fencing, and the desired finished surface texture. The answers depend on effective communications between the manager, the tennis professional, the tennis committee, and the architect or engineer.

Third, those concerned with building the tennis courts must be aware of current construction standards. Sources of this information include:

1. U.S. Tennis Court and Track Builders Association, 63 Wall Street, Suite 3000, New York, NY 10005
2. The Asphalt Institute, Asphalt Institute Building, College Park, MD 70740
3. U.S. Tennis Association, 707 Alexandra Road, Princeton, NJ 08540
4. Local tennis court builders, pavers, resurfacers, and material suppliers. "Let your fingers do the walking!"

Old Court Repair and Resurfacing

Some of the same general considerations mentioned in new court construction apply to old court repair or resurfacing. The most important issue is for the manager to know how much repair work is needed and to have a realistic notion of what problems can and should be solved. The repair process may involve consulting several different professionals or experienced people.

REPAIRS FOR CEMENT OR ASPHALT COURTS.   The following are some examples of major repair work.

1. Surface cracking caused by the court stresses
2. Surface cracking caused by settling of the foundation
3. Surface cracking caused by roots from nearby trees
4. Large depressions caused by wash-out (these are particularly frequent in the case of asphalt)

Little can be said for major repair work other than it is costly and no easy solutions or remedies exist. The solutions usually fall into two categories: tearing out and starting all over again or rebuilding over the existing pad, and finding temporary solutions that buy some time before the problem occurs again.

Minor repair problems for concrete and asphalt courts include:

1. Nicks in the surface caused by tennis rackets
2. Minor flaking or peeling of the old surface
3. Minor "bird bath" holes ⅛ inch deep or less
4. Slick surfaces in high-use areas

These problems can usually be repaired satisfactorily by any surfacing company.

RESURFACING CEMENT OR ASPHALT COURTS   When cement is being resurfaced, the following steps should be followed:

1. Remove all existing surface material by sand blasting.
2. Clean courts with acid.
3. Cover entire court area with a good cement primer to assure adhesion.
4. Recolor with the chosen coating system.
5. Redo the white lines.

When asphalt courts are being resurfaced:

1. Clean courts off and remove all existing loose material.
2. Apply at least one coat of a sand-filled asphalt emulsion to old rough-textured surfaces.
3. Apply the color coating and the white lines.

Court Lighting

The art of illuminating sports areas came into its own in the late 1920s. Previously, when someone wanted to light up a tennis court, indoor lamps were often hung over the center of the court. Later, very simple flood lights were developed in an effort to protect lamp bulbs from the weather. Eventually floodlights of modern design were produced. Now a multitude of lights have been designed, providing specialized light sources.

The first lamps commercially available were incandescent, most of these furnishing a very compact light source. Later, the incandescent quartz lamp made its appearance. Being a comparatively long light source, the quartz lamp required special parabolic reflectors to produce different types of vertical beam distributions. Various beam patterns had already been developed for the regular incandescent lamps.

The mercury lamp arrived about the same time as the quartz lamp was introduced. Although it was twice as bright as the incandescent lamps, the color of the mercury lamp's light was not acceptable, nor was the size of its light source. With filaments as large as 5 inches or more in length and 4 to 7 inches in diameter, it could not produce the medium or narrow beams that are best for outdoor lighting.

When the metal halide lamps, which are basically mercury lamps with metal additives in the arc stream, came along with their smaller light sources, floodlights producing practically all types of beams became available. The color of metal halide lamps is quite similar to daylight, which does not distort color reproduction. (Sodium lamps are not discussed because their monochromatic yellow beam distorts colors and makes their use objectionable to many people.)

Tables 6.2 and 6.3 provide information on lamps including modern lamp sizes and the minimum efficiency (useful light output compared with total energy input) that may be expected from various well-designed floodlights.

As demonstrated in the tables, the 1000- and 1500-watt incandescent lamps offer the best lighting sources. Comparing these lamps to a 1000-watt metal halide lamp, however, reveals that the metal halide produces approximately five times as much light on a watt-for-watt basis. A floodlighting installation at normal voltage requires only one metal halide flood to produce the same results as three 1500-watt incandescent lamps. The incandescent floods, furthermore, use 4500 watts compared with only 1100 watts for the metal halide lamps. From an operational standpoint, metal halide lamps can reduce electrical costs by 75 percent or more. In this day and age, that kind of fuel savings can be crucial. When considering lamp replacement cost, too, the metal halide offers greater long-term economy. The incandescent, with its 1000-hour life, will have to be replaced ten times within the 10,000-hour life of the

TABLE 6.2 Floodlight Sizes

Beam Spread (in degrees)	Type	Effective Revolter Area in Square Inches				
		Under 227 (1460)*	Over 227 (1460)*	Under 227 (1460)*	Over 227 (1460)	Any Other
10–18	1	34	35	—	—	20
18–29	2	36	36	22	30	25
29–46	3	39	45	24	34	35
46–70	4	42	50	35	38	42
70–100	5	46	50	38	42	50
100–130	6	—	—	42	46	55
130+	7	—	—	46	50	55

*By percent.

TABLE 6.3 Floodlight Efficiency Levels

Watts	Volts	Hours of Life	Approx. Lumens
		Incandescent	
500	120	1000	10,445
1000	120	1000	23,100
1500	120	1000	33,620
1500	132	300	45,000
		Quartz (Incandescent)	
500	120	2000	9300
1000	240	2000	21,500
1500	208	3000	29,000
		Clear Mercury	
400	24,000	20,500	12.50
1000	16,000+	55,000	34.70
		Metal Halide	
400	15,000	34,000	31.25

metal halide lamp. This replacement cost will total $75.10 over 10,000 hours, which is more than the cost of a metal halide lamp. In addition, the labor cost of replacing nine incandescent lamps points up the greater savings that ultimately are realized by metal halide installation.

Many factors influence selection not only of the lamp but also of the type of floodlight. Some of the most important considerations are installation cost, line voltage, wire sizes, and controls. Other important features include light utilization, flooding distribution, mounting height, shadows and light direction, pole locations, light loss factors, type of area, and total acreage to be covered. For best results a competent lighting engineer should be consulted for careful assessment of these details.

The number of lighting fixtures necessary for any particular area can vary greatly, depending upon lamp sizes, lumen outputs, and floodlight design. Years ago, the Illuminating Engineering Society (IES) publications specified the number of incandescent floodlights required for a given sports area. Now this information is obsolete because of the many different types of lamps and floodlights available.

The quantity of light for different areas can be determined by an experienced engineer. The quantity in each case is determined by the size of the area, type of sports activity, and required illumination.

Research into the requirements for tennis court lighting, which took both indoor and outdoor lighting into consideration, has confirmed that illumination must come not only from the sides of a court but also from the back corners so that the vertical intensities, so necessary at the baselines, are provided. Floodlighting five tennis courts using these new principles proved successful. Eight 1000-watt metal halide 4-

by 5-inch general-purpose floodlights, produced over 30 footcandles of light. The location, mounting, and aiming of the floodlights, along with the very necessary horizontal louvers to provide cutoff, assured that players at the baselines would not experience any direct glare from floodlights opposite them. The horizontal louvers also protected the residents of the surrounding neighborhood from the very high candlepower produced by the 400 floodlights for the five courts.

Actual costs were little more than those necessary for an installment of ten regular floodlights. The big difference between this installation and a similar incandescent one is the lower power demand of 8800 watts per court for the metal halide lamps, as compared to twenty-four 1500-watt incandescent lamps for the same footcandle intensity. The reduction in floodlights also decreases the wire size and the cost of controls, poles, and other equipment, which in turn reduces labor costs. A similar analysis could be made for other sports areas and the results would be about the same. With a continuing fuel shortage facing the United States, it makes a lot of sense to decrease energy usage while installing better lighting and at the same time providing better playing conditions.

Each outdoor installation must be considered a separate project. In every case the services of an electrical engineer specializing in illumination is an absolute necessity.

Tournaments

Tournaments are an essential activity for every club with tennis courts. A tournament can have as many parts as the members desire, the usual ones offering men's and women's singles (the men play against men and the women against women), men's and women's doubles (two men play against two men and two women play against two women), and mixed doubles (a man and a woman play against another man and a woman). The basic considerations for operating the big tournaments are:

1. When and for how long can the courts be closed to players who do not participate in the tournament.
2. What is to be the entrance fee and will the players receive extras, such as new balls, refreshments at courtside, and perhaps a banquet.
3. Has the tennis department budgeted for the tournament and what is the club's share of total expenses, include, for example, officials' fees.

Because setting up and operating a tennis tournament is complicated, the tennis pro will need the full cooperation of the tennis committee to make the tournament a success. The first order of business is to appoint a tournament director. Some of the details that might be handled by the pro or the director are:

1. Making sure the date does not conflict with other club events.
2. Confirming whether or not the tournament will be sanctioned by the United States Tennis Association.
3. Deciding which courts will be used for the tournament and what hours they will be available on tournament days for other players.

4. Arranging publicity and giving the tournament a name. The name should be one that has significance for club members, honoring, for example, a well-loved deceased member. The tennis pro will work with the tennis committee and the general manager in setting up a plan to advertise the tournament to all interested club members. A photographer should be called in during some part of the last day of the tournament to provide a lasting record.
5. Ensuring that entry blanks and information letters are available at least six weeks in advance of the tournament.

Preparation of the Tournament

The information letter sent out to club members should include such details as dates, starting times, entertainment, parties, and banquet details if planned, costs, entries, officials, the dress code, and when members can call their own matches. Also, information should be provided on the scoring method to be used—two out of three sets or the pro's method of three out of five.

The entry form should include information on the time to register and the deadline for registration (usually 2 to 5 days before the tournament begins). If the tournament will include players from other clubs, the entry blank should include remarks from their coach as to their experience and playing ability so that proper seeding (ranking of their ability) may be made. The best tournaments are always those in which players of almost equal ability play each other.

The draw—matching the players—should be made soon after the deadline with no changes allowed other than withdrawals. The time for forfeiture and warm-up is set in advance and is usually 15 minutes for each.

When the players report for registration, they should be given a draw sheet and a court assignment sheet telling them where and whom to play. They should be told how long a match will be delayed before a forfeit is called (usually 10 to 15 minutes). At this time the committee should confirm all entries, get the names of any new doubles teams, and try to collect all entry fees.

The next step in planning the tournament is for the tennis pro and the tennis committee to appoint a tournament director. Along with the pro, this person will run the tournament.

Scheduling and operation of matches are the major responsibilities of the director. Much can be accomplished from the tournament headquarters, which may be nothing more than a large desk, sometimes inside a tent. A large copy of the tournament draw should be posted here so that the match scores can be recorded and released to the interested members and players immediately.

When the tournament has started, the director should periodically check that the players know the courts they have been assigned and that the officials are on the courts and regulate the warm-up time.

Whenever players take a court, the time should be recorded. This will prevent them from warming up for more than the allotted period. As soon as a match has been completed, the director records the score on the large official draw sheet and calls for the next pairing to take the court.

A public-address system is a valuable aid. So is a portable bullhorn.

Finally, consideration should be given to holding a banquet at the club to make the awards to the winners.

Tennis for Children

Every club manager must give serious thought to children's tennis programs. This entails encouraging the tennis professional to hold regular teaching clinics where children can be taught the game as a group. The pro will charge each parent for the classes. In addition, group games assist in holding the youngsters' attention and maintaining the interest of the beginner.

New players welcome low-key competition. It takes a long time before the average beginner is able to serve and play a full game. Meanwhile, spirited contests make the instructional period more fun.

Where facilities are limited, games are an invaluable teaching aid, even for the intermediate player. A lively elimination contest against a wall can keep many students happily occupied and at the same time enable them to practice tennis skills.

In selecting contests for a particular class, it is advisable to choose activities every participant can enjoy with ease. For example, relay races, although a popular training exercise, require students to perform five successive forehands against a wall and may be frustrating to a group of young beginners if each member of the class is not yet ready to hit five forehands in succession.

Thus, goals must be within everyone's reach. It is better to plan a team game for points rather than individual games. If students have trouble, they may not earn any points for their team, but at least they are less likely to berate themselves or their teammates with their failure to perform.

Games are used to teach agility, to speed reaction time, and to improve hand, eye, and foot coordination and teamwork.

Prizes are usually not necessary. In fact, they detract from the educational value of informal competition. Too much early emphasis on winning often defeats the slow learner or reluctant participant. A better method is to impose penalties on the losers. For example, a team that comes in last has to run laps, pick up all the balls, or do five push-ups.

Group Games

STATUES   Students stand in open formation. The instructor calls signals for forehand, backhand, or serve. Periodically, in the middle of a stroke, the instructor calls "freeze." Everyone must stop and hold their exact grip, stroke, and foot position. Anyone caught with an error gets a point. At the end of the game, each student has to do a push-up, jog around the court or some other minor penalty for each point earned.

SIMON SAYS   Students stand in open formation. The instructor calls out the signals as follows: "Simon says do a backhand." "Simon says do a forehand." "Do a low forehand." If anyone follows a command not prefaced by "Simon Says," they get penalized a point.

FOLLOW-THE-LEADER   Students stand in open formation. The instructor, at the front of the group, calls signals aloud while performing forehands, backhands, and serves and moving about as if in actual court play. The group must follow. Anyone who misses a cue and takes a step or swings the racket in the wrong direction earns a penalty point.

Relay Races

POTATO RELAY   In line formation, students are divided into two or more teams. A circle is drawn about 20 or 30 feet in front of each team. On signal, the first player in line places a tennis ball on the "sweet spot" of his or her racket and races to place the ball in the center of the circle. The next player runs to the circle, picks up the ball, and places it on his or her racquet, then runs back to give the ball to the third in line. Any player dropping the ball from their racquet must chase and retrieve it. Play continues until each player on the team has successfully handled the ball. The team finishing first is declared the winner.

DRIBBLE RELAY   In line formation, students are divided into two or more teams. The goal is to bounce the ball with the racket to a designated mark and back. The team finishing the exercise first, wins.

FOOTWORK RELAYS   Any combination of footwork drills can be applied to a relay race, such as skipping, running, or shuffling sideways to a designated mark and back.

BALL RELAYS   Depending on the capabilities of a class, goals can gradually be upgraded to appeal to the better players. For example, two teams are formed of as many players as desired. Each team then faces the other across the net, forming into a single straight line behind the baseline. A player on team A starts the volley with a forehand stroke across the net and goes to the end of the line. The front player on team B returns the shot and retires to the end of that line. The players continue to alternate. Any player who misses a shot leaves the game. The team having the last player wins.

Rallying

The final stage in learning ground strokes is rallying. If the class is large and only a few courts are available, it will not be possible for the entire class to rally at the same time.

The tennis professional will divide the students by the number of courts available. For example, if there are two courts available and twenty-four students, twelve would be assigned to each court. Six players, three at the baseline on each side of the net, would rally for a specific number of minutes, then the other six would play.

Another method is the use of "stations." Some students continue to work on various segments of the strokes and tossed-ball drills while as many students as can safely do so practice rallying.

In the early stages of rallying, it may be best to permit students to stand a step or two inside the baseline. Either player may start a rally with a feeder stroke (a bounce-and-hit). Players attempt to rally (not to cause a "miss") by providing easy-to-handle first-bounce shots for one another. Balls may be returned after any number of bounces, but the objective is to hit accurately enough to provide a one-bounce hit. When the teacher thinks any two students are ready for advancement, they are encouraged to hit harder and to play from the conventional rally location, one step behind the baseline.

Giving Individual Attention

THE STATION METHOD   The use of stations, at which students work on separate drills at each different station, allows the teacher to make personal contact with every individual in the class. According to this method, players move from station to station, one of these being the teacher's station, where personal observations and comments can be given to each student. If the group is large, naturally the amount of personal attention teachers can give, even in this way, is limited.

THE "BUDDY SYSTEM"   Another kind of personalized instruction is possible using the "buddy system." With this technique, students work in pairs and coach each other. This requires that the students be instructed in and have knowledge of specific checkpoints relating to the mechanics of strokes. It is not usually difficult for someone to recognize whether a racquet is held and swung properly after seeing the teacher demonstrate the swing and observing the swing of other students. "Racquet head up," "elbow bent," "point toward the fence," these are examples of the kinds of simple expressions often used by group teachers in the buddy system. Teachers can multiply their instructions by the number of buddies coaching at any particular time.

HITTER-TOSSER-RETRIEVER METHOD   Large groups can also be accommodated by using the "hitter-tosser-retriever method." Students are arranged in three lines on the court, then rotated as follows: after the tosser throws a designated number of balls (not too many, as rotation should be fast if the group is large), he or she becomes the hitter. When the hitter has finished, he or she becomes the retriever; then the retriever becomes the tosser, so that everyone in the group gets a turn. This leaves the instructor free to rotate attention.

Providing Play Experience

Finally, after several periods of instruction, teachers must provide the actual play experience students want and should have. Actual play, however, for a large group presents problems, so full-scale competition is precluded. The best teachers can do is simply to provide drills that simulate actual competitive-play situations. Again, assigning stations for practice and play enables everyone to participate.

Segments of a particular court, or gym or blacktop area, are designated stations or, if space permits, each court may be designated a separate station. Several members of the class are assigned to a station to practice one particular skill or one particular shot. One group on a court may practice forehand cross-court shots while another, on the same court, may hit backhand cross-courts. At another station, students may serve and return serves and, at a fourth, students may try rallying.

Groups are rotated from time to time so that eventually every player is assigned to each of the stations and to the full courts for play. During all of these drills students are working at stations appropriate to their levels of ability. Meanwhile, teachers move from station to station, dividing their time carefully so that all the hitters get some individual attention.

AQUATIC SPORTS

Man's interest and fascination with water and the sea dates back further than recorded history. Sufficient evidence is available to show that prehistoric man could swim. Pools are known to have been used by civilized man as early as the first historic mention of the Seven Wonders of the World; pools decorated the Hanging Gardens of Babylon. Pools were also a daily part of the lifestyle of the ancient Greeks and Romans.

For a club without access to an ocean, lake, pond, stream, or river, aquatic sports consist of wading, swimming, diving, water polo, water ballet, snorkeling, and scuba diving. All of these activities, with the exception of wading and diving, can be performed in the club's central pool or pools.

Wading Pools

A wading pool, with a maximum 12-inch depth, is a must in any family-oriented club. If the club does not have one, management might consider purchasing a few plastic portable children's pools. If there is sufficient space on the pool's apron, this would be the best location for them. Members could be asked to reserve the pools in advance so that they would be ready on their arrival. If the apron cannot accommodate the pools, consideration might be given to pouring a small concrete slab over the grass area (the children's splashing and the emptying of them soon turns the club's grass into mud). Another alternative is for families with very small children to bring their own pools. A hose must be available to fill them.

The club may wish to have rules for the wading pool that are distinct from those for the swimming pool. The aquatic director could meet with a mothers' group to formulate the rules.

Swimming and Diving Pools

Swimming pools can be constructed in any size and in any shape. They can have diving boards, diving towers, sliding boards, snack bars (for both food and beverages), and poolside furniture. Many clubs have removed diving boards and slides because they can be dangerous to even the most experienced divers and swimmers in the pool. Research has shown that 66 percent of all recreational spinal injuries are a result of diving accidents. Statistics are not available as to what percentage of these injuries occur in pool tanks.

Slides are dangerous in a narrow pool if their exits are aimed at the opposite wall; also the ladder and handrails get slippery and can cause bad falls. In order to accommodate divers, some more daring clubs, like the Breton Bay Country Club in Maryland, have built separate diving pools of various sizes and depths, the minimum depth being 20 feet. Other clubs reserve a small part of the deep end of the pool for divers by using a buoyed rope. (*Note:* Most liability policy premiums are higher for clubs with diving boards and/or slides in their pool.)

Club management should consider the following safety hints in pool areas:

1. Slips and falls on pool aprons are a major source of accidents. A covering of indoor-outdoor carpeting can enhance safety while providing a more comfortable surface for bare feet as well as a decorative effect.
2. Check the covering on the diving boards for worn or torn spots that may trip the diver.
3. Adjust the boards so that is is not tilted or too springy. A board even slightly

twisted could send the diver off to either side and cause even the experienced diver to land wrong or be catapulted off the board.

4. Frequently check the depth markings on the side of the pool to verify that they are bright and clear. This protects swimmers diving from the side of the pool.
5. Prohibit double-bouncing, which may cause a diver to slip.
6. Make sure divers check that the landing area is clear.
7. Do not allow divers to wear goggles or face masks. They can cause eye and nose injuries.
8. Club swimming pools should not be operated without a lifeguard on hand. Hire a lifeguard even for parties where no swimming is meant to take place but where a pool is present and an accident is possible.
9 No running or horseplay is allowed in the pool or in the pool area.
10 At times the pool apron will be slippery. Urge everyone to walk with care.
11 Children under 12 must be accompanied by an adult to enter the pool area.
12 Floatable toys and rafts are only allowed in the pool when an area of the pool has been roped off.

Water Ballet

Water ballet is synchronized poses and movements done to music by one or more persons in the pool. The water should be a minimum of 6 feet deep. The sport is very difficult but has gained in popularity since becoming part of the Olympics.

Water Polo

Although an Olympic sport, water polo is not played very frequently in family-oriented clubs because the game utilizes a considerable portion of the pool. The game has become primarily a swimming club activity. At some clubs however, such as the Riviera Country Club in Florida, there is a demand and the club designates a time and a space for the sport.

Pool Management

The aquatics department can be organized in many different ways, the two most common place either the general manager or the manager for recreation directly over the aquatic director, who oversees the lifeguards.

The duties and responsibilities of the aquatics director are as follows:

1. Supervise the operation of the club's pools.
2. Train and supervise the lifeguards.
3. With the general manager, prepare the pools operating regulations for approval by the board. These would include both the safety and social rules, in addition to the days and hours that the pool is open for the members' use:
4. Make sure the pool and the pool area are only open when a lifeguard is on duty.

5. Keep the pool and the pool area clean.
6. Check and maintain the proper balance of chemicals to keep the pool sanitary.
7. Keep the pool safety equipment in a readily accessible place. This will include a phone, a first aid kit, ring buoys with restraining lines, shepherd's crooks, whistles, lifeguard chairs (one for each 2000 square feet of pool surface area), and gas·masks.
8. If the pool is heated, maintain the water temperature between 73 and 75 degrees Fahrenheit.
9. Keep indoor pool air temperatures 5 degrees warmer than the water.

Most states require that all swimming pools be enclosed by a fence with a gate that can be locked when the pool is closed. In swimming pools managed by the Special Services Department of the United States Navy, a wading pool must also be enclosed by a fence at least 3 feet high with a latched gate. Clubs should consider these two safety precautions even though not legally bound to meet these requirements.

Given the importance of the club's lifeguards, management should also consider the following precautionary measures:

- All guards should be at least 18 years of age.
- The absolute minimum qualifications for guards should be both senior lifesaving and first aid certificates. To be extra careful, management may also wish to have their swimming ability tested by the aquatics director. In addition, lifeguards should be trained at the club to perform cardiopulmonary resuscitation (CPR) if they have not been certified.
- Actual rescue drills should be held at least once each month when the pool is open.
- All lifeguard training should be fully documented to prove, in the event of an accident, that the club took "reasonable care." Proof of reasonable care is the best defense a club can have in a lawsuit.
- All guards should wear a distinctive uniform.

REVIEW QUESTIONS

1. What are the various sources of golf course revenue?
2. What are the possible sources of income for the golf professional?
3. What are the duties of the golf pro?
4. What is the value of a turf nursery to a club?
5. Discuss why and how golf carts should be promoted by club management.
6. Why should both the golf and tennis professionals be encouraged to hold clinics for children?
7. What is the role of the tournament director in operating tennis tournaments?
8. What is the biggest advantage of an automatic irrigation system?
9. What factors must be considered to effectively illuminate a tennis court?
10. What measures should be taken to ensure safety at every club pool, with or without slides or diving boards?

CASE STUDY

The Idaho Sunset Golf and Country Club is having a great many problems with the club's golfers. Although there is a cap of 300 on membership which the board reluctantly passed (as there are over forty potential members on the waiting list), there still is a long wait for a tee time. The board cannot reduce the cap any further, as the club needs new members to survive. The club has only one type of membership although it has eight fine tennis courts and an Olympic-size pool.

The board has asked the general manager to do a survey and get answers to the following questions:

1. What is the average length of time it takes our members to play eighteen holes? How many players can our course accommodate daily?
2. How many players can the other clubs in our area, with eighteen-hole golf courses, play in a day?
3. Is there any method we can use to get additional members without raising the cap?

The survey furnished the following facts, which management and the board should be able to use in solving the problem.

- The course, at this time of the year, receives 12 hours of daylight, from 7 A.M. to 7 P.M. The average time it takes our members to play eighteen holes is 5 hours and 10 minutes. Because of this, players teeing off after 2 P.M. cannot play the entire eighteen holes and in order to play nine holes, they must tee off by 4:15 P.M.
- At three other courses surveyed, the average time for players to finish eighteen holes was 4 hours 30 minutes.

Given this information, answer the following questions:

1. How many eighteen-hole and nine-hole rounds can our club members complete in a day?
2. How many eighteen-hole and nine-hole rounds can the other clubs' members complete in a day?
3. How can the Idaho Sunset speed up play?
4. Is there any way the club can take in new members without raising the cap?

7 Merchandising the Club and Its Activities

Basic differences distinguish advertising, marketing, promotion, and merchandising activities: *Advertising* is a scattergun approach in which promotional material is sent to all eligible club members and persons recommended by members. An example would be the monthly bulletin or flyers. *Marketing*, in the club business, refers to selecting a particular concept and contacting specific members to sell them on the idea. Limiting the field of contacts is called "knowing your market." An example would be contacting only tennis players with information about a tennis tournament if the club has no space for spectators. In the event the club had a center court with a grandstand, then advertising could be used. *Promoting* is marketing in much greater depth. This could be on-site posters in the pro shop, a pretournament cocktail party, a display of prizes for the winners, a wine display in the dining room, and so forth. *Merchandising* is the complex art of using advertising, marketing, and promotions to turn services and products into money. In the club business, services could be more rounds of golf or more members dining at the club. The volume of services and products the club sells and sound management are the hallmarks of a successful operation.

Merchandising to some extent is a trial-and-error process, depending on individual aspirations and inspirations. Club managers must continually seek new ways to market and promote services and products, using their own imaginations and any suggestions staff and members may provide. Methods must constantly change as new and better ideas come forth.

Club members, like most people, hunger for novelty. This is particularly true at a club that members frequent on a regular basis. Therefore, it is necessary to be original in the introduction of innovations as well as consistent in the use of proven ideas.

Successful club merchandising starts by selling the members on the idea that they have the best management and staff in the club business. Use all available tools to further this concept, particularly the club bulletin.

In addition to selling the idea of a talented and loyal staff there are a number of basic principles management should be aware of:

209

1. Keep abreast of the times in choosing products and equipment. Join CMAA and attend the local chapter meetings to discuss club business. Also plan to attend the local or national restaurant and hotel shows at least once every 2 years, setting specific times when you can meet representatives of major purveyors.
2. Keep the clubhouse livable, maintaining temperature, lighting, and sound at comfortable levels. The distinctive atmosphere a club develops, if agreeable, will sell itself.
3. Design is a key merchandising concept. The caliber of the club is expressed by the decor of the clubhouse, the pro shop, the locker rooms, the health club, the restrooms, and any other public area. An air of orderly, spacious elegance should be management's benchmark.

PROMOTIONAL TOOLS AND PRODUCTS

In undertaking advertising, marketing, and promotions, the club manager must first determine what tools are available and what products are to be promoted. Some of the tools are:

Monthly bulletins
Fliers
Posters
Party brochures
Menus
Menu clip-ons
Table tents
Personal contacts

All these can be used to promote the following services, each requires that certain questions be addressed.

Dining Room. Can this facility use additional business every time it is open or just for certain meals? Are the hours of operation satisfactory to the members? Could the sale of cocktails, appetizers, desserts, and after-dinner drinks be increased? Could wine sales by the glass and bottle be increased in the dining room?

Additional Club Parties. Does the club need and would the members attend additional club parties?

Bar and Cocktail Lounge. Could the club accommodate additional bar and cocktail business?

Pro Shop. Could sales in the pro shops be increased with better advertising, promotions, merchandising, and lighting?

Game of Golf. Could the rounds of golf be increased without disrupting the membership? Could the use of the driving range and the practice green be improved?

Other Recreational Facilities. Could the usage of the other recreational facilities be increased without disturbing the membership?

The answer to all of the above questions, for the purpose of this text, is yes. These services and their promotional media will be discussed at length throughout this chapter.

However, before promotions of any sort can begin, management must find out which classes of members are using which club facilities to effectively target appropriate markets. Classes are defined according to:

1. *Age Group*. This class may be subdivided into teenagers, young couples, the thirty-to-fifty group with and without children, and the fifty-and-above group. Each of these groups may have different ideas as to what they wish the club to provide.
2. *Employment Status*. Time constraints, desires, and needs are sometimes different for members who work and retirees, who no longer engage in a daily regimen.
3. *Single Status*. This class not only includes unmarried persons but also unaccompanied women or men.

Monthly Bulletins

All clubs find it necessary to contact the general membership at regular intervals. One method is to publish a bulletin or newsletter, which can be circulated on a regular basis or at infrequent intervals. Most clubs use the mails for bulletin delivery, and bulk mailing at a reduced price is available. The bulletin is more useful if the member receives it prior to the first of the month. This allows the member planning time.

The basic editorial content of the bulletin should be a reporting of the recent interesting events and coming attractions. Announcements could include tournament winners and runner-ups with pictures; special events in sports, such as a hole-in-one in golf; members appearing at special parties; etc. Future events could be advertised by means of a monthly calendar, illustrated differently each month (Fig. 7.1).

In preparing the bulletin, the following suggestions may be of assistance in helping to make it interesting:

FIGURE 7.1 *Monthly club bulletin.*

1. The bulletin should be used to impart information to the membership. It is not a sounding board for the manager, the directors, or any special group. If members' opinions are desired on a specific subject, the proper form is a separate questionnaire (see Appendix 3).
2. Each month the bulletin should look different. This can be accomplished in many ways. For example:

   • Vary the color, paper, and print.
   • Use different sizes and styles of print.
   • Vary the size and/or the shape of the stock used.

3. In reporting the same events that will occur on consecutive days, use a series of blocks (days or dates) instead of repeating the items over and over.
4. To vary the calendar, display the days of the week vertically instead of horizontally.
5. Every party planned should be published in the bulletin. The employee planning the party would have to receive the host's or hostess's permission in advance. Once a party appears in the club bulletin almost every party host/ hostess will want to be mentioned in the bulletin.
6. Management should highlight events it particularly wishes to bring to the membership's attention. This can be done by boxing the item, using different style letters, underlining, or using a picture to illustrate the item.
7. Use the same techniques as are used in designing the menu—the same reading principles will apply.
8. Everyone likes personal attention. Print a photograph of the new board of directors annually, establishing a club tradition. Throughout the year print pictures of the various committees. Use pictures of the various sports committees at the start of the particular sports season. Also, pictures of individual members participating in club activities are of interest to members and their friends.
9. Plan an "Employee of the Month" program with a picture and a short write-up of the employee's background and his or her value to the club.
10. Brag a little. Use the bulletin to advertise that new delicious menu item, the new carpet in the dining room, the new piece of equipment that the club has recently purchased, and so forth.

Fliers

Fliers are used as single-sheet advertising for any special event (Fig. 7.2). The cost is very low and distribution can be by mail or if practical, by hand. Some clubs located in housing areas have used newsboys/girls to hand-deliver fliers.

Also, have fliers available at the reception desk, bar, and cocktail lounge, and in the various shops.

REMINDER. . . .

Monday,
January 1st

ORANGE BOWL / SUGAR BOWL

Notre Dame	Miami
vs.	vs.
Colorado	Alabama

Pregame Buffet $15.00++
4:00–7:00 P.M.
Big Screen Television
Buses Depart 7:00 P.M. Limited Seating

Wednesday,
January 17th

GET ACQUAINTED COCKTAIL PARTY

Complimentary Hors d'oeuvres—7:00 P.M.

Friday,
January 19th

ITALIAN BUFFET EXTRAVAGANZA

Dinner–Dance

Complimentary Wine—$20.00++

Sunday,
January 28th

SUPER BOWL PARTY B.B.Q. BUFFET

5:00 P.M.—$15.00++

FIGURE 7.2 *Club flyer.*

Posters

Posters in the clubhouse, the pro shops, and other areas that members may frequent should only be used to sell members on using one or more of the club's facilities. In preparing the message to be communicated to the members, written words and pictures must have sales appeal, holding viewers' interest long enough for them to read and absorb the message. A picture is almost always an attention-getter, so try to plan to have photographs available for each poster. For example, a picture of last year's Christmas tree surrounded by members would be a fine addition to the poster announcing this year's Christmas party.

In designing posters, some of the following ideas may be of assistance:

1. Spotlight the poster either from overhead or from the side. If a picture is used, the words could be illuminated. Cut out and cover the words with translucent paper for a really unusual effect.
2. Vary the size and shape of the posters used. Two or more boards can be taped together to make a self-standing table display. When using this type of poster, also consider a static display in front of it.
3. Vary the language, print, and spelling. An October Fest could be advertised in German as long as every employee could translate the poster for the members.
4. Use colored slides to project pictures of previous parties.

Party Brochures

Create a printed brochure listing all of the services the club is capable of performing:

- Weddings
- Birthdays
- Anniversaries
- Celebrations of any kind
- Special events

Emphasize the professionalism and talent of the club staff and that it is available to stage any type of affair. In fact, use the word *stage* frequently in the brochure. Use color for both the paper and the print. The paper used should be 8 inches by 8 inches or smaller, so that when folded it would fit into a standard business envelope. Mail these to the entire membership with the October or May monthly bulletin.

In the brochure stress the ease of entertaining at the club without having to shop, cook, serve, and clean up. Note the unique menu items available, including foreign dishes and a complete gourmet menu.

Menus

The menus used for each of the club's meals is an excellent advertising medium. Their contribution to the overall appearance of the dining area must not be overlooked. The menu should be bright and sparkling but above all clean. Many clubs have discovered that the menu may be left with the member after the order has been taken without fear of the member changing his/her mind. The menu sells the "bill of fare" but it also can be used to sell other items. Even on that rare occasion when an order is changed because the menu was left at the table, if the staff is taught to handle this gracefully, the club can boost itself.

The first item for sale is the menu itself. The club could include, as a preface, a history of the club and drop a few names of its outstanding *deceased* members. A perfect host or hostess, having guests and knowing that the menus are for sale from information in the club bulletin, might offer to purchase one for the guests.

The menu can also serve as a simple wine list. Try when preparing a new menu to use the words "The Manager's Wine Selection for this Entree is . . . " and select both a white and a red. No longer do sophisticated diners follow the traditional concept of white wines with fowl and seafood and red wines with red meat, so a choice between a white and a red is indicated. Select good-quality but modest-priced wines and watch the wine sales grow. The club should also have a fine-wine list.

Use the dessert and after-dinner drink menu to advertise entertainment in the bar and cocktail lounge.

Menu Clip-Ons

A small rectangular printed piece of cardboard clipped to the menus in both the dining rooms and the cocktail lounge is a very effective means of not only advertising special food items but also special events (Fig. 7.3).

Table Tents

Another effective advertising medium is a "tent," a folded piece of cardboard, printed on both sides. Only one tent should be used at a time, but two items can be advertised, one on each side. The tent would be used to suggest a new drink, a special event of any kind, a special wine, or a new dessert.

Make Your Reservations Early For
GALA CHRISTMAS PARTY
December 15th

Dinner at 8 P.M.
Dancing and Entertainment at 10 P.M.

FIGURE 7.3 *Menu clip-ons.*

Personal Contacts

Word-of-mouth recommendations are probably the best advertising tool of all. Introduce any new food item by first serving it to the dining room employees. Their approval of a dish practically ensures its popularity with the membership. Encourage employees to learn as much as they can about the food the club serves.

Of course, some of the best publicity is provided by members who enjoy coming to the club.

Marketing Survey

One way to find out the needs and wants of the membership is through a marketing survey. The club sector does not need to use commercial pollsters to gather information; it simply mails surveys directly to its membership. Additional information may be gathered by person-to-person contact.

The survey could be inaugurated by a questionnaire sent to the entire membership (see Appendix 3). The survey must reflect a very positive attitude on the part of management: "We know we are good but we are striving to be even better."

PROMOTING THE DINING ROOM

Promoting the dining room is promoting the club. Members may join for many other reasons, but it is the dining room that imparts the social atmosphere of the club. It is vital to the financial success of a club that the dining room gain a reputation for innovative ideas, fine service, and good food.

PROMOTING CLUB PARTIES

A successful party usually consists of the following steps:

1. *Theme*. New and innovative ideas are fine, but simply adding a new twist to an old idea may create a very attractive theme. Parties should be more than food, a flood of alcohol, and live music. Members will appreciate the effort on the part of management to please them on different levels, and more members will attend the club's parties as a result. It takes management involvement to make a truly well-planned party work for the club. If a theme party is planned, the manager may wish to be the star performer.

2. *Planning*. The planning for the party includes four stages:

   - What the club is going to do. This includes the broad scope of the party
   - What is being celebrated
   - The theme
   - Day, date, and time

3. *Ingredients*. Details to be considered include:
   - Advertising
   - Other printed material
   - Costumes and decorations
   - Music
   - Special props
   - Menu and wines
   - Price

4. *Methods*. Working with the entertainment committee, management ascertains whether a special committee is to be formed for the event. Management then determines who will be responsible for what. The manager enlists the assistance of each department of the club and assigns individual responsibilities.

5. *Implementation*. It is now the manager's responsibility to follow through and ensure that all of the tasks are accomplished.

Types of Parties

All parties can be celebrations. Following are ideas, new and old, for days to celebrate in every month.

January

January 1: This is New Year's Day, but it is also the day of the Tournament of Roses Parade in California and the Rose Bowl Football Game. Consider having late morning tournaments and a late afternoon light western buffet with a wide-screen television set on hand so that members can watch the games.

Also La Salle's expedition reached Peoria, Illinois, in his exploration of the West in 1618. A western buffet would be appropriate to celebrate this event.

Other "first" events include Paul Revere's birthday in 1735 and Betsy Ross' in 1752, and the United States flag "The Grand Union" was displayed for the establishment of the Continental Army in 1776. The latter could be celebrated as Patriot's Day. A Boston Baked Bean Dinner at a modest price (after that wild New Year's bash) might please club members.

If later in the month a party is desired, other memorable events that took place in January were:

January 24: In 1848 gold was discovered in California.
January 31: Robert E. Lee was appointed commander in chief of the Confederate forces, and Zane Grey, the great author of Western stories, was born.

February

February 2: France recognized Americans' right to rebel against England and started assisting in the fight.
February 3: Prince Mutsuhito became Emperor of Japan in 1867.

February 10: France and England ended the French and Indian War and Canada became British.

February 14: Valentine's Day.

March

March 1: In 1638 the first Swedish settlers arrived in America and built the first log cabin.

March 17: St. Patrick's Day.

March 24: William Penn founded the colony of Pennsylvania in 1680.

April

April 1: April Fool's Day.

April 4: Los Angeles was incorporated as a city in 1850.

April 15: San Francisco was incorporated as a city in 1850.

Easter Sunday.

May

First Friday: Arbor Day in Rhode Island and Idaho.

First Saturday: The Kentucky Derby.

Third Saturday: Armed Forces Day.

Third Sunday: Mother's Day (see below).

May 1: Labor Day is celebrated in Central American and communist countries.

June

Third Sunday: Magna Carta Day and Father's Day (see below).

June 2: First Italian immigrant arrived in New York in 1635.

July

July 1: The Era of the Olympiads begins in Greece in 776 B.C.

July 4: Independence Day.

July 14: Lewis and Clark were the first Europeans to enter the state of Washington from the East in 1806.

August

August 1: First cable car ran in San Francisco in 1873.

August 4: The United States purchased the Virgin Islands from Denmark in 1916.

August 21: Hawaii became a state in 1959.

September

First Monday: Labor Day (see below).

Second Saturday: Miss America Contest winner is announced.

September 16: Mexico's Independence Day.

October

Second Monday: Columbus Day.

Fourth week: National Pretzel Week.

October 19: The British surrendered at Yorktown in 1781.
October 31: Halloween.

November
Fourth Thursday: Thanksgiving Day.
November 11: Veterans Day.

December
December 25: Christmas Day.
December 31: New Year's Eve (see below).

In addition to holding parties on traditional holidays, some innovative planning may satisfy club members' longing for something new when a holiday has no traditional theme. A theme could be developed for Mother's Day, Father's Day, Labor Day, and New Year's Eve.

Mother's Day
In many clubs this day is a complete sellout, with dining reservations booked solid with multiple seatings. Even then, all of the members cannot be accommodated. The answer might be to hold a May Fair to celebrate this wonderful day. The fair could be held both inside and outside the club in tents if necessary. Rent rides for the children, have games and contests for all ages, and set up the dinner buffet style in the club with the dining out of doors. Members could eat anytime they choose within certain hours, say, 2 to 8 P.M. Another idea is to hire an orchestra and the local high school baseball team to attend the dinner and after each seating have them ask the mothers to dance. Have volunteer hosts and hostesses introduce the boys. A meal and minimum wage will be sufficient pay, as many mothers will tip their escorts.

Father's Day
This is the day to make Dad feel important. Have a special menu for the dinner. Keep it limited and allow only the head of the table to get a copy. Make sure all the entrees are explained so that the person with the menu can discuss the items with each person. Serve the vegetables in bowls so the head of the table may serve them or the diners may help themselves. In other words, make this meal different from the ordinary club fare.

Or simply include a cordial for Dad in the price of the meal. This can be handled with a little ceremony, then food orders can be taken at the table.

A third suggestion is to take reservations so that the club will know the name of the father and have a small gift and a place card ready for him. Calculate the price of the gift into that of the meal. For example, for 100 reservations with twenty dads, raising the price of the dinner a dollar would allow for twenty $5 gifts from the pro shop or any store.

Labor Day
Labor Day traditionally has been a day to spend at the club. In trying to make the celebration different and more interesting, remember that the original purpose of the holiday was to honor working men and women. A picnic could be held during the day

with international cuisine at dinner. Have three or more tables honoring the workers of several countries. These could include the United States, Canada, Mexico, and the Central and South American countries. For posters, recipes, and other materials, contact the local ministries of the countries selected.

New Year's Eve
This is traditionally a night to have fun, to shed one's concerns, and look forward to a happy and prosperous new year. Therefore fantasies are in order!

Celebrate the turn of the century, either 1900 or 2000. Make the occasion a costume party and set up the club in accordance with the theme. If 1900 is selected, members could wear dress of the period instead of formal attire. The staff could also be in costume. If 2000 is to be the theme, then the entertainment committee could establish the dress code. What will people wear to a ball in the year 2000? It's anyone's guess.

PROMOTING GOURMET DINING

A club dining room should have special events for its members that might not be available in other establishments. Gourmet dining is one such event, which can be promoted in many different ways. One way is for a Gourmet Club to be established within the club membership. In a Navy officer's club, for example, the members have formed an association called the "East India Company," the eighteen members of which dine elegantly once every 3 months. In their experience a minimum of six persons is needed to warrant serving an authentic gourmet dinner, and the maximum that can be accommodated when the regular menu is being served to members in the dining room is twenty.

Another way to promote gourmet dining is to establish a Gourmet Corner in the dining room. By request and with noncancellable advance reservations only, the club will serve a gourmet dinner to six to twenty persons.

PROMOTING THE SALE OF COCKTAILS, APPETIZERS, SALADS, DESSERTS, AND AFTER DINNER DRINKS

If the club has à la carte items on its menu, an easy way to increase sales without additional dinners is to promote items not included in the à la carte offerings. The following steps, if implemented, may assist in doing this:

1. Sell the serving staff on the importance of this sort of menu promotion. One sales incentive could be money. If the club has a service charge and it is shared with the servers, make up a chart with their share of a number of sample items. For example, a country club in Texas, with a 15 percent service charge shares 10 percent of it with the servers. The chart could look like this:

à la Carte Reimbursements Chart

For Each of These Items You Sell		You Receive
Bar Cocktails	@ $2.75	$.28
Shrimp Cocktail	@ 5.95	.60
Lobster Cocktail	@ 7.95	.80
Caesar Salad	@ 5.95	.60
Desserts	@ 2.50	.25
Brandies	@ 3.50	.35
Irish Coffee	@ 3.50	.35

Sell a party of four shrimp cocktails and earn an additional $2.40.

1. Another sales incentive is pride. Keep track of the individual items, not dollars, that each server sells. Publish the statistics for the employees each month.
2. Establish and implement a uniform policy of presentation. Some of the methods might include:

   - A dessert cart at the entrance to the dining room or wheeled to the member's table
   - A dessert menu presented to diners just after the dinner plates have been cleared
   - A club specialty dessert that can be presented by the staff, trained in the presentation: for example, "We have a homemade white chocolate mousse that is absolutely delicious"; the server pauses to see if there are any takers, then announces, "We also have a complete selection of cakes, pies, and ice creams."

3. Train the employees not to be "pushy." A simple request suffices: "Would you like to have a cocktail or a bottle or glass of wine?" or "We have fresh jumbo shrimp cocktails tonight."

PROMOTING THE SALE OF WINE

The sale of wine with food is another way to enhance members' enjoyment in dining at the club. Some of the things that management can do after the wine cellar has been established and the wine list printed are:

1. Work with the distributor to build a wine display at the entrance to the dining room. The display should feature a particular wine and should be changed at least every 2 weeks.
2. Have every wine on the list, with the exception of sparkling wines, available by the glass. Use Ventmaster, available from the wine distributor, to seal the wine after the bottle is opened. This seal will keep the wine in its original condition for as long as 3 months. Have champagne and other sparkling wine in splits.

3. Store wines at the proper temperature. Red and other types of wine that are not to be refrigerated cannot be served warm.
4. Teach the serving personnel the proper way to uncork the bottles and properly serve the wine.

PROMOTING THE COCKTAIL LOUNGE

An attractive cocktail lounge can be an asset to any club even if the members are not particularly heavy drinkers. Often the lounge is used as a meeting place for parties. Such meetings increase potential sales for drinks, so it is incumbent upon management to create an attractive atmosphere. Ways of attaining this objective could include:

1. Create a club, not a bar, atmosphere. Furnish the lounge with lounge furniture, coffee tables and side tables, not booths, tables, and chairs. Bar stools should be comfortable, with backs to them.
2. Create a soft glow with the lighting, eliminating any harshness. Stay away from individual lights on the coffee tables. Check frequently that the room temperature is pleasant and that the ventilation system is keeping the air fresh.
3. Become known for having different stock than the commercial or hotel lounges, such as a complete line of foreign beers. Beers from at least fourteen countries are available in the United States today, and this number is expected to increase to twenty or more by the year 2000. Most distributors will give the clubs a sampling to get started. In the event the club is going to feature foreign beers, print up table tents allowing members to review what is available.
4. Have an hors d'oeuvre menu in the cocktail lounge. The menu could start with the appetizers the club offers and be supplemented with other types of snacks the members might desire.
5. Serve any drink to a member at half price on the presentation of any proof that a dinner has just been eaten. The proof could be a token from the server or a tear-off sheet from the bottom of the guest check, etc.
6. An elegant touch, if the lounge decor permits, is to serve coffee, dessert, and after-dinner drinks in the lounge using the cocktail staff and a separate guest check. This should be done on unannounced occasions when business is slow in both the dining room and lounge.

PROMOTING THE GAME OF GOLF

The golf course is often the primary reason people join a club. It is of extreme importance, therefore, that there be sufficient time for all golfing members to play. The ideal maximum number of players for an eighteen-hole course is 300. This number is frequently exceeded because of the high cost of maintaining the course. In the early nineties the annual cost of maintaining an eighteen-hole course is close to half a million dollars. Thus any means of making the course more available, without upsetting club members, could be financially rewarding.

First, light the course. This might sound uneconomical, but it has proved very practical for some West Coast courses. These are mostly municipal courses, but the idea merits serious study by private clubs. In the southern states where the game can be played year round, the number of additional rounds lighting could make possible may justify the cost. Most electric companies will install any outdoor lighting without a down payment and with a very small rate of interest or none at all.

Second, form a 4-hour club. With a golf cart, eighteen holes can be played in 4 hours if the golfer plays steadily and takes 110 strokes or less. Many golfers, however, use the tees and the greens to socialize and take more than this amount of time. Honor the members who play the course in 4 hours. A lapel pin, their name on an honor roll, and other recognition would be appropriate.

Third, many courses give the player the option of using a cart or walking. Limit the walking option to days when the course is not being used to capacity.

The driving range and the practice green are also places where utilization may perhaps be increased. The following ideas may be useful:

1. Light the range. This gives working members, during the winter months, an opportunity to fine-tune their game. If the club charges for a bucket of balls, this could be a self-supporting effort.
2. If there is heavy demand, with long waiting periods, and the driving range is at least 350 yards long, consideration could be given to using both ends of the range.
3. Borrow a Japanese idea. Because of their severe shortage of land, they have built multiple-story driving pads.
4. Practice greens and chipping areas can be lighted to increase their availability to members.

PROMOTING THE PRO SHOP

Whether the professional is operating the shop as a concessionaire or the shop is being operated by the club, it is still, in the members' minds, a club facility. Thus management must take an interest in its operation and assure it meets the club's standards.

The shop should be treated as if it were a very high-class boutique and always have something new to display. With the change of seasons, sales should be held to turnover the previous season's merchandise. Management should try to entice members into the shop for reasons other than shopping. Ways to encourage impulse buying are to:

Display club trophies in the shop.
Install one or more public telephone booths in the shop.
Place the check-out counter well into the shop so that shoppers on their way to the counter will see as much of the merchandise as possible.

Proper lighting is another important consideration in promoting shop sales.

Merchandise Display: Lighting

The effective use of lighting is an often overlooked aspect of merchandise display. It probably does more harm than good to light an ineffective display since the lighting tends to emphasize its shortcomings; it is equally harmful to illuminate a good display ineffectively. The more complete the presentation, the more attractive to the eye, and the better the chances of selling.

The purpose of lighting tends to be obscured in the pro shop. It becomes a source of vision, rather than a visual magnet. The light fixtures are usually set to flood the selling area, giving equal light throughout, with the most light either deliberately set on the counter with the cash register or in the middle of the room. This evenness of light tends to create a collage, which requires the members visually to isolate the elements in which they might be interested. The net effect is distraction and detraction. Instead of enhancing the merchandise, this type of lighting makes it resemble a sea of shapes and colors.

The first principle of effective display is to understate. One outstanding item effectively stated draws more audience attention than several diffused "specials." It is often a good idea to focus the prospective customer's attention on a single bargain and then use graduated lighting to draw attention to the item next to it, then the item next to that, and so on.

Colors are an important part of clothing. They must leap out and grab the attention of the buyer. A sure way to do this is to highlight the dominant color of the fabric. Poor lighting dulls a color, can even change it, but properly selected colored lights will dramatize the manufacturer's carefully created concept. A yellow light on a yellow shirt can be most effective, especially if the yellow is flanked by darker colors, say, blue or stripes.

Lighting can produce many subtle effects. Light can come from above or below by means of a spotlight, flashing lights, and displays that use motion. Again, the general rule is not to overdo. Use different types of lighting on different types of merchandise. This tends to give them an identity.

Lead the buyer through the shop with displays and lighting. Nothing should detract from, or conflict with, the main display. Some element in that primary display should match up with something in the next display, the one that you want the buyer to go to next. If a shirt-and-slack ensemble is being featured, direct the buyer's attention to color-coordinated shoes. Let him or her *glimpse* the shoes in the background as the ensemble is viewed while highlighting the color in the shoes that matches the outfit. An added benefit to graduated lighting is that many times the buyer will pass other *related* items moving between dominant and secondary objects.

Indirect Lighting

Bulbs set behind a valance or a baffle mounted on top of the display will throw light downward. In the same fashion, lighting can be directed upward by the use of floodlights or footlights. Indirect side lighting can also be achieved by using upright panels behind which bulbs are mounted so that the viewer cannot see them from the front. To hide lights totally from view may be too costly an expense. Set panels so that the lights are hidden from a distance, or use soft lights that are themselves enclosed. Top shelves should be top-lit, middle shelves side-lit, bottom shelves bottom-lit.

Lighting from Below

Set a small lamp in an opaque box and cover the top of the box with a ledge of frosted glass. Place the object to be displayed on this glass ledge, centered but slightly back, so that the light will both illuminate the object and throw interesting shadows on the wall behind it. Be sure to put some holes in the back of the box so heat can escape.

Spotlighting

Spotlighting, as the name implies, is used to project a circle of light on a single important element. If one color of a colorful display is to stand out, spotlight that color with a matching light. Spotlighting with articulated lamps is very effective. These are desk lamps with joined and segmented floating arms or clamp-on lamps with brackets which easily clamp to a shelf or ledge. Also ball lights or globe lights are effective in half-flooding, half-spotting objects.

Motion Display and Lighting

Although certain eye-catchers are an excellent means of presenting a great number of items, motion displays are complicated and expensive. The cheapest way to get this type of display is to consult with the vendor who supplies the club with alcoholic beverages, as these types of displays are used to merchandise the beverages and, though still operative, are replaced every so often. The motor from a discarded beverage display can be used to propel a display at the club.

REVIEW QUESTIONS

1. What is the basic difference between advertising and promotion?
2. What are the tools the management of an equity club can use to advertise club activities?
3. When and how could a flyer be used to advertise a club party?
4. Describe how a club bulletin can be varied and made interesting from month to month.
5. What are three ways that impulse buying could be encouraged in the pro shop?
6. Explain how a display can be arranged so that a golf bag presentation might also sell golf clubs.

CASE STUDY

A club in the northern part of the United States had a very bad summer season. During 3 months of unusual weather when it was not raining, the temperature would sometimes drop into the low fifties. Approaching the fall season the pro shop inventory of summer clothing was $10,000 compared to an average of $1000 in years past.

The club normally priced its clothing to realize a 20 percent gross profit. Develop a complete merchandising plan, including price reductions, advertising, and a diagram of the proper lighting and display for the pro shop. Because the plan must not lose money for the club, any funds expended must be added to the selling prices of the merchandise. In all calculations, assume that the sale will be successful and that all the old inventory will be sold.

8 Managing the Club's Entertainment

WHAT TO CONSIDER WHEN CHOOSING ENTERTAINMENT

The purpose of club entertainment is to get the members to use the facilities and to help the club gain a reputation as a fun place to be. In order to do this, entertainment must amuse, divert, give pleasure to the members, be vivid enough to be remembered, and meet the financial goals set by the club. It is "fond memories" that bring the members back. One way to accomplish this objective is to provide a souvenir for the member to take home after every big affair.

Entertainment can be divided into two broad types: in-house and external. Entertainment that is in-house is completely self-contained in regards to personnel. Equipment may be rented or purchased, but the members or club staff provide the people needed. In contrast, external entertainment involves hiring persons outside the membership and staff.

The types and styles of entertainment that can be offered to club members are limitless. There is apparently no clearly defined established pattern to guide management such as age, social position, profession, education, sex, or ethnic background. Certain considerations, however, may be helpful that are used in advertising, in particular, in regard to age. The ages at the two ends of the spectrum are the most difficult to satisfy. Teenagers are difficult to please because the entertainment they enjoy is limited, much of the music is "fad," and it is part of the status game to dance and listen only to an "in" group. When planning entertainment for teenagers have a good representation of youngsters on the entertainment committee.

The older members are often more interested in their own conversation than in dancing, and most music is an annoyance. The manager must explain this to the reservations clerk so that tables at a distance from the band or in another room may be offered. Music for the over-fifty group should be nostalgic and, except for special occasions such as New Year's Eve, not highly amplified.

The entertainment that is offered by the club is the acid test of the manager's imagination and professionalism. All entertainment is budgeted and approved by the various club committees, but the success or failure of any facet of the club's business is the manager's sole responsibility. Effective organization is of paramount importance and will make or break an event (see "Promoting Club Parties" in Chapter 7).

Ideas for the entertainment of the members come from many sources. The CMAA publishes the party ideas of club members in *Club Management* magazine and then reprints them in pamphlet form. The pamphlets, which sell at a nominal price, are called "Ideas for Parties." Club purveyors are another source of party ideas:

1. The U.S. Brewer's Association has a free booklet, "Beer Party USA," available through local beer distributors.
2. Most distillers publish one or more party idea books.
3. Marketing plans are available from many equipment manufacturers.
4. The National Restaurant Association publishes a booklet entitled "Ideas for Profit for Food Service Operators."

IN-HOUSE ENTERTAINMENT

The Christening Breakfast or Luncheon

A christening party can celebrate anything from a baby's baptism to the launching of a special project to the purchase by the club of something new. The party is usually planned as a rather elegant breakfast or luncheon affair. An array of chilled juices are set on the tables. The food, designed to go with the champagne, includes individual pastry shells filled with chilled poached eggs plus scooped-out tomato shells heaped with herbed scrambled eggs—served cold, in a grand French manner.

A Pool Party

No Hawaiian theme, no hula dancers, no flowers floating in the pool, and no tiki torches: The pool party in question here requires only casual dress and offers swimming if the members care to. This is the time and place for a barbecue. Make it different by not having a buffet line but serve from the kitchen, using paper plates and plastic knives, forks, and spoons. Have an outside bar, using paper cups. Hire a disk jockey who has outdoor equipment and a collection of various types of music. Start the party at around 7 P.M. so anyone who wishes may take a dip before dinner. This may sound very ordinary, but many members will enjoy the relaxed atmosphere.

The We-Got-Something-Back Party

For a do-away-with-the-blues, tax spree party for April 15, the theme is green. Perhaps a keg of green beer left over from St. Patrick's Day, a month ago, could be served with the regular menu featuring green vegetables. Cocktail napkins are play money and paper placemats over the regular linen are a xerox sheet taken from an

IRS tax form. The dessert could be a "U.S. Mint Mousse," made with green creme de menthe, and the after-dinner drink (at a special price) a grasshopper. This is the night for a full orchestra.

The Retirement Party

A retirement party can be a very solemn affair or a grand frolic. It is the opinion of the author (who tried retirement one time but could not stand it) that at this sort of party a good time should be had by all. The club works out the details with the member planning the party. The following ideas may make the party a delight: Decorate the club party room as an office. Move some equipment so that it will not disturb normal operating routine. (If filing cabinets are used, they should be locked.) Use office memos as place cards with a "From" and "To" line and the mandate: "Please read carefully, this is an order, CONGRATULATIONS AND HAVE A GREAT TIME."

When wine is served, have a monogrammed lunch box delivered to the retiree with a split of wine in it. The server could make a great display of presenting the box and opening the wine. After the meal has been finished, and the speeches given, before the real gift is presented, as a gag have the largest potted plant in the room placed in front of the retiree. Now this is the time the ordinary party starts to break up, but this is not an ordinary party. A pianist can be hired and song books rented for a close-out song fest with a pay-as-you-go bar. The party will be long remembered.

The Honeymoon-Isn't-Over Party

A Honeymoon-Isn't-Over party is a great idea for celebrating a wedding anniversary be it the first or the fiftieth. The title itself sets the tone. The party should be kept very informal and a good time planned rather than a ceremony. For post-fifth anniversaries memorabilia are appropriate, such as wedding and honeymoon pictures. If the couple plan to renew their vows, then a bower and a wedding cake may be ordered. Otherwise, this is not a wedding but an event to celebrate a happy one.

The Back-to-the-City Party

A few weeks after the big Labor Day bash, a very casual hot dog and hamburger type of party could be planned. The kids have been back in school a while, and many families will be eager for a family event.

The Member-of-the-Cast Party

If the club members have a drama club, they may wish to have a surprise party for their star. Set up the room as for an after-theater party, with posters and balloons and the staff, including the manager, in costume. After-theater food is usually of the breakfast type, so the low food cost will compensate for the cost of the props.

The High School Graduation Party

High school graduation parties have become a serious problem for some localities because they tend to last all night. Clubs could hold this type of party with minimum staff, the supervision ensuring the parents of the teenagers a good night's sleep.

A special committee of interested parent members could be formed to work with management and assist with the decorations. The price that the club will charge must be approved by the parents and the house committee. Students, however, will make the final decision as to where their graduation party will be held. The club's minimal expenses will be the following:

1. Overtime or double time for the staff involved. If the club's locker rooms are to be used, they must be fully attended. If the pool is used, lifeguards must be hired.
2. An orchestra. It should be stipulated in the contract that only a local band will be provided, which the students will choose.
3. Party room decorations.
4. Rental of a large-screen television set and at least two movies selected by the student committee.
5. Hot dogs, hamburgers, soft drinks, and a full breakfast.
6. Interior and exterior security guards. Many managers hire off-duty police officers as guards for special events.

The party must be held on graduation day. Do not serve, or allow to be brought into the club, any alcoholic beverages regardless of state laws. To further enhance fun and safety:

- Identify the party areas and lock up the rest of the club.
- In setting up the room, make sure the area for dancing is as large as possible.
- Use buffet service for the two meals.
- Hire a photographer.

Then a timetable must be worked out, including the following information:

1. When the party is to start (suggestion: 8 P.M.).
2. Availability of the pool and locker rooms. If affordable, suggest that an attendant be present in the women's locker room who can assist the girls with their wet hair. The pool party could run from 8 to 10 with music, perhaps live, at the poolside for dancing.
3. Pool closing (10 P.M.).
4. 10 P.M. to midnight: Hot dogs, hamburgers, french fries, and soft drinks are served. Midnight to 3 A.M.: soft drinks.
5. Dancing in the ballroom (10:30 P.M. to 2:30 A.M.).
6. Motion pictures (2:45 A.M. to 4:30 A.M.).
7. Breakfast (4:45 A.M.).

BUILT-IN ENTERTAINMENT

Certain kinds of entertainment are available to club members whenever the club is open and can be seasonal as well as year-round:

1. Outdoor facilities—the golf course, tennis courts, and pools.
2. Television facilities—The set could be in the bar, reading room, or have a space of its own. Some clubs are having some success purchasing or renting large-screen sets for major television events.
3. Game devices—pool and billiard tables, slot and pinball machines, shuffleboard, air hockey and ping pong tables, electronic games, etc. These could be placed throughout the club or confined to special rooms.
4. Card, reading, and writing rooms.
5. Library.
6. Weather station—A push-button weather radio station would be very useful to a club that has both indoor and outdoor activities. They are relatively inexpensive for the service they provide and do not require an antenna.
7. A computer that quotes stock market prices can be leased for a very modest price. The installation is via telephone lines and is not expensive or complicated.

SPECIAL ENTERTAINMENT

Special entertainment is the one-time or cycle event that is completely self-contained, involving only club members and staff.

Bingo and Keno, where legal, are still very popular with the older club members. Motion picture race games have become popular and satisfy some segments of club membership. The race games come under many names. A few of the best known are Armchair Races, Cinema Races, and A Night at the Races.

Member and staff talent is there; it just takes a lot of work by management to uncover it. Most normal club members are gregarious—this means there is some amount of "ham" in their makeup. Management may be able to start a drama club, prose- or poetry-reading club by just stimulating interest and rehearsal space. Musicians might be had for the looking. Classes in dancing, art, and crafts might also be of interest to the members. Management must take the initiative and personally seek out interests and talent, eventually forming a pool of special entertainment that can be drawn upon and that could stage, for example, a play or musical, a pantomime show, a trio or band performance, or prose or poetry reading.

ENTERTAINING THE CHILDREN

A new dimension in graceful dining has been added by providing dining facilities for mother and dad separate from those for the children. This answers the need of working parents to have some quiet time for themselves.

A club can begin by setting aside a small room on the slowest night in the week (only offer the service one night a week to start). Equip the room with a television set, a video cassette recorder, children's tables and chairs (these can be rented), coloring books, and crayons. Next select the person who will be responsible for the children, generally ages two to eight. One of the places to recruit could be a local college or university that has education courses. Two other things to be considered are licensing and insurance. Child care centers in most states require a license, and the club's liability policy must cover this activity.

BOOKING ENTERTAINMENT

In booking entertainment for the club, three bureaucratic requirements must be considered: (1) liability insurance, (2) contracts, and (3) performance bonds. Whether a fashion show, a demonstration of flower arrangements, an orchestra, or a disk jockey show, this type of entertainment requires special management attention when persons other than club members or staff are involved.

Liability Insurance

Whether the entertainment is free, voluntary, or paid, the club has an obligation to protect hired personnel by ensuring that both working equipment and conditions are safe. The same liability also concerns the entertainers. If an act can be hazardous to the members, management must insist that liability insurance be carried and paid for by the performers.

Contracts

Most clubs will need to contract for the music they use. All of the music written by American composers is copyrighted and two associations monitor copyright fees, the American Society of Composers and Publishers (ASCAP) and Broadcast Music Incorporated (BMI).

A written contract with the entertainer or agent will not, in itself, guarantee a successful performance, but it is a start. A contract puts the parties on notice that certain expectations must be met before payment can be made of the amount stipulated in advance. The following specifics may be of assistance in negotiating a contract.

1. Note the date of the contract and the place, time, day, and date of the performance. A provision as to penalties for lateness or a "no show" may also be included.
2. Specify the length of the performance—one, two, or more hours.
3. If the club is hiring a "name" group whose reputation will attract a large crowd, the club should take the following precautions. Give in the contract the exact

name of the entertainment group and the names of the persons involved, and include a picture of the persons who will be performing at the club. It will be too late to take action if management thinks they are hiring a famous band, but only the leader shows up on the night of the performance with a picked-up local group.

4. The contract should specify the exact number of minutes they will play each hour. Management should determine this based on economics. If the party has an open bar, for instance, playing time should be longer and intermissions shorter. If drinks are on a "pay-as-you-go basis," the number of intermissions is increased.
5. Note any equipment the club must furnish.
6. Note any transportation needed for the performance.
7. Detail the food, drinks, and/or lodging to be furnished for the performers.
8. Specify how payment will be made.
9. Define how contractual disputes will be handled. Usually the club representative who signs the contract is the final arbitrator in all disputes.
10. The conduct of the entertainers must remain subject to the control of the club manager at all times. The contract should specify that:

   • Food and drink are not allowed on the bandstand.
   • Smoking is not permitted on the bandstand.
   • All personnel must conform to the dress rules of the club, except while in costume.
   • All personnel must at all times conduct themselves as ladies and gentlemen.
   • Drunkenness or the use of any narcotics or drugs is a just cause for canceling the contract with no reimbursement.

11. The management reserves the right to control the volume of sound of any and all pieces of electronic amplifying equipment.
12. The management reserves the right to insist that no lyrics, movements, or gestures be indecent, obscene, or in poor taste.
13. The principal entertainer must carry liability insurance to protect the club from any injuries that may result from the act either to an actor, a club member, a club guest, or a club employee.
14. The contract can be terminated, without penalty, by the club until 24 hours before the performance is scheduled if for any reason the club cannot stage it.

Performance Bond

A performance bond is an insurance policy, purchased by the entertainer, that guarantees he or she will appear at the time, date, and place specified or the club will be reimbursed for their loss. An easy way to enforce the requirement is to pay an advance deposit. This is an essential part of the contract, as some performers do not allow sufficient time for travel delays between appearances and risk seriously inconveniencing the club.

Management Control

The manager must exercise careful judgment in the control of entertainers because of the fine line that exists between employees and contractors. If detailed supervision is given, the entertainer could be considered an employee under Internal Revenue Service regulations. The club could then be responsible for withholding tax, Social Security, worker's compensation, and other taxes. The manager must have a very complete idea of the performance to be given, for however specific a contract, not all details can ever be covered.

FINANCIAL ANALYSIS

The purpose of a good entertainment program is to cultivate membership and increase business at a predetermined profit or loss. The manager must be able to analyze the financial impact of the scheduled events to avoid overextending the club's budget.

One easy way to compute the dollars involved is to use the net profit percentage generated by a particular department, which tells the manager when the dollar sales become profit. For example, the food department works on a 5 percent net profit, the bar on a 25 percent net profit. A dinner dance is planned for the normal attendance of 100. Additional costs are represented by the band and the club labor needed to rearrange the room and clean up; this is computed to be $750. The bar may conservatively plan on selling two drinks for every additional diner. The food check average is $10 per person, and the two drinks are $3. Therefore, a $1.25 profit can be expected from each member at the dance:

$$5\% \text{ of } \$10 \ (= \$.50) + 25\% \text{ of } \$3 \ (= \$.75) = \$1.25$$

If the normal dinner crowd is 100, then 600 additional diners would be needed to break even:

$$\$750 \div \$1.25 = 600 \text{ members}$$

Thus if entertainment is to be used to increase business, other plans must be made. Perhaps a package deal could be established so that part of the cost would be paid by all diners. An admission fee or cover charge could be exacted so the club would break even or maybe make a small profit. The manager must analyze every event, be it a clubhouse affair or an athletic tournament, to determine whether the club can make a profit, break even, or arrange for subsidies.

REVIEW QUESTIONS

1. What are the two broad types of entertainment? Explain each type.
2. What two age groups are the most difficult to entertain? Why?
3. What specifics should an entertainment contract cover?

4. List the expense items a club must consider in planning a high school graduation party.
5. Prepare the planning schedule for a television party, held at a club to view some very interesting event.
6. What sort of talent could management hope to find among its members and staff in seeking to provide in-house entertainment? How might a talent search be conducted?
7. What is the purpose of ASCAP and BMI? Why are they necessary?
8. What is "a performance bond"? Why is it necessary?

CASE STUDY

The management and the entertainment committee have planned the biggest and grandest party of the year to celebrate the club's fiftieth anniversary. They have scheduled a "name band" and an off-Broadway musical show as the evening's entertainment, reserving a total of 200 seats. The entertainment requires two separate contracts, both calling for performance bonds, which have been submitted. Part of the band's contract includes a clause specifying they will play the required music for the show. The all-inclusive fee for the band is $4000 and for the show $8000. The club paid 50 percent of each fee when the separate contracts were signed and the performance bonds delivered.

One hour before the band is to arrive at 6 P.M. to start setting up for the show, a telephone call is received by the club's receptionist, stating that the band leader is ill and that the band will be unable to come. The caller hangs up before the receptionist can call the manager.

The performers for the off-Broadway show are already in the club with their manager, and the club manager's first action after hearing the bad news is to consult with her. The show cannot be presented without music. Both the manager of the troop and the actors standing close by moan in horror.

The 200 members arrive at around 8 P.M. to have a wonderful time.

Management has a number of options to choose from in trying to make this party a success. Describe two of them in detail.

9 Insurance, Construction, Renovation, and the Club Development Professional

INSURANCE

Insuring the club properly is a very complicated task. A major challenge is presented by the efficient coordination of insurance program expenditures. Cost-effective handling and proper identification of insurable risks require a systematic approach. Each insurance policy is a separate contract with its own conditions, limitations, and exclusions, and each claim is a separate occurrence with unique characteristics that will be evaluated by either the insurance company or the courts based upon determinations of fact.

An insurance program consists of two parts: the coverage that the club needs and where to purchase it. A club can retain the services of a professional insurance consultant, or if this is not possible, it can deal with an insurance agent or insurance broker. Agents are employees of a specific insurance company but may sell insurance from any company with which they have a state license. Brokers are usually single entrepreneurs who are licensed by several companies. Management should treat insurance like any other purchase. Once the insurance needs have been established, it is advisable to shop around. The club is not only purchasing coverage but also service, and an insurance agent or broker can only be judged by the service that is given.

The club must arrange and maintain a broad, competitive program. The ultimate decisions rest with management as to how much insurance, what portions of the property and business not to insure, and which deductible levels best fit the particular situations.

The agent or broker is a direct representative of the insurance markets. After the agent or broker has been selected, the professional competency of the agency should be assessed and its existing relationship with recommended markets should be evaluated, just as coverage and pricing of various parts of the insurance program are considered.

The policies and coverages referred to in this chapter will vary between jurisdictions and insurance providers, and the lists and insurance information presented are not intended to reflect all coverages available or to fully describe any coverage.

Property Insurance

Besides buildings and their contents items that may be eligible for insurance coverage are golf courses and irrigation equipment. Replacement cost should be assessed at whatever the insurance contracts permit, in addition to obtaining the broad, or all-risk, coverage provisions. The phrase "all-risk," however, in insurance contracts usually does not mean that all risks are insured against but merely that the coverage statement is very comprehensive, making the list of exclusions in the policy very long in contrast to that of a stated-peril policy. Business interruption insurance (loss of business income resulting from peril to insured property) is also an important part of a good program.

Following is a list of some important considerations in establishing property insurance coverage for a club:

1. Building values should be checked to ensure adequate replacement cost estimates. This can be done by consulting a qualified independent realtor or at least current construction values per square foot for similar buildings can be obtained through a contractor. Reevaluate property values annually and review them with the insurance agent or broker.
2. Adequate values of building contents should be verified by appraising inventory lists at current replacement cost levels.
3. Some equipment (computer systems, golf carts, golf course equipment) may need to be insured on special policies to be properly insured.
4. Special coverages are also available for accounts receivable and valuable papers and records.
5. Spoilage from damage to an electrical system can be included in a boiler and machinery policy.
6. Business interruption values are calculated according to a formula, and care should be taken to furnish accurate figures in arriving at the amount of insurance needed.
7. Swimming pools and tennis courts (including fences) are usually included on the property insurance schedule.

Casualty Insurance

Casualty insurance pertains primarily to a club's liability in terms of bodily injury and property damage arising from some form of negligence (tort liability). This includes general liability, liquor liability, automobile liability and physical damage, excess liability (called "umbrella" liability), and worker's compensation. Worker's compensation insurance includes the employer's liability and differs from the other policies in that it applies to the club's employees only. The policy incorporates in its provisions applicable state laws for the handling of medical and other compensation in on-the-job injuries of employees. Another difference in this policy is that the amount of insurance paid is limited by state law.

General liability (bodily injury and property damage liability) insurance for club operations is divided into several categories. Premium levels are determined by rates applied to total sales. *Premises/Operations general liability* applies to third parties on the premises—a customer tripping and falling, for example, or customers suffering injuries or death from a catastrophic occurence such as fire. Liability does not extend to on-premises products. *Products/Completed operations liability* applies to third-parties consuming food or drink on the premises. Products liability usually applies to bodily injuries or property damage that occur away from the insured premises, but is modified by policy endorsement for club operations because the product is consumed on premises.

General liability insurance is written under two types of policies: occurrence and claims made. Occurrence is generally the preferable coverage form, but market availability results in some coverages only being offered on a claims-made basis.

Automobile liability and physical damage coverage insures for the hazard of liability claims from third parties arising out of the use of insured automobiles and damage to insured vehicles.

Employers are responsible for checking the driving records of employees who operate club vehicles or use their own vehicles in company business. In the case of an accident, negligence may be imputed to an employer who assigned driving duties to an employee with a poor driving record.

All automobiles should be reported for listing on the policy, and any changes should be promptly reported to the insurance representative.

Savings on premium levels for physical damage insurance on owned vehicles can be maximized by setting deductibles on a single claim as high as the club can afford. High deductible levels keep small physical damage claims from needing to be handled by the insurance company and prevent unnecessary claim reporting of claims that could have an adverse impact on insurance premiums. In fact, unless the employer is an extremely large club with the ability to have a properly staffed department to manage defense of liability claims, it is generally better to have no deductible applicable for the liability portion of the insurance program.

Often it is difficult to make a preliminary determination as to the potential exposure of a liability claim, thus the insurance company claim department is in the best position to handle, defend, and evaluate liability claims from the very beginning.

Prompt reporting of claims to the respective insurance carrier is extremely important, not only from the standpoint of proper handling of claims but for the continuing relationship with the insurance provider. Claims reported late are sometimes already unnecessarily out of hand by the time they are reported.

Excess (umbrella) liability policies provide extremely high catastrophe limits of liability insurance protection. In essence an umbrella policy adds $1 million or more additional liability protection to the primary limits provided by the general liability, automobile liability, and employer's liability portion of worker's compensation policy.

Umbrella policies should be carefully reviewed, as there is no industry standard, and forms and rates can vary considerably between different insurers. Inclusion of products liability and liquor liability in the umbrella policy coverage must be specifically addressed, as these exposures are frequently excluded from the umbrellas.

Pollution liability is generally excluded from primary and umbrella insurance policies, and requires special handling to determine availability of markets if the exposure exists and coverage is desired.

Safety engineering and loss control services are provided by most insurance carriers. Proper utilization of these services and additional support when needed can significantly help in promoting the safety of the club's premises as well as improve operational efficiency. Insurance companies take their safety recommendations very seriously, and noncompliance with or disregard of these can sometimes result in cancellation of an insurance program.

Liquor liability insurance applies to claims arising from alleged negligence in the selling, serving, or furnishing of alcoholic beverages that results in injuries or damages to third parties. For example, if a person served alcoholic beverages at a club is involved in an automobile accident driving away from the club, a court may find the club liable if damages against the club are sought by the member and injured third parties. Liquor liability is excluded from coverage of general liability policies for certain operations involving the furnishing or serving of alcoholic beverages.

Owners' protective liability insurance provides protection for the club owner when a construction project is contracted for with an independent contractor. The insurance program of the contractor should be required to be extended to include the owner as an additional insured party and have an indemnification agreement holding the owner harmless in the event of liability claims arising from the construction project. Owners' protective liability provides liability insurance for the club within their own general liability insurance program for the contingent liability of the construction operations being performed by the contractor, and also provides a separate set of liability limit protection.

It is important that a general liability insurance program be extended to product liability, liquor liability, and the club's protective liability, as these are not automatic inclusions.

Bond Programs

Bond programs include the areas of fidelity bonding and security bonding. A *fidelity bond* is for the protection of an employer against the financial infidelities of an employee, i.e., embezzlement of funds or property. Fidelity bonds, however, exclude inventory shortage, or other mysterious disappearances, which continue to be a business risk. A pension or profit-sharing plan should also be part of the bond.

Proper handling of fidelity exposure controls is extremely important, requiring frequent counts and inventories, separation of functions in bookkeeping and accounting for receipt and disbursement of funds, and countersignatures on checks.

Surety bonds are often required by various governmental agencies that oversee licensing and the collection of taxes by business. Examples of this type of bond requirement are the mixed-beverage bond sometimes necessary to obtain and retain a liquor license. In addition, the sales tax bond is needed in some jurisdictions to get a sales permit.

Surety bonds hold the bonding company liable for payment up to the amount of the bond for taxes that a business is supposed to collect. Therefore these bonds are in essence financial guarantees of the business that is bonded, and a requirement of obtaining this type of bond is proof of financial stability (primarily cash liquidity) and a favorable credit history.

The club applying for a bond agrees on signing the bond application that the bonding company will be indemnified and held harmless by the applicant and indemnitors of the applicant from any liabilities that the bonding company may incur as a result of its suretyship, including legal fees. Thus the club needing the bond must have sufficient financial stability and liquidity to convince the bonding company that reimbursement could readily be made to the bonding company should it be called on to honor the bond obligation.

A club with minimal capitalization will usually need to bring in individual indemnitors that are financially acceptable to the bonding company in order to be able to qualify for the bond. If the customary financial underwriting requirements cannot be met by the club or available indemnitors, bonding sources are sometimes available that charge higher rates according to the financial risk involved.

Making a conscious determination not to insure certain exposures should be entertained only after due consideration has been given to the total potential financial risk being assumed along with the ability of the club to withstand and survive under worst-event projections.

Employee Benefit Plans

Employee benefit plans comprise the group insurance programs available to employees and their dependents. These generally include some combination of life, medical, dental, and disability insurance. Frequently certain parts of a plan will be paid by the employer and are called "noncontributory," meaning the club pays for it. Federal law makes it mandatory that this apply to all employees. Other parts, called "contributory," apply to elective coverage and may be paid for by the employee. Pensions (retirement plans) and profit-sharing plans fall within this category.

Worker's compensation and employer's liability policies apply only to job injuries, including occupational disease of employees. Claim payments are determined according to a schedule of benefits that varies by state. Insurance premiums are measured by a rate being applied to payrolls that reflects the injury exposure of specific jobs performed. An experience modification based on prior claim experience is also applicable on a mandatory basis to qualifying risks, and this can greatly influence the net premium cost result.

Payrolls are audited at the end of each policy year, and the advance policy premium paid is adjusted to reflect the actual payroll exposure developed during the year for each job classification, resulting in either an additional or refund premium due.

Specialty Insurance

Specialty coverage is usually an extension of a primary insurance program and may include some of the following:

Liability for directors and officers
Fiduciary liability (for trustees of employee benefit plans)
Boilers and machinery
Flood, earthquake insurance, mudslide, and pollution liability
Equipment rentals
Sports arenas and activities
Watercraft and aircraft

CONSTRUCTION

Into every club manager's life a little rain must fall, and if the rain had a name it would be "construction." A manager can do certain things, however, to provide a little waterproofing. The following steps, if taken slowly and one at a time, may assist management in getting the job done.

Any major construction project needs an architect to draw the plans and specifications for the contractor. Do not make the major mistake of having an architect start the project—this is management's responsibility. For assistance the manager might request that the board appoint a Special Construction Committee. The project must be clearly defined by management and the committee prior to the employment of an architect. The following questions will assist in this task:

1. What new construction is contemplated?
2. Why is the contruction needed and when is it to be completed?
3. What affect will the new project have on subsidiary facilities such as parking, and water and sewage capacities?
4. If the project is a new kitchen, is a food consultant available to work with the architect?

Architects charge a percentage of the total cost of the project for their fee. For this fee the club receives a complete set of construction plans, an estimate of the cost, and continued inspections to ensure that the contractor builds in exact accordance with the plans.

The next step is to hire an interior design firm to work with the architect so that the finish of interior floors, walls, and ceilings can be incorporated into the construction plans.

The Contract

The plans should now go out to reputable contractors for bids. The fees will range from 6 to 10 percent. Some important items for management to consider in the invitation-to-bid letter include:

1. The number of days the contractor estimates the construction will take.
2. The daily penalty if the project takes more days than the contractor estimated.
3. Whether the contractor has studied the plans and the project can be completed in accordance with the architect's drawings. This is very important because if contractors find a flaw in the architect's plans, they can bid lower, knowing that "change orders" will make them a substantial profit. In the meantime the architect will have been paid, forcing the club to file a law suit, which may take years to resolve.
4. Any precautions that are needed to protect existing property or equipment.
5. The method of payment and the method of arbitration that may be necessary.

When the various contractors' bids have been received, the following items should be considered.

- The club is under no obligation to accept the lowest bid. The contractor bidding lowest may take longest to complete the project.
- One contractor may wish to substitute materials for those called for by the architect. In this case the architect must be consulted.

RENOVATION

The same preplanning used in a construction project applies to any club renovation. The important difference in a renovation project is that it may seriously interrupt the normal business of the club. The ideal time for any major renovation—new carpeting in the club, major repairs, etc.—is when the club is closed. If this is not possible, then plans must be made to use alternate facilities. The board must appoint a Special Renovation Committee to assist management with the project.

Now the club holds a design contest, a normal procedure, which does not cost or obligate the club in any way. The successful interior designer will expect that if new furnishings are required, they will be purchased from him or her. The design contract should specify:

1. Prices for all items.
2. Whether the price includes uncrating, installation, and setting up.
3. If any renovation includes a sports area, whether the professional in charge has been consulted.
4. The proposed delivery date for the new items.

THE CLUB DEVELOPMENT PROFESSIONAL

The planning, development, and construction of a golf course project is a formidable task that challenges even the most experienced developer. With over 150 new courses being constructed by real estate developers each year, it is clear that, when designed and developed properly, golf course projects make sound financial sense.

Most courses today are developed as part of a PUD (Planned Unit Development) and generally represent the primary amenity for these master planned communities. Because the golf course will most likely represent the single most important marketing tool for the sale of residential properties, its development and long-range disposition must be exceptionally well planned.

Developers must consider more than just the delivery of a certain number of playable holes of golf. They must look at the initial requirements to operate effectively and the future demands that will need to be met to become profitable. This requires continual analysis of the trends and developments of the market and a thorough knowledge of the technological innovations that will satisfy the market demand.

The time from the conceptualizing of a golf course amenity to its delivery may be several years, and the successful developer realizes that during this time numerous critical changes in the market and in industry technology can and will occur. In order to stay abreast of these changes and react effectively to them, the successful developer is now recognizing the "economy" and good business practice of hiring a Club Development Professional (CDP) as early in the planning as possible. It is the CDP's business to know the latest market trends impacting the industry and the procedures and equipment which are available to expedite development. Taking advantage of a more efficient irrigation system on the market or simply adapting the pool for aquatic exercise classes could save the developer thousands of dollars and greatly improve the marketability of the club, enhancing the revenue base of the entire operation.

Another area where the CDP's expertise has proven invaluable is in the long-range planning for the operation and disposition of the club. Most golf facilities initially operate as daily-fee courses but convert to private status once the real estate development provides a sufficient number of members to support the facility. Often the ultimate goal of the developer is to sell the facility to the membership. Providing the basis for the smooth transition of the club through these planned phases should be done at the outset. The club bylaws and membership categories should be developed with this ultimate goal of the developer in mind. If not addressed at the onset, an equity conversion or buy-out can be an agonizingly complicated transaction that can erode anticipated profits.

The use of a CDP greatly reduces the risk of failure and offers effective insurance against costly mistakes and financial setbacks. The CDP can provide the resources and assistance necessary to deliver an exceptional facility that will operate effectively today and in the future.

The following list provides an overview of the consulting services offered by a CDP:

1. Club concept development
   Club and amenity conceptualizing
   Project and amenity integration planning
   Feasibility studies and market analysis
   Financial pro forma development
   Membership strategy and structure determination
   Clubhouse design and construction

2. Club business plan development
    Budget planning-preopening; capital, start-up and operational
    Cash flow planning and analysis
    Standards of operation
    Operational manuals and detailed job descriptions
    Purchasing specifications
    Accounting and control systems
    Employment policies and legal requirements
    Employee staffing and compensation plan
3. Membership matriculation and marketing
    Design of membership collateral materials
    Board of directors development and orientation
    Membership director recruitment and training
    Comprehensive sales and marketing programs
4. Local/regional competition study
5. Member surveys, questionnaires, and focus group assistance

Having determined how the CDP may assist the club developer, management should consider the following points when selecting one:

1. *Credentials.* Does the individual/firm have the appropriate background and experience?
2. *Reputation.* What is the reputation of the individual or firm in the club industry?
3. *Network.* Does the individual/firm have the resources to draw upon? Can the full scope of services be provided? The team approach can prove beneficial.
4. *Flexibility.* Does the individual/firm have the ability to tailor services to meet the needs, methods, and rates and adjust these as necessary?
5. *Location.* If the individual must travel long distances (generally over 4 hours), the travel expenses could become prohibitive.
6. *Contract.* Does the individual/firm provide a written agreement and does it address clearly the responsibilities and the various types of work to be performed?

Working with a CDP is both challenging and rewarding. Productive use of a CDP in the planning of a project can ensure its viability into the future. The CDP is likewise challenged to maintain an effective relationship with the developer, his or her committees, and the other technical advisors and subcontractors providing services. The CDP must also remain sensitive to any budget restrictions that may impact the delivery and implementation of his services.

REVIEW QUESTIONS

1. In the insurance business, what is the difference between an agent and a broker?
2. What are the areas of the club business that are covered by "bonding programs"?
3. If the club held a poolside buffet dinner and swimming was part of the program, which of the various types of insurance would protect the club?

4. Under what circumstances would an interior designer become involved in a construction contract?
5. In determing the successful contract bidder, what factors must a club take into consideration?
6. How would a club development professional (CDP) be of assistance to an equity club in financial difficulties?
7. What details should be included in a contract with a CDP?

CASE STUDY

The Raging Waters Yacht Club had a major disaster. A 60-foot motor yacht moored to its pier caught on fire. The fire was in the engine room, where a lot of combustibles were stored, including paint. The yacht's owners were not on board and a fire alarm was not part of the boat's protective system.

The fire was on a weekday and only a small number of the members were at the club. The dining room overlooked the marina and one of the members dining there noticed the smoke. When the member shouted, "Fire on the dock," the hostess rushed to a telephone and called the volunteer fire department. In the meantime the member ran out on the dock, followed by one of the cooks with a fire extinquisher. The boat exploded just as the member ran up, killing him instantly. The cook was blown into the shallow water and was knocked unconscious. The explosion had thrown burning debris into the air and caused the pier and the clubhouse roof to catch fire.

In spite of the flying debris and sparks, the rest of the members and staff were able to get the cook to a safe spot and launch a small rowboat to search the water for the missing member. Unfortunately, it was the harbor master's day off, but the manager was doing a fine job organizing the rescue operations. He had a member of his staff use a garden hose on the blazing roof while he went inside to call for an ambulance and the paramedics.

The fire truck arrived without the tanker because of the club's proximity to the water. The pier ablaze, a fireman had to wade out with the intake nozzle. Not only was the large yacht on fire, but the wind had blown flaming embers onto three other boats, which were now burning.

The outcome of the disaster was as follows:

The member's body was recovered.
Seven yachts valued at over $1 million were destroyed.
The cook suffered a broken collar bone and was out for 3 weeks, after which he was able to return to light duty.
The clubhouse roof and all of the dining room furnishings had to be replaced.
The pier had to be completely rebuilt.

The club has complete insurance coverage.
Question: Which insurance policies cover each of these events?

Country Club Membership Bylaws for a Corporate Club

The following bylaws are adopted and issued by the Board of Directors of the Country Club, herein called the "club" pursuant to Article IX of the Corporate Bylaws, and these Membership Bylaws are subject to change, amendment, or repeal in whole or in part at any time and from time to time by action of the Board of Directors.

ARTICLE I   ORGANIZATION AND OBJECT

Section 1.   This club is organized pursuant to the laws of the State of California, as the _____ Country Club.

Section 2.   The object for which this Club is formed is to promote and encourage outdoor sports, particularly golf, tennis, and swimming.

Section 3.   The principal office of the Club in the State of California shall be located in the unincorporated area of San Diego, California.

ARTICLE II   MEMBERSHIP

Section 1.   The classes of membership hereinafter set forth confer upon the holder thereof the privileges of the use of the Club facilities only. Membership does not confer any ownership or interest in the assets of the Club. The Club reserves the right to operate Club facilities, or through license, lease, or otherwise, to operate said facilities through licensees or leases or other arrangements.

Section 2. Fees.   Dues, transfer fees, and any other charges for use of the Club facilities for services rendered or food, beverage, or merchandise offered for sale, are subject to change at any time without previous notice provided, however, as an accommodation to members, an effort will be made to give advance notice of changes in initiation fees, dues, and/or transfer fees.

Section 3.   The membership of the Club shall consist of the following classes:

A. General
  1. General Golf and Tennis
  2. General Golf
  3. General Tennis
  4. General Special
  5. Junior
B. Annual
  1. Annual Golf and Tennis
  2. Annual Golf
  3. Annual Tennis
  4. Annual Special
  5. Annual Corporate
  6. Annual Nonresident

Section 4. General Golf and Tennis Membership.   There shall be two (2) types of General Golf and Tennis memberships, i.e., single and family. A single membership includes all Club privileges for the designated member only. A family membership includes all Club privileges for all members of the immediate family (living at home and unmarried) under twenty-one (21) years of age.

Persons entitled to General Golf and Tennis membership privileges shall have and enjoy all the rights and privileges of the Club, subject to such restrictions, limitations, and regulations as may be imposed by the Board of Directors from time to time.

General Golf and Tennis memberships shall be transferable only as hereinafter provided.

Section 5. General Golf Membership.   There shall be two (2) types of General Golf memberships, i.e., single and family. A single membership includes all Club privileges for the designated member only. A family membership includes all Club privileges for all members of the immediate family (living at home and unmarried) under twenty-one (21) years of age.

Persons entitled to General Golf membership privileges shall have and enjoy all the rights and privileges of the Club, except use of the Club tennis facilities, subject to such restrictions, limitations, and regulations as may be imposed by the Board of Directors from time to time.

General Golf memberships shall be transferable only as hereinafter provided.

Section 6. General Tennis Membership.   There shall be two (2) types of General Tennis Memberships, i.e., single and family. A single membership includes all Club privileges for the designated member only. A family membership includes all Club privileges for all members of the immediate family (living at home and unmarried) under twenty-one (21) years of age.

Persons entitled to General Tennis membership privileges shall have and enjoy all the rights and privileges of the Club, subject to such restrictions, limitations, and regulations as may be imposed by the Board of Directors from time to time.

General Tennis members, subject to revocation at the discretion of the Board of Directors, shall have limited and provisional use of the Club golf course under regulations established by the Board of Directors from time to time.

General Tennis memberships shall be transferable only as hereinafter provided.

Section 7. General Special Membership (formerly General Social). General Special membership shall consist of single membership and family membership. Single membership includes all Club privileges excepting use of the Club golf course and the Club tennis courts for the designated member only. Family General Special membership includes all Club privileges excepting use of the Club golf course and the tennis courts for all members of the immediate family (living at home and unmarried) under twenty-one (21) years of age. Existing social memberships shall be automatically reclassified to General Special memberships. Persons entitled to General Special membership privileges shall have and enjoy all the rights and privileges of the club, except use of the Club golf course and Tennis facilities, subject to such restrictions, limitations, and regulations as may be imposed by the Board of Directors from time to time.

General Special members, subject to revocation at the discretion of the Board of Directors, may have limited and provisional use of the Club golf course under regulations established by the Board of Directors from time to time.

General Special memberships shall be transferable only as hereinafter provided.

Section 8. Junior Membership. Junior membership includes all Club privileges for a single person between twenty-one (21) and thirty-one (31) years of age. Persons entitled to Junior membership privileges shall have and enjoy all the rights and privileges of the Club, subject to such restrictions, limitations, and regulations as may be imposed by the Board of Directors from time to time.

Junior memberships are nontransferable, provided, however, they may be converted to another class of membership. In the event a Junior member applies for and is granted another class of membership, the amount of the initiation fee paid for the Junior membership shall be credited toward the initiation fee for such other class of membership.

The class of Junior membership was closed as of February 1, 1975, and no additional Junior memberships will be issued.

Section 9. Annual Membership. As set forth in Article II, Section 3, above, Annual memberships shall consist of the following: Annual Golf and Tennis, Annual Golf, Annual Tennis, Annual Special, Annual Corporate, and Annual Nonresident.

Annual memberships are for one year only. Renewal of Annual memberships is in the sole discretion of the Board of Directors. Annual fees and monthly dues are subject to change at any time, without notice, subject to the provisions of Article II, Section 2, above. Annual memberships will be issued for one year on a fiscal year basis, commencing March first and ending the last day of February of the following year. Persons applying for Annual membership on or after August first will be entitled to a fifty percent (50%) reduction of the annual fee.

Annual memberships are not subject to sale or transfer and are for the sole use of the person or family to whom they are issued.

Section 10. Annual Golf and Tennis Membership. Annual Golf and Tennis memberships (single and family) shall have the same privileges to use the Club facilities as is conferred upon General Golf and Tennis memberships.

Annual Golf and Tennis members shall have and enjoy all the privileges of the

Club, subject to such restrictions, limitations, and regulations as may be imposed by the Board of Directors from time to time.

Section 11. Annual Golf Membership. Annual Golf Memberships (single and family) shall have the same privileges to use the Club facilities as is conferred upon General Golf memberships.

Annual Golf members shall have and enjoy all the privileges of the Club, subject to such restrictions, limitations, and regulations as may be imposed by the Board of Directors from time to time.

Section 12. Annual Tennis Membership. Annual Tennis memberships (single and family) shall have the same privileges to use the Club facilities as is conferred upon General Tennis memberships.

Annual Tennis members shall have limited and provisional use of the Club golf course under regulations established by the Board of Directors from time to time, which use is subject to revocation at any time at the discretion of the Board of Directors.

Section 13. Annual Special Membership. Annual Special memberships (single and family) shall have the same privileges to use the Club's facilities as is conferred upon General Special memberships.

Annual Special members shall have limited and provisional use of the Club golf course under regulations established by the Board of Directors from time to time, which use is subject to revocation at any time at the discretion of the Board of Directors.

Section 14. Annual Corporate Membership. Annual Corporate memberships shall have the same privileges to use the Club facilities as the Annual Golf and Tennis Family membership, with the right to select three (3) designees, single or family. If a designee is single, then the privileges are limited to the designee only. If a designee is married, then the designation includes all members of the designee's immediate family (living at home and unmarried) under twenty-one (21) years of age. The designees of the Annual Corporate membership shall have all the privileges of the Club, subject to such restrictions, limitations, and regulations as may be imposed by the Board of Directors from time to time.

Section 15. Annual Nonresident Membership. Annual Nonresident members shall have the same privileges to use the Club facilities as Annual Family Golf and Tennis members, with the exception that Annual Nonresident members shall be required to pay golf course and tennis court fees at the rates prevailing for guest privileges for the use of said facilities. Annual Nonresident membership shall be available only to nonresidents living outside a seventy-five (75) mile radius from the country club. And the use of the Annual Nonresident membership shall be limited to a total period of three (3) months only during each fiscal year, to be designated in advance by the nonresident member.

Annual Nonresident members shall have all privileges of the Club, subject to such restrictions, limitations, and regulations as may be imposed by the Board of Directors from time to time.

Section 16. Other Memberships. The Board of Directors may at any time and from time to time establish such other classes of memberships as said Board shall determine desirable.

Section 17. The Board of Directors shall have the power and authority to prescribe such rules and regulations governing each of said classes of membership and all of the terms and conditions pertaining thereto as said Board shall determine from time to time.

The memberships granted hereunder are a license to use the facilities of the Country Club and a privilege which must be respected. Misconduct or obscene behavior will not be tolerated and may result in the revocation of membership for cause shown. Delinquency in payment of dues and/or hours accounts, resignation, death, or expulsion for cause will result in the termination of the Annual Membership without refund for any unexpired term.

Section 18. General Membership Conversion Option. General members shall have the option to convert to Annual memberships pursuant to regulations established by the Board of Directors.

ARTICLE III TRANSFER OF GENERAL MEMBERSHIPS

Section 1. The transfer and sale of general memberships, i.e., General Golf and Tennis, General Golf, General Tennis, General Special (formerly General Social), and Junior shall be made only by the Club. Upon resignation or death of a member, the membership may be surrendered for cancellation, and upon such surrender the liability for dues shall cease, or upon the resignation or death of a member, the member, his executor, administrator, or personal representative may offer in writing to sell said membership to the Club. The Club shall within fifteen (15) days after receipt of said written offer accept or reject said offer. In the event the Club does not accept said offer, the membership shall be placed on the list of memberships for sale in order of receipt. All memberships offered for resale shall be offered at the then current price established by the Board of Directors for the sale of new memberships. If new memberships are available for sale, the Club shall endeavor to maintain the value of the memberships offered for resale by offering said memberships for resale on a one-for-one basis (for each new membership sold the Club will offer receipt memberships for resale in the order of priority of those offered for sale). Upon the resale of memberships offered for resale, the Club shall receive a transfer fee, which shall be fixed from time to time by the Board of Directors at the sole discretion of the Board of Directors. A member desiring to list his or her membership for sale shall deposit said membership with the Club, duly endorsed, together with his or her membership card, and at the time of resale of said membership the Club shall remit to the member, or his executor, administrator, or personal representative, the purchase price received therefor less any transfer fee, taxes, and/or any dues or other charges owing to the Club. A general member who has elected to resign and place his or her membership for sale shall be and remain an active member of the Club until his or her membership has been sold and shall remain and shall continue liable and responsible for the payment of monthly dues and other charges as levied upon the membership by the Board of Directors. The effective date of his or her resignation shall be the date of the resale of membership, provided, however, that in the event of the death of a single general member who has been a general member for at least six (6) months prior to his or her death and paid dues for the last six (6) months from the date of his admission to the Club, then dues shall cease upon such membership upon the last day of the month during which such death occurs until the resale of such membership.

ARTICLE IV   APPLICATION FOR MEMBERSHIP

Section 1. Applications.   All applications for membership of any class shall be in writing and in form and content as the Board of Directors shall prescribe. Applications shall be processed by such persons and committees as the Board of Directors may from time to time specify. Applications must be approved by a majority of the membership committee and ratified by a majority of the Board of Directors. All proceedings taken by the Board of Directors with respect to the election of members shall be secret, confidential, and final. Each application shall be acted upon separately.

Section 2. Waiting List.   A waiting list of applicants for membership shall be kept by the Secretary of the Club. No applicant shall be placed upon the waiting list until his or her application has been tentatively approved by the Board of Directors. Any membership which the Club may hold and desire to sell shall be offered at the price asked by the Club to the applicants on the waiting list in the order of their priority. The order of priority shall be in accordance with rules established by the Board of Directors from time to time.

Section 3. Qualification for Membership.   A person approved for membership shall qualify and become a member of the Club by:

a. Signifying his or her acceptance in writing and

b. Paying, in cash, or making arrangements satisfactory to the Board of Directors for payment of required fees, taxes, if any, and any accumulated dues, charges, etc. If any accepted applicant fails to qualify, as aforesaid, within thirty days after notice of election has been mailed to him or her, he or she shall be deemed to have withdrawn his or her application for membership.

ARTICLE V   DUES AND CHARGES

Section 1.   The dues for all members shall be paid monthly in advance.

Section 2.   Subject to such limitations as may be herein provided, the Board of Directors shall at all times have the power to fix and increase or decrease the initiation fees and dues payable by all classes of members.

Section 3.   All dues and indebtedness by members shall become due and payable on the first day of the month and shall become delinquent on the fifteenth day of the month. The Board of Directors may from time to time impose such rules or regulations as it deems proper with respect to members whose accounts with the Club are delinquent, including suspension of membership or expulsion from the Club.

ARTICLE VI   TERMINATION OF MEMBERSHIP

Section 1.   Any member who shall be found guilty by the Board of Directors of violating the Bylaws of the Club or any rules or regulations adopted by the Board of Directors or conduct injurious to the reputation of the Club, may, after an appropriate hearing, be suspended for any period of time or expelled from membership. Any suspension or expulsion of one person entitled to exercise the rights and privileges of a family membership shall not affect the other persons entitled to enjoy the same family membership.

Section 2.   Any member who shall have been suspended or expelled shall immediately and automatically forfeit his or her membership to the Club and shall thereafter have no rights or privileges in the Club unless and until he or she shall have been reinstated to good standing in the Club and his or her membership rights and privileges reinstated to him or her.

Section 3.   Members may resign from membership in the Club at any time upon payment of all their indebtedness to the Club. Such resignation shall be in writing delivered to the General Manager of the Club. Any members who so resign their membership shall not be entitled to any refund or other compensation except as herein specifically provided for in Article III hereof.

ARTICLE VII   MEMBERSHIP CERTIFICATES

Section 1.   The Secretary of the Club shall keep a membership book containing the names and addresses of each member. Termination of any membership shall be recorded in the book, together with the date on which the membership ceased.

Section 2.   Certificates of membership shall be issued by the Secretary to each member of the Club.

Section 3.   Upon resignation, termination, or transfer of the membership, the membership certificate and the membership card of such member shall be returned to the Secretary of the Club for cancellation.

Section 4.   All members shall advise the Secretary of any change of address and whenever any notice is required or permitted to be given to a member pursuant to the Bylaws or rules and regulations of the Club, such notice addressed to such member at his or her last address as shown on the Secretary's records shall be deemed to have been properly given.

ARTICLE VIII   GUESTS AND NONMEMBERS

Section 1.   Guests are defined as persons who are not members, but who are personally escorted by a member.

Section 2. Guests Without Cards.   Any member may introduce a guest to the Club for the purpose of getting acquainted by having such guest personally sign the Guest Register. No member shall make a practice of repeatedly introducing the same person who is eligible for membership; and no member shall at any time introduce any former member who was expelled or whole membership was terminated. Each guest may enter said Club only when accompanied by the host member.

Section 3. Visitor's Card. A Visitor's Card may be issued at the written request of a member in good standing upon such terms and conditions as shall from time to time be determined by the Board of Directors. Such visitor's card grants regular privileges and is valid for two weeks.

Section 4. Nonmembers may enjoy the use of the facilities of the Club upon such terms and conditions as the Board of Directors may impose.

Section 5. Guests whose manner, appearance, or deportment are not within the standards of membership or who offend or disturb other members may be asked to leave.

Section 6. No guest shall be permitted to contract any indebtedness. Guest fees as posted will be charged to the member for such guests.

ARTICLE IX   GRATUITIES

Employees are prohibited from receiving tips or remuneration from the members, and members are prohibited from giving the same except as may be permitted by the Club for services other than food and beverage. Tips as determined by the Board of Directors will be added to food and beverage chits.

ARTICLE X   RIGHTS AND OBLIGATIONS

No member shall, merely by virtue of such membership, have any rights of ownership in any of the assets of the Club, nor shall any such member have any liability of any kind, solely by virtue of such membership, except for the payment of dues, house accounts, and other obligations to the Club and for the observance of rules and regulations as provided in the Bylaws and Club and Ground rules. It is expressly stipulated and understood that no property rights or vested rights of any kind accrue to the benefit of any member solely by virtue of membership, except the right to use the facilities of the club so long as he or she is a member in good standing. The members are not liable for the debts or other obligations of the club, past, present, or future.

ARTICLE XI   BOARD OF DIRECTORS

Section 1. General Powers. The affairs of the Club shall be managed by its Board of Directors.

Section 2. All rights and privileges of members are subject to rules and regulations adopted from time to time by the Board of Directors.

ARTICLE XII   COMMITTEES

Section 1. Committees not having and exercising the authority of the Board of Directors in the management of the Club may be designated by a resolution adopted by a majority of the Board of Directors present at a meeting at which a quorum is present. Except as otherwise provided in such resolution, members of each such committee shall be appointed by the Board of Directors. Any committee member may be removed by the Board of Directors whenever in its judgment the best interest of the Club shall be served by such removal.

Section 2.   Each of said committees shall consist of at least three (3) members. A member of the Board of Directors shall be an ex-officio member of each of said committees.

Section 3. Term of Office.   Each member of a committee shall continue as such until the next annual meeting of the members of the Club and until his or her successor is appointed unless the committee shall be sooner terminated or unless such member be removed from such committee or shall cease to qualify as a member thereof.

Section 4. Chairman.   One member of each committee shall be appointed Chairman by the Board of Directors.

Section 5. Vacancies.   Vacancies in the membership of any committee may be filled by appointments made in the same manner provided in the case of the original appointments.

ARTICLE XIII   MEMBERS' REPRESENTATION ON BOARD OF DIRECTORS

The Corporate By-Laws of the Club provide for a Board of Directors of nine (9) members. A majority of the Board of Directors (5) shall be elected from persons nominated by the shareholders of the corporation, and four (4) members of the Board of Directors shall be elected from persons nominated by the majority vote of the members of the following classes of membership, to wit: General Golf and Tennis, General Golf, General Tennis, General Special, Annual Golf and Tennis, Annual Golf, and Annual Tennis.

ARTICLE XIV   AUXILIARY GROUPS OR ASSOCIATIONS

Any Auxiliary group or association that may be formed with the Country Club will function under the rules and regulations established by the Board of Directors.

ARTICLE XV   RECLASSIFICATION OF MEMBERSHIP

All requests for reclassification of membership (i.e., change from Golf to Tennis, Tennis to Golf and Tennis, or Tennis to Social, etc.) shall be submitted in writing to the General Manager of the Country Club and shall be subject to the approval of the Board of Directors based on quotas established from time to time for the various classes of memberships.

Note: These Bylaws are a sample of what a real estate developer would use while operating the Club prior to an "Equity Conversion."

Club Membership Rules

HOUSE RULES

1. The General Manager of the Club, or his designee, shall have full and complete charge of the clubhouse and grounds at all times.

2. The hours of operation of the clubhouse, pro shop, locker rooms, snack bars, and pool shall be determined by the General Manager and will be adjusted as Member usage dictates.

3. The Club will be closed on Monday of each week, except when a national holiday (as determined by the General Manager) is observed on that day of the week, in which case the Club will be open on Monday and closed the following day.

4. The Business Office will be open from 8:30 A.M. to 5:00 P.M., Tuesday through Friday.

5. Attire for both men and women should be in good taste, and appropriate for the season. Proper attire excludes such items as cut-offs, tank tops, and tee shirts. Swimming attire is permitted only in the pool area. Except in the pool area, men are required to wear shirts with collars. The appropriate staff members have the responsibility of enforcing the appropriate attire and all Members are expected to report any infractions noted.

6. Guests: Members may introduce guests to the Club subject to the following conditions:

    A. Members may entertain guests who are not members of the Club provided that they accompany their guests and arrange for payment of the appropriate fees as may be established from time to time by the Club. Visiting house guests of the Club do not have to be accompanied by a sponsoring member, but must be issued a temporary guest card while using the Club facilities and pay the appropriate fees.

B. Members are responsible for the conduct, dress, and charges accrued by their guests.

C. The General Manager, or his designee, may at any time, without stated reasons, deny guest privileges to any individual when, in his opinion, it is in the best interest of the Club.

7. Reciprocal privileges with other country clubs are subject to the rules of those clubs. For our Members who desire to use the facilities of other clubs, the General Manager will provide a card or letter of introduction and a request for extension of their guest privileges.

8. Lockers are rented to Members on an annual basis, payable in advance. The lockers are secured through the Business Office and billed on the Member's statement. The locker rooms are for the exclusive use of Members, their guests, and their children who are of legal age and have permission to use their parents' locker. Golf clubs, except for extra or odd clubs, are not to be stored in lockers. The Golf Pro Shop offers club storage and cleaning service.

9. No food or beverage may be consumed on the Club premises unless purchased from the Club.

10. Liquor law violations are prohibited on the premises; i.e., Members and guests are not permitted to bring intoxicating beverages on the premises. Members and guests not of legal age may not consume intoxicating beverages on the premises. Members and guests who are intoxicated may not be served intoxicating beverages on the premises, etc.

11. A 15 percent service charge is added to all food and beverage checks. These sums are distributed to food-and-beverage personnel.

12. Members shall be liable to the Club for the value of all Club property which is damaged or removed by them or their guests. Conversely, the Golf Pro Shop is liable to the Members for golf clubs, bag, and contents for which a fee is paid for storage and cleaning.

13. No children the age of twelve (12) and under are allowed at the Club unattended.

14. Strict observance of any Federal, State, County, and City regulations with respect to gambling of any nature on the premises is required.

15. All personal or private property, while on or about the Club's premises, is strictly at the owner's risk, except for golf clubs, bags, and contents, which are stored for a fee in the Golf Pro Shop as provided in House Rule 12.

16. Parking must be within the marked spaces. Parking is not permitted in the circle drive at any time.

17. Members of the Club shall not reprimand any Club employee. Complaints should be reported immediately to the General Manager or the appropriate Supervisor for assessment and rectification. More serious complaints should be made in writing and directed to the General Manager.

18. Any person creating a disturbance may be requested to leave the Club's premises and may be refused service by the General Manager.

19. Any Member having given a special order for a luncheon or a dinner, including Club functions, and wishing to countermand that order, must give the Club at least 24 hours notice. Otherwise, they will be charged with the amount of that order.

20. Reservations for all clubhouse activities are to be made with the Business Office.

21. Members and employees of the Club are requested to report any violation of Club rules or bylaws. Members in violation will be subject to disciplinary action or expulsion as set forth in Section 4.6(C) of the Club Bylaws.

22. When one or more Members cause a room or facility to be kept open after the regular closing hours and have not made previous arrangement with the General Manager, such Member or Members shall be charged for no less than one hour, nor no more than the total hours such room or facility is kept open by them for their personal use, at a rate commensurate with the total cost to the club for staffing and heating or air conditioning the room or other facility.

23. The accounting period for charge to Member accounts closes on the 20th of each month and statements are mailed to the Members on or about the first day of the following month. Payment is due upon receipt of said statement and will be considered delinquent on the 20th day of the month (30 days). Members will receive with their statements an envelope for mailing payment. All Member charge tickets will be held at the Club for a period of 90 days. If a Member's account becomes delinquent by 60 days, he or she will be notified by letter of his or her suspension and the posting of his or her name on various bulletin boards at the Club. A 1.5 percent per month finance charge (which is an annual rate of 18%) will be added to all delinquent accounts not paid by the 20th of the month.

24. No fishing, hunting, or possession of firearms is permitted on Club premises. No swimming or wading in the Club's lakes is permitted.

25. No subscription lists may be circulated and no articles other than those offered by the Club shall be sold in the Club unless specifically approved by the management of the Club.

26. No pets are permitted on Club property.

27. Only Members and their guests and children of legal age are permitted in the 19th Hole.

GOLF COURSE RULES

Weather permitting, the golf course will be open at either 7:30 A.M. or 8:00 A.M., as seasonally determined by the Golf Pro, Tuesday through Sunday and Holidays. Play may not commence before these hours.

1. All Members and guests must register in the Golf Shop prior to play.

2. Guests may play the course accompanied by a Member or Members who shall register themselves and their guests and sign for the applicable guest fees.

3. An in-town guest (resident) may only play the course once a month and must be accompanied by a Member. A guest living within a 50-mile radius of the Club is considered a resident or in-town guest.

4. All matches must start from no. 1 tee, unless permission is obtained from the Golf Shop to start from no. 10 tee or other starting point as approved or directed to accommodate the Members.

5. Any group not proceeding directly from the no. 9 green to the no. 10 tee will lose its position on the course and must check with the Golf Shop before resuming play.

6. No group larger than a foursome will be allowed on the golf course without the express permission of the Golf Shop.

7. Groups less than a foursome may have additional players assigned during heavy play at the discretion of the Golf Shop.

8. Members, when practicing, are to use the driving range and practice green areas only. Under no circumstances are the regular greens, tees, or fairways to be used for practice. Only driving-range balls may be used on the driving range. Putting and chipping is allowed on the practice putting green, but no pitching is permitted.

9. Riding carts are available for Members and guests. Riding carts are limited to two bags and two persons. Riding cart regulations are more fully explained under Riding Car Regulations.

10. All riding carts shall follow the cart paths except when the 90-degree rule has been invoked by the Golf Shop. Avoid areas newly planted or under repair and approach no closer than 20 yards from any tee, green, bunker, or its shoulder. Avoid all wet areas.

11. Slow Play: If a group falls one clear hole behind the group in front of it, the slow group must invite the group behind to play through. In case play is delayed on account of a lost ball, the group playing behind shall be invited to play through. Should the above conditions prevail and the trailing group is not invited through, it shall be the right and the privilege of the group following to ask permission to play through.

    Whenever, under this rule, the group ahead is required to invite the trailing group to play through, then, after issuing the invitation to play through, the players in the slow group shall take a position on the course out of the line of play and shall remain stationary until the invited group has played through. The invited group must play through once the invitation has been received, in order that groups which may be following will not be delayed. A group must step aside and let the groups behind play through any time a course marshal so requests.

12. A single player, twosome, threesome, or fivesome has no standing at any time and shall give way to foursomes.

13. Each player must have his own set of clubs.

14. All players shall exercise care to prevent damage to the course by observing the following rules:

    A. Under no circumstances should a ball be played from any putting surface with a club that will damage the green.

    B. Golf bags should not be placed on the putting surface of the green.

    C. Turf, cut or displaced by a player, should be replaced immediately and pressed down with the foot. All ball marks made in the green should be repaired immediately.

    D. After any play from sand traps, the sand must be smoothed and raked.

15. Proper attire: Attire for both men and women should be in good taste and appropriate for the season. Proper attire excludes such items as cut-offs, tank tops, tee shirts, and swimming wear. For males, shirts with collars are required, and the Golf Shop will ensure that all golfing participants are properly attired prior to beginning play.

16. Children under 6 years of age are not permitted on the golf course at any time.

TEE RESERVATIONS

1. Tee reservations will be taken 2 days in advance daily beginning at 7:30 A.M.

2. On Thursdays and Fridays from 7:30 A.M., tee times will be made by telephone only.

3. Monday Holiday tee times will be taken on Friday.

4. For Saturday, Sunday, and Monday Holidays, only one tee time per day per call will be taken.

5. Players requesting tee times must provide the names of the other players in their match. If the players' foursome is not complete and the Golf Shop staff is not advised of the names of all players by tee-off time, the foursome may be filled by players from a standby list.

6. Players who cannot use their tee times should call in advance to give notice of cancellation so that tee times may be reassigned.

JUNIOR PLAY

1. Juniors are defined as any son, daughter, or guest who has reached the age of 6 and is under 16 years of age.

2. Juniors under 16 and over 12 years of age are permitted to play golf on weekends and holidays only after 3:00 P.M. during daylight savings hours and from noon forward during standard time.

3. Juniors 12 and under are permitted to play golf when certified by the Golf Pro and accompanied by an adult golfing Member, subject to the restriction set forth in 2 above.

4. Children under 6 years of age are not permitted on the golf course at any time. See Golf Course Rule 16.

5. Juniors shall not be permitted to ease or operate a riding golf cart.

6. Juniors shall, at all times, conduct themselves in a gentlemanly or ladylike manner. Temper displays, damage to Club property, and so forth shall be cause for suspension.

7. Members are charged with the responsibility of acquainting their junior children of guests with the rules and etiquette of the Club before permitting them to play.

GOLF CART REGULATIONS

1. Privately owned golf carts are not permitted on Club property.

2. Operators of riding golf carts must be 16 years of age or older and possess a valid operator's license.

3. Each riding cart is restricted to two riders and two golf bags.

4. When seated in a riding golf cart, keep both feet within the cart at all times.

5. All types of golf carts must at all times be kept at least fifty (50) feet from the approaches to the greens and shall not be driven or pulled onto the green and tee slopes.

6. The use of any type golf cart is subject to the determination of the Golf Pro and the Course Superintendent based on weather and course conditions.

7. When riding golf carts are permitted on the course, they must be kept on the cart paths at all times. When weather and course conditions warrant, the Golf Pro and Course Superintendent may allow riding golf carts to leave cart paths

by invoking the 90-degree rule, which permits the cart to leave the cart path by driving at a 90-degree angle to the player's ball and directly returning at a 90-degree angle to the cart path.

8. Operators of riding golf carts shall observe safe driving principles at all times and must obey signs, stakes, and other markings used to guide carts.

9. Every effort should be made to avoid bare spots, wet or soft areas, or areas under construction.

10. Players using carts are not entitled to any privileges in playing through other players except as stated under "slow play" etiquette under Golf Course Rule 11.

11. Players renting riding golf carts from the Golf Shop are responsible and liable for any damage to the cart.

TENNIS RULES

The Tennis Professional, or his or her designated assistant in his or her absence, shall have the full charge of the tennis facility and shall be the first authority as to the interpretation or enforcement of the following rules.

1. All Members, except Special, may use the tennis courts without payment of fees.

2. All Members and their accompanied guests must register at the Tennis Shop before play. The full names of all players shall be plainly recorded. Court fees for guests must be paid before entering the courts.

3. All Members and their guests must leave the court promptly when their reserved time expires. If they desire to continue playing, they may report to the Tennis Shop to see if the courts are available.

4. Courts are available for play from 8:00 A.M. until 10:00 P.M., Tuesday through Sunday. When the Club recognizes a Monday Holiday, courts will be available on that day but not on the following Tuesday.

5. Only participating players will be allowed on the courts.

6. Appropriate tennis attire must be worn at all times.

   A. Shoes must have soft rubber soles and be specifically designed for tennis (no cleated shoes).

   B. Shirts and socks will be worn at all times.

   C. Cut-off jeans or jams, school jerseys, gym-type shorts and tee shirts, golf slacks, and swim wear are not considered to be acceptable tennis attire.

7. Guests must be accompanied by a Member of the Club or must hold a guest card which has been issued by the Business Office.

8. No abusive or profane language is permitted.

9. No racquets are to be thrown at any time while on the courts.

10. Smoking is not permitted inside the court areas.

11. All metal racquets must have bumper guards attached for the protection of the courts.

12. No food or beverages may be brought onto the Club premises unless purchased from the Club.

13. No food or beverage is permitted inside the court areas.

14. Players shall abide by the rulings of the Tennis Pro when questions arise on such matters as tournament rules, courts to be used, length of play, courtesy, etc.

15. Members are responsible for the observation of Club rules by their guests.

COURT RESERVATIONS

1. Court reservations may be made two (2) days in advance by calling the Tennis Shop.

2. Failure to appear within ten (10) minutes of the reserved time will result in forfeiture of the reservation.

3. Reservations shall be for a maximum of 1½ hours.

SWIMMING POOL RULES

1. The use of the swimming pool is restricted to Members, members of their household family, and their guests.

2. The swimming pool will be open daily, except Monday, beginning Memorial Day weekend and closing after Labor Day weekend. The pool will also observe any Monday Holiday openings observed by the Club, in which case it will be closed on the following Tuesday. Hours will be from 10:00 A.M. until 8:00 P.M. unless weather conditions make it necessary to close and except as posted for special events.

3. Conduct at the pool must be such as to provide the greatest safety for all Members and their guests. The Swimming Pool Supervisor is given the full authority to enforce all swimming pool rules and regulations.

4. All Members and guests must register before entering the pool area. A charge will be made for guests and they must be accompanied by the Member inviting them.

5. No person shall enter the pool at any unauthorized time or when a lifeguard is not on duty. The pool is officially closed when a sign is posted.

6. Running or scuffling in the pool area is prohibited. No spitting or spouting water in the pool will be permitted. There will be no horseplay in the pool or pool area.

7. Do not talk to the lifeguards unnecessarily. The guards are on duty for your protection.

8. The lifeguard in attendance will assist the Swimming Pool Supervisor in enforcing swimming pool rules and regulations and, in the Supervisor's absence, will have full authority.

9. Children under 8 years of age, and all children who cannot swim must at all times be attended by a parent or other adult person (18 years or older) having them in charge.

10. Children from 8 to 12 years of age must be accompanied by a parent or other adult person (18 years or older) at all times, unless they have passed the Club's required swim test.

11. The use of body-holding devices, such as floating tubes, life jackets, etc., will be restricted in the pool at the discretion of the Swimming Pool Supervisor or lifeguard in attendance.

12. No cut-offs or shorts will be allowed in the pool.

13. Persons with skin disorders or other infections must not enter the pool.

14. No glassware will be permitted in the pool area at any time.

15. In case of emergency, the pool must be cleared immediately.

16. The Club is not responsible for stolen or misplaced items.

17. State regulations require that a shower be taken prior to entering the pool.

18. Swimmers must remove all hair pins from their hair before entering the pool or wear a bathing cap.

19. No food or beverages are permitted in the pool area unless purchased from the Club.

Membership Questionnaire

Dear member:

Will you do us a favor?

Your Club is conducting a survey of its membership to gather information and opinions on the facilities and quality of service that you are provided. Your answers will enable the Board of Governors and management to be aware of member requirements in specific areas, and this in turn will help them to respond more accurately to the needs of the overall membership.

It will take only a short time to answer the simple questions on the enclosed questionnaire and to return it in the stamped reply envelope.

Your answers will be kept confidential and used only in combination with others to provide a composite picture. They are essential to the accuracy of our research.

Thank you for your valuable assistance.

Sincerely,

PRESIDENT

P.S.   If you care to, please include your address with the questionnaire so that we can send you a complimentary guest greens fee certificate as a token of our appreciation.

By requesting the club members' names and offering something if the following questionnaire was filled out, 73 percent of the forms sent were returned, some with valuable suggestions. Of the responses, 13 percent had complaints, whether justified or not, but all of the respondents received a personal letter from the president and a guest card.

SURVEY OF COUNTRY CLUB MEMBERS

1. What is your age?
   under 25 years ___   35 to 44 years ___   55 to 64 years ___
   25 to 34 years ___   45 to 54 years ___   65 or over   ___

2. What type of membership do you have?
   _____

3. How long have you been a member?
   ___ under 1 year   ___ 4 to 6 years
   ___ 1 to 2 years   ___ 6 to 8 years
   ___ 2 to 4 years   ___ 8 or more years

4. a. Was your membership originally purchased for business, personal, or combined use?
   _____

4. b. What do you use the club for now?
   _____

5. What factor was most important in your decision to join the country club?
   ___ location   ___ facility
   ___ price   ___ golf course
   ___ friends
   ___ other:_____

6. If you are a member of other private clubs, please list them.
   _____
   _____
   _____

7. Please rank the clubs listed below by their image in the community (#1 as best, #2 as second, etc.).
   ___ A Country Club   ___ E Country Club
   ___ B Country Club   ___ F Country Club
   ___ C Country Club   ___ G Country Club
   ___ D Country Club   ___ H Country Club

8. What do you like most about your country club? _____
   _____
   _____
   _____

9. What do you dislike most about your country club? _____
   _____
   _____
   _____

10. Please use the rating scale on the left side to indicate how you feel about the club's performance in each of the following areas. Ratings may be based on your personal experience, or on anything you may have seen or heard about them.

Excellent	10	_____ Golf shop facilities
	9	_____ Golf shop service
	8	_____ Golf cart operations
	7	_____ Course supervision of play
	6	_____ Bag storage and service
Average	5	_____ Golf activities and tournaments
	4	_____ Men's golf association
	3	_____ Women's golf association
	2	_____ Driving range
Poor	1	_____ Golf course

_____ Golf course condition

_____ Halfway house

_____ Tennis shop facilities

_____ Tennis shop service

_____ Tennis court condition

_____ Tennis activities and tournament

_____ Swimming pool facilities

_____ Swimming pool staff and service

_____ Swimming pool activities

_____ Locker room facilities

_____ Locker room service

_____ Food and beverage facilities

_____ Food and beverage service

_____ Food and beverage prices

_____ 19th-hole facilities

_____ 19th-hole service

_____ 19th-hole prices

_____ Club-sponsored parties

_____ Overall club operation

11. Have you had occasion to use the club's facilities for a private function:
Yes ___   No ___

12. Using the same rating scale as before, how would you assess the club's performance at your private function?

___ Assistance in planning

___ Quality of food served

___ Quality of service provided

13. What major improvements do you feel are essential to the success of the country club?

_____

_____

_____

14. How responsive is management to your suggestions or requests?

_____

_____

_____

15. Additional Comments:

_____

_____

Name and address:

_____

_____

Job Descriptions

TITLE: BACK WAITER

> *Reports to:* Dining Room Manager
> *General Duties:* Assists front waiter in carrying out the dining room procedures to ensure member satisfaction.
> *Specific Duties:*
>
> 1. Serves bread and butter.
> 2. Take members' orders into kitchen.
> 3. Upon request of the front waiter, returns to kitchen and picks up all orders, checking each against the dupe, and delivers them to station.
> 4. Removes soiled dishes to the kitchen.
> 5. Checks constantly bread, butter, water, and ashtrays.
> 6. Assists the front waiter/waitress.
> 7. Always is attentive to the members' needs.
> 8. Cleans up. Performs other duties as may be assigned.

TITLE: DINING ROOM WAITRESS/WAITER

> *Reports to:* Dining Room Manager
> *General Duties:* Prepares dining room for service and serves the members. He/she must know the general rules of etiquette in order to provide gracious service. The waiter/waitress is responsible for prompt and proper service at his/her station.
> *Specific Duties:*
>
> 1. Sets table.
> 2. Pours water for members.
> 3. Takes cocktail orders.

4. Serves cocktails on show plates.
5. Coordinates ordering, serves courses.
6. Removes dishes and silverware following each course (when everyone at the table has finished).
7. Removes everything from the table following main course except flowers, candles, water glasses, napkins, and ashtrays.
8. Crumbs table.
9. Takes order for coffee, tea, and other beverages.
10. Presents dessert cart or menu. Serves desserts.
11. Performs coffee service.
12. Presents check when asked.
13. Changes ashtrays, pours water, etc.
14. Always is attentive to members' needs.
15. Cleans up. Performs any other duties delegated by the supervisor.

TITLE: POOL SNACK BAR COOK

Reports to: Executive Chef
General Duties: Ensures the proper functioning of the pool snack bar, including guest checks, inventories, presentation, and member satisfaction.
Specific Duties:
1. Ensures the availability of all required menu items.
2. Preportions all cold meats and cheeses.
3. Prepares and serves all items, sandwiches, and salads, in accordance with the established portions, presentation, and operating methods.
4. Prepares and serves all fruits, beverages, snacks, and ice cream in accordance with the established portions, presentation, and operating methods.
5. Prepares and records all employee meals.
6. Prepares in advance designated items for the following day.
7. Requisitions items for the following day.
8. Obtains guest checks from office.
9. Is responsible for the proper execution of the service procedure.
10. Keeps daily log book of complaints, weather, and food-and-beverage volume.
11. Implements the charge procedure.
12. Returns daily checks to the office.
13. Responsible for maintaining cleanliness of work areas, storage areas, equipment, and member dining areas.
14. Secures food and equipment.
15. Does special assignments as requested by the chef.

Suggested Readings

Bridenbaugh, Carl. 1981. *Early Americans*. New York: Oxford University Press.

Club Managers, eds. 1986. *Club Management Operations*. Kendall-Hunt.

Dittmer, P., and G. Griffin. 1984. *Principles of Food, Beverage and Labor Cost*. 3d edition. New York: Van Nostrand Reinhold.

Fulmer, Richard M. 1987. *The New Management*. 4th edition. New York: Macmillan.

Grossman, Harold L. 1989. *Grossman's Guide to Wines, Beers and Liquors*. 7th, rev. edition. New York: Scribner's.

Hodgetts, Richard M. 1989. *Modern Human Relations at Work*. 4th edition. New York: Dryden Press.

Kotschevar, Lendal H., and Charles Levinson. 1988. *Quantity Food Purchasing*. New York: Macmillan.

Lejeune, Anthony. 1979. *The Gentlemen's Clubs of London*. London: Dorset Press.

Ninemeier, Jack D. 1986. *Planning and Control of Food and Beverage Operations*. 3d edition. Edited by Marjorie Harless and John Glazer. East Lansing, Mich.: Educational Institute of American Hotels.

Ward-Thomas, Pat. 1980. *The Royal and Ancient*. Edinburgh, Scotland: Scottish Academic Press.

Index